Equity and How to Get It
Rescuing Graduate Studies

Edited by
Kay Armatage

Inanna Publications and Education Inc.
Toronto, Ontario

Published by:
Inanna Publications and Education Inc.
operating as *Canadian Woman Studies/les cahiers de la femme*
212 Founders College, York University
4700 Keele Street
Toronto, Ontario M3J 1P3
Telephone: (416) 736-5356, Fax (416) 736-5765

Printed and Bound in Canada
by University of Toronto Press, Inc.

Cover Design/Interior Design: Luciana Ricciutelli

Canadian Cataloguing in Publication Data

Main entry under title:
Equity and how to get it: rescuing graduate studies

ISBN 0-9681290-2-1

1. Universities and colleges – Graduate work. 2. Educational equalization.
3. Discrimination in Education.
I. Armatage, Kay.

LB2371.E64 1999   378.1'55   C99-930430-5

Contents

1. Equity

2. Re-Loading the Canon

3. Pedagogy

Equity and How to Get It

Acknowledgements

This collection of articles found its beginnings in a conference sponsored by the Graduate Collaborative Program in Women's Studies, University of Toronto. The conference was suggested by then Dean of the School of Graduate Studies, Jon Cohen, as an undertaking for the newly founded Graduate Collaborative Program in Women's Studies. Dean Cohen had initiated a study of gender inequities at University of Toronto some years earlier and proposed a conference on gender equity in graduate studies as a followup. Graduate Women's Studies, however, saw it as no longer appropriate to isolate gender from other related equity issues, and began planning the more inclusive "Rescuing Graduate Studies: Equity and How to Get It."

There had been a number of local and national conferences on gender and pedagogy, including Women In Graduate Studies in Ontario, COU/OCGS, 1989; York University, 1992 and 1995; Educational Equity in Graduate Studies, 1993. There are also several publications which deal with the theme either wholly or in part: *Report of the York University Conference on Gender and Graduate Studies*, 1994; *Pedagogy and the Personal*, 1995; *The Gender Question in Education Theory, Pedagogy and Politics*, 1996. Since the early 1990s we have seen an accumulation of data as a result of studies undertaken by individual scholars and specific units at post-secondary institutions. The Status of Women Committees of the Royal Society of Canada (1989), OCUFA (1991) OCGS (1993), COU (1993) and CAUT (1993) have also provided important documents.

Most of these studies concentrate on undergraduate education. The OCUFA Final Report on the Status of Women in Ontario Universities, for example, devotes only three pages to the experience of graduate students.

Gender issues remain significant foci of research and theory in all disciplines. In tandem with this is the exciting and ground-breaking scholarship that is currently being undertaken on the more wide-ranging and inclusive gender-related topics of class, race/ethnicity, disability and sexualities. The issues of graduate teaching and research needed to be placed in this broader, global context. "Rescuing Graduate Studies: Equity and How to Get It" aimed not only at enhancing this new interdisciplinary research agenda but at refocusing the dialogue specifically on graduate level education.

Preliminary discussions with a wide range of faculty, students, equity officers and administrators indicated an extraordinary level of enthusiasm and commitment. Little effort was necessary to recruit an organizing committee, a committed and capable group representing a diversity of interests, expertise, and sectors. Graduate students took substantive positions in the conceptualisation and organisation of the conference.

The committee identified the following themes as the architectural foundations for the conference. 1) Pedagogy and the Disciplines: questions of interdisciplinarity and new fields of research; the traditional canon as disciplinary paradigm; pedagogy and research that are sensitive to cultural, gendered and class differences; teaching from a feminist, racialized or other explicit perspective. 2) Supervision and Mentoring: relations between supervisors and students; micro-inequities of power; gender and race harassment; politics and responsibilities of role models; mentoring; the politics of co-authorship. 3) Funding, the Temporal Agenda and Support: hierarchies in funding, teaching and research assistantships; the four-year Ph.D. and relations to family care; parental leaves, deferred fellowships; differential funding by gender and division; "life" in graduate studies; counselling and social support services; athletics and cultural life; information technology; family and child-care; housing; safety. 4) Transformations: Challenges and Effects of Women's Studies: the history and challenges of the institutionalisation of women's studies; transformations of institutional culture; resistance and challenges.

The three-day event attracted over 130 graduate students and faculty registrants from the University of Toronto and neighbouring institutions, including students from other provinces. The participants numbered more than eighty, including key-note speakers, respondents, panelists, interactive facilitators and presenters. A final informal plenary session, attended by more than fifty speakers, registrants and organizers, offered general recommendations of the conference.

A commissioned report on the conference, including executive summary and recommendations, followed a few months later. This report makes it clear to the University of Toronto and other institutions that significant work will be necessary to reach the goal of equity in graduate eduation and that students, faculty and administrators are committed to seeing its implementation.

For assistance with the conference, there are many people and offices to thank.

Planning discussions involved University of Toronto faculty from Women's Studies, Political Science, Philosophy, Education, Information Studies and Computer Science; administrators from the School of Graduate Studies; University of Toronto equity officers (Status of Women, Family Care, Race and Race Relations, Native and Aboriginal) and graduate students. The organizing committee consisted of Rona Abramovitch (Status of Women Officer), Kay Armatage (Director, Women's Studies), Fabienne Baider (French/Women's Studies), Rodney Bobiwash (Director, Aboriginal Programs), Pia Kleber (Director, University College Drama Program), Rhonda Love (Community Health; Grievance Officer, UFTA), Anna Pelkner (Sociology/Women's Studies, Humboldt/University of Toronto), Ruth Perkins (Executive Assistant, Graduate Students' Union), Ruth Pierson (History, OISE/University of Toronto), Roger Simon (Curriculum, Teaching and Learning, OISE/University of Toronto), and Paul Tsang (Physiology; Services Advisory Board). Specifically for the portion of the conference that was marked as the Humboldt/Toronto Sociology/Women's Studies Exchange, organizers were Kay Armatage (Director, Women's Studies, University of Toronto), Margrit Eichler (Sociology of Education, OISE/Univesity of Toronto), Pia Kleber (Director, University College Drama Program, University of Toronto), Hildegard Maria Nickel (Director, Zentrum fur Frauenforschungen, Humboldt University-Berlin), and Vappu Tyyska (Sociology, University of Toronto).

For help with general questions and methodology, I must especially thank Joy Parr for materials and advice, and Ceta Ramkhalawansingh (City of Toronto) for continuing and always excellent support. Thanks also to Patricia Seaman for her contribution to the organization of the conference, its subsequent report and the collection of these papers. Principal John E. Browne, Roger Rendeau, and Audrey Perry of Innis College also made generous contributions of their time and expertise.

The financial sponsors of the conference were University of Toronto

School of Graduate Studies; Vice-President, Research and International Relations; Vice-President, Provost; Graduate Collaborative Program in Women's Studies; Humboldt University-Berlin; German Academic Exchange Service (DAAD); Lufthansa German Airlines; Consulate General of Germany; Ontario-Quebec Exchange; Innis College; City of Toronto; Drama Program, University College; Faculty of Law; Graduate Students' Union; Dean, OISE/ University of Toronto; SAC Women's Commission; Department of Sociology; New College; East Asian Studies; German Department; Philosophy Department; French Department; and Department of Spanish and Portuguese.

Throughout the process of organizing the conference and editing this collection, I have repeatedly called on two colleagues and friends. June Larkin (Women's Studies and Equity Studies, University of Toronto) has been unstinting in her support, hard work, good sense, editing savvy and excellent outfits. Kass Banning (Cinema Studies, University of Toronto) has generously contributed her exceptionable knowledge and analysis of substantive issues along with regular drives home and meticulous hair-dying.

Finally, Luciana Ricciutelli has done first-class work with editing this book.

Introduction

Kay Armatage

It was a conference on Black Popular Culture held at The Studio Museum in Harlem and the Dia Center in Soho (December 1991). All the honchos of postcolonial studies were there—Stuart Hall, Cornel West, Paul Gilroy, Kobena Mercer, Isaac Julien, bell hooks, Angela Davis, Coco Fusco. The conference rolled along through the first night and the second day, with one exciting speaker after another—each one talking longer than the last. By the end of the second day, the conference was a half day behind schedule. On the last day, session chairs were exhorted to adhere strictly to the allotted time for their panels, and so began the ritual of passing notes to the podium (three minutes left, one minute, please finish up now). Each speaker in turn received the notes, nodded politely, and scrambled to finish on time. Everyone was cooperating beautifully.

But not Hazel Carby. A young fair-skinned and fair-haired woman with a soft Scottish burr of an accent, she was on a tear. Her paper, "The Multicultural Wars," addressed the contradictory nature of the black presence in North American universities. The culture industry had discovered the black woman writer as a highly profitable enterprise, and some black male professors were garnering major media attention. Meanwhile, numbers of black students were steadily declining, and the value of affirmative action in faculty hires, student recruitment, and curriculum transformation was being hotly debated under the "political correctness" banner. At the same time, universities every-where were jumping on the "diversity" bandwagon—at least in their student handbooks, catalogues and publicity materials. "Departments and programs in many private universities, for example, will proudly point to an 'integrated' curriculum while being unable to point to an integrated student body—except in the photographs in their student handbooks, photographs that contrive to demonstrate 'diversity' by self-consciously including the pitiful handful of black/Latino/Asian/Chicano and perhaps even fewer American Indian students on campus" (191).

As I recall, Carby was about a third of the way into her paper when the first note was passed to her. She looked at it briefly and kept on going. The second note arrived, which she ignored. When the third note was placed on the podium, she immediately crumpled it into a ball with her left hand and threw it to the floor. She kept going. This was a topic in which she was passionately engaged. Seven years later, I can still recall the dramatically sarcastic cadence to her voice as she read an extended quote from Nicolaus Mills' survey of 1990 college publications, her rhythm pausing each time over the word diversity, which she pronounced with an extended rising long "eye" in the first syllable, and a short falling staccato triplet for the last ones: "deye-versity." I'll quote the passage; you'll have to imagine Carby reading it aloud:

> "Diversity is the hallmark of the Harvard/Radcliffe experience," the first sentence in the Harvard University register declares. "Diversity is the virtual core of University life," the University of Michigan bulletin announces. "Diversity is rooted deeply in the liberal arts tradition and is key to our educational philosophy," Connecticut College insists. "Duke's 5,800 undergraduates come from regions which are truly diverse," the Duke University bulletin declares. "Stanford values a class that is both ethnically and economically diverse," the Stanford University bulletin notes. Brown University says, "When asked to describe the undergraduate life at The College—and particularly their first strongest impression of Brown as freshmen—students consistently bring up the same topic: the diversity of the student body." (529-531)

A few weeks later on a university presidential committee on racism and anti-racist initiatives, a large group sat in the intimidatingly vast Council Chamber around the extremely grand table, trying to bash out a new credo, a new mission statement for the University of Toronto. I brought up Carby's/Mills' point, and suggested that the University of Toronto might heed this critique. Today, from the University of Toronto website, we find "recognition of the diversity of the University community" to be the second of the four principles to which our institution is committed, well ahead of "fiscal responsibility and accountability," but just trailing "respect for intellectual integrity, freedom of inquiry and rational discussion." In 1999, the college where I teach has a student body that is 80 percent white, middle-class, from two-parent families who own their own home. Its faculty is 100 percent white. In fact, in the Faculty of Arts and Science (with a professoriate of tenured and tenure-track 740) there is only one black woman tenured faculty member.

So it was Hazel Carby who alerted me to the trend towards idealizing diversity in our universities as a marketing tool. To the concept of diversity has been appended "equity and justice." At a recent symposium inaugurating an Equity Studies program at the University of Toronto, Rodney Bobiwash fielded a new term, also coated with cynicism. He spoke of the "equity industry," the hosts of counselors, equipment manufacturers, ramp experts, lawyers, advocates, report writers, conference organizers and human resource managers/officers who were making their living "servicing" and "accommodating" "special interest groups" who, like black American undergraduates, are increasing neither in numbers nor in access to institutions. He introduced his talk with the following anecdote:

> A few years ago, in an effort to create access for people with disabilities, a major public institution in Toronto decided to install a wheelchair ramp. After several weeks of construction and some promotional fanfare, the ramp was ready to be unveiled at a ribbon-cutting ceremony. A wheelchair-bound client was recruited to wheel up the ramp and cut the ribbon. To the embarrassment of all assembled, the door at the top of the ramp opened in such a way as to prevent the wheelchair's access once it reached the top of the ramp. This story has always symbolized to me the major problem with access and equity programs—you get to the top of the ramp and you still can't get in. (Rodney Bobiwash, unpublished paper, 1998).

This collection of papers came together at least in part bathed in the light of consciousness and knowledge of the current questioning of the discursive field of diversity/equity. The central tropes of equity discourse have become familiar, even doxalogical: special topics programs, access, pipeline statistics, role modeling, chilly climate, institutional aporia. This volume challenges the equity doxa from a variety of political (is personal) perspectives, and from a range of disciplinary bases.

The first section, Equity, offers critiques—and the occasional optimistic exhortation—of the current state of equity in post-secondary educational institutions, specifically at the graduate level.

The book begins with William Haver's response to the now infamous text, Bill Readings' *The University in Ruins* (1996). As Haver attests, Readings' analysis devolves on the assertion that the university has come not merely to resemble, but to be in fact, a transnational corporation consecrated to sustaining and reproducing the metamorphoses of an inescapable postindustrial capitalism. While many of us fear this trend, and rebuke it in protestations such as the recent walk-out at the University of Toronto convocation conferring an honorary degree on George Bush (1998), Havers challenges Readings' assumptions by what he calls the "insistence of the social" and argues that a serious, existential engagement with the essential difficulty of thinking is the most practical and most revolutionary of proposals. He emphasizes that the social does not exist, but happens, and thus interrupts our epistemological and political business as usual. With many of the writers in this anthology, Havers argues from his own experience, specifically with the Asian and Asian American Studies Program at Binghamton University. His students are the "1.5 generation": "this is the place of an ontological stammering, where to speak is always to speak of the impossibility of communication." In this pure interruption there is "nothing other than the very movement of thinking." On the contradictions of cultural studies, Havers' position is firm: "Let me be blunt. I do not think there has been, is, or ever can be, an equitable institution....And this because the institution of institutionality—that is, the act of foundation that enables the institution as such—is always the instauration of a certain power relation that it is the task of the institution as such to reproduce."

In "Educational Equity: No Turning Back," Juanita Westmoreland-Traoré calls for a "return to basics" in the discussion of equity. Working from her knowledge of equity legislation, case law and the current climate in the courts, she charts a brief history of the constitutional protection of equality, with a special note on the significant implications of the shift in terminology from "affirmative action" to "equal opportunity." She argues that this shift signals a fundamental change in the governmental approach to these issues. Specifically in relation to equity-seeking groups within the university, she reviews the current status of the effort to remove historical and ongoing disadvantage, concluding with a discussion of the tenets of inclusive teaching and learning environments. In the final section of the paper, Westmoreland-Traoré summarizes the strategies and issues addressed by the other articles in this text: curriculum offerings and teaching methodologies, including evaluation methods; broader definitions of research; policies and bylaws on student admissions and faculty searches; debates about academic freedom and excellence; and the inextricable connection between employment equity and educational equity. She cites Harriet Tubman's motto, "No turning back," which kept people moving on the Underground Railroad, often in daunting circumstances when they wanted to quit. Westmoreland-Traoré calls for "the same steadfast determination to face the work on equity issues and social change that lies ahead of us."

In "Linking Employment and Educational Equity," Allison Young responds to Westmoreland-Traoré's rallying cry, reiterating her insistence on "the inextricable connection between employment equity and educational equity." Young uses her experience in the Graduate Students' Union at Dalhousie University (Halifax) to apply the employment equity processes at universities to issues of educational equity in the graduate student environment. Unlike employment equity, she argues, the main focus of educational equity is not on the range of employees in an institution, but on the nature of the programs and the climate in which they are delivered. However, Young points out that employment equity depends on an equitable educational environment, since without such an environment, there will never be a large enough pool of qualified designated groups to form a diverse faculty and staff.

In "Race and Equity in the Academy," George J. Sefa Dei uses the discourse of race to illuminate the way equity issues problematize the core of privilege, power and justice in institutional knowledge. Although mindful of the trajectories of difference and the interlocking nature of oppressions, he focuses on race to guard against that easy slippage into a bland talk of social justice for "all" that fails to name race and difference in stark terms. With Westmoreland-Traoré and Young, Dei is optimistic about the surmountability of equity challenges in the academy. He sees education itself—the kinds of questions educators ask and address in school settings—as potentially transformative, capable of producing schools as sites which serve the multiple interests, desires and aspirations of a diverse body politic.

Kathleen Rockhill is considerably less sanguine about the potential for equity for the disabled in universities. "In these mean-spirited times," she writes in "Symbolic Equity: Disability in Higher Education," "I have my doubts about how far we can move the university in the direction of greater equity." And without such movement, "participation is impossible for all but the most privileged amongst the disabled." Rockhill asserts the necessity to confront the contradictory regulatory functions of the university as the gatekeeper of privilege: "As the arbiter of what counts as expertise in our society, the university determines which bodies get to perform expertise upon other bodies—that is the distinction between who gets interpolated as one who knows and/or has the capacity to learn to perform that knowledge—and who gets interpolated as not having that capacity of knowledge."

With Patricia Monture-Angus, we move to the other end of the spectrum of responses to the possibilities for equity specifically for First Nations peoples. "Selected University Experiences: A Preliminary Discussion of Equity Initiatives for Aboriginal Peoples" uses traditional techniques of Aboriginal pedagogy to examine the marginalization of Native students and of Native Studies programs in the university. To "speak softly about equity" from within the discourses of Aboriginal epistemology, she tells her own story: her decision to leave the teaching of Law for Native Studies, her analysis of the problems of Native Studies as defined and practiced and her discussion of the ongoing relationship of paternalism and colonialism which dominates the experience of Aboriginal students.

The discussion of Native Studies in Patricia Monture-Angus's article forms a bridge to the second section of the anthology, Re-Loading the Canon. The challenge to the patriarchal Eurocentrism of the traditional academic canon has been a cornerstone of equity theory. Central to this challenge has been the founding of new, often interdisciplinary programs of study which not only interrogate the scholarly canon and its disciplinary methodologies but also develop new knowledges and new objects of study. Twenty-five years ago in North America, Women's Studies programs struggled to be born, and then struggled to grow, and then struggled to survive against a widespread institutional and media backlash, and then, quietly, deliberately and forcefully began to build. Now there are Women's Studies and Gender Studies programs at most of the respected universities in North America, and graduate programs, research institutes and canonical and methodological/disciplinary debates are beginning to emerge. Women's Studies in many ways provides a model for the debates about institutionalization of special topics—the spaces posited by and through identity—as a strategy for achieving equity.

From a background in feminist scholarship, Jodi Jensen and Erica Meiners examine curricular strategies to address equity and diversity within the natural sciences and medicine in "Making Que(e)ried Bodies? The Politics and

Practices of Special Topics." Their discussion emphasizes two central points: the necessity of rethinking inter-intra disciplinary coalition work, and the necessity of theory as inseparable from practice. The politics of special topics are queried in light of their flourishing in the U.S. during the era of Reagan and Bush and in Britain under Thatcher. While special topics achieve the creation of additional academic and intellectual space, they also may serve to contain political challenges within disciplines and allow institutions to respond to the consumer demands of students without introducing fundamental changes. They may well also assist in creating the illusion of equal access and proportionate representation of minorities.

"Institutionalizing Postcolonial Studies" is the topic of Kofi Asare's paper, in which he addresses one of the new kids on the block. Although in the United States Black Studies and African-American Studies have been established for some time, in Canada Postcolonial Studies and Queer or Sexual Diversity Studies are the most recent of the new identity-based fields to seek legitimation in the academy. Unlike Women's Studies in its founding stages, however, Postcolonial Studies has a significant and well-developed body of scholarship to draw upon, as it has been built on the foundations of the feminist, psychoanalytic, poststructuralist, commonwealth literary studies and other new interdisciplinary fields of the past two decades. Thus, Asare points out, Postcolonial Studies enters the field at a full gallop: "the debate around postcolonialism as an oppositional practice is being staged as a contest of theories." Asare briefly summarizes and critiques the positions of Edward Said, Gayatri Spivak, and Homi Bhabha, and unapologetically claims Postcolonial Studies as an act of recuperation. Although Postcolonial Studies must be posited as an ongoing and active negotiation with its own protocols of engagement, Asare cautions (quoting Spivak) that "knowledge and thinking are halfway houses...and that they are judged when they are set to work."

The last two papers in this section return to Women's Studies and Gender Studies not as a model for the re-loading of the canon, but in the fledgling moments of institutionalization in other parts of the world. University of Kharkhov scholar Irina Zherebkina brings new light to the question of equality/equity, as these terms were foundational for communist discourse. Now, in post-Soviet Ukraine, a variation of utopian social space is being developed, in which a new ideology of social inequality appears to be the guarantor of happiness. "Women's Studies in Post-Soviet Totalitarianism: Between Institutionalization and Realpolitics" outlines the current contours of feminism, women's position in the state and in the academy, and the official political discourses concerning women in the new Ukrainian state of national independence. Zherebkina draws on the experience of North American Women's Studies in comparison with the traditional Ukrainian women's movement: "Ukrainian women truly have grounds to fear that western feminism will remain a hegemonic modern women's discourse in publishing, mass-media, education and the economy, and that this type of feminism cannot be adopted by women who live under different social conditions." Moreover, the fractured oppositional women's movement has lost its ground in these reinvented nations. Multiple contradictions are emerging. Under the socialist regime, feminists had a specific utopian sphere of privacy, created to elude Party control, that made possible a very particular kind of agency and enjoyment that does not exist in democratic society. Feminists in these nations seek to return to that privileged space by developing women's studies programs in universities. In Russia, the field of Women's Studies and Gender Studies is experiencing rapid development. Chairs of "feminology" are actively forming. However, the chairs emphasize that they are not connected with western feminism, but rather with establishing "the high role and predestination of women," in which the maternal nation-building function is the top priority. The very notions of women's rights have lost their established meaning since communism collapsed, and have been replaced by new state policies regarding racism and social inequality. Zherebkina notes that, unaware of these contradictions, western feminists optimistically imagine that the collapse of communism confirms the political and theoretical project of feminism and women's studies. Thus the challenges of "re-loading the canon" are extremely vexed for myriad reasons; such a doxalogical strategy is doomed to be "performative and simulative" in the post-Soviet reality.

Hildegard Maria Nickel faces somewhat different ideological and scholarly questions in East Germany since the fall of the Berlin wall in 1989. Universities in Berlin boast thirteen chairs in Women's Studies or Gender Research, a significant number of research professorships in the field and women on the teaching staff, commensurate numbers of graduate students, and at Humboldt University-Berlin, a Centre for Interdisciplinary Research dedicated to women's studies and gender research. With Zherebkina, Nickel sees nothing to be gained from looking back with nostalgia to the academic system under socialism. She dismisses past research on women as "collaborat[ing] in the creation of myths about the successful advance of equal rights...[and] in the atrophy of women's consciousness and public desensitization to the gender question." The current situation, after reunification and restructuring, is hardly better despite established fields and numbers of professorships to the contrary. Nickel's dissatisfaction is evident:

> I can gloss over the irritating interplay of cooperation and competition which this unequal constellation entails, and over the mechanisms of specific exclusion or inclusion in the framework of informal relationships. I shall concentrate instead on 'institutional resistance' to [gender research] which is regarded as ridden with conflict, which arouses uncomfortable feelings, and which places stones in the path of what Merton calls 'sociological euphemism'. Sociology's 'institutional resistance' to the gender theme is implemented not only by means of isolation and marginalization, but also by means of delegation and cordoned-off enclaves.

Nevertheless, Nickel manages to close with a hopeful note as she looks forward to the establishment of the first degree in Gender Studies (as opposed to special themes within other disciplines) in Germany. And in that context, the discussion about women's and gender research and the development of appropriate disciplinary theory can continue.

The section on Pedagogy takes up issues related to special topics curricula and teaching and identity-based strategies for servicing diverse student bodies. Some of the fundamental notions of equitable pedagogy are researched, reconsidered, re-evaluated and retheorized here.

Theoretical dimensions of chilly climate issues are encountered and explicated in Terry Provost's meta-linguistic "The (Un)Specified We: (Re)Creating (Di)Visions Through Words." With philosophical and linguistic tools, Provost offers a personal, theoretical, and scholarly examination of the ramifications of the use of personal pronouns in the classroom. Provost's voice is equally at ease with affective expression ("Absorbing and interpreting these terms has chased me into different emotional realms—anger, fatigue, anxiety, resignation, and finally resistance") and with disciplinary terminology ("Is there really an inclusiveness experienced with the utterance of these words? Or do they act as linguistic agents that result in excluding and recolonizing the marginalized subject?"). Her text is scarred with cleavages, emphatic slashes and parentheses which suggest the multiple angles of ambiguity and allegory contained in "ordinary" as well as formal language. Her (re)definition of the chilly climate reflects "the (im)palpability of discourse relations, namely that of their (in)visible implicit/explicit occasioning of power and subjugation, which creates ranks by sieving out subject from non-subject." Particularly in classroom settings, "where academic discourse ideology is kinetic, intense and peaking," Provost sees discourse involving the personal pronouns we, us and ours as "an ongoing obstacle in basic communication and in academic interlocution." Through classroom utterances, such "discourse rituals" become reified and progress as follows: "professors lecture; students listen, wait, interiorize theory, internalize vocabulary, debate intrasubjectively, and then respond.... In this light, the use of these terms in academic contexts is perpetuated partly by a lack of critique concerning their ethnocentric referencing to the speaking subject, partly by subliminal persuasion and militant conditioning, and partly by the facility in lingually surrendering and conforming to the expressions used by the majority."

From the other side of the pedagogical dyad, Jamie-Lynn Magnusson studies the potential for resistance to special topics curricula and teaching through the process of student evaluation. Although the frequency with which university professors who 'teach against the grain" endure stress in their academic environment as a result of student hostility to course material has been explored quite extensively in critical pedagogy literature, the scholarship on student evaluation of teaching has not dealt with this topic. In "The Evaluation of University Teaching: Exploring the Question of Resistance," Magnusson argues that current methods of evaluating university teaching have evolved within a positivist psychometric paradigm that supports conventional pedagogical practice, and further, that it reproduces these institutionalized practices. Effective teaching comes to be defined in terms of structural categories that are ostensibly empirically grounded and validated. This means that "the technical discourse of psychometrics, situated as it in within a positivist framework, is closed off from a scholarly examination of these definitions of effectiveness as socially constructed and institutionally mediated categories. Similarly, there is no scholarly examination of evaluation as a social practice within academic organizational culture, with meanings that are constituted socially and politically." It is significant that definitions of excellence have become institutionalized within Eurocentric patriarchal academic cultures and have the effect of regulating those elements of education: "they are discursive practices...that legitimate certain conceptual practices and delegitimate other conceptual practices. In order to address the question of equity in graduate education, then, one must understand how our evaluation practices tend to delegitimate precisely those conceptual practices grounded in the epistemological frames of groups that have been marginalized or excluded within the academy."

In "'I Never Really Thought About It': Master/Apprentice as Pedagogy in Music" and in "Be Like Who? On Race, Role Models and Difference in Higher Education," Roberta Lamb and Warren Crichlow respectively take on another of the foundational theories of equity, the effectivity of mentoring and role modeling for students as a means of achieving equity in education, professions, and business.

Music education in the classical western tradition has employed mentoring/ apprenticeship as standard educational practice for hundreds of years not only in universities but in choir schools, convents or monasteries, and royal courts. Yet, says Lamb, despite a sizable percentage of women professors and students at all degree levels, "the music discipline remains a male-dominated and Eurocentric field." There are still only a handful of symphony conductors, music directors, recording company executives, featured soloists and so forth who are not male, white, able-bodied, straight or closeted. Such disadvantages of mentoring instigated Lamb's study of mentoring as an equity strategy, particularly in relation to undoing patriarchal relations. Using a qualitative sociological methodology, Lamb collected and analyzed anecdotal data from female and male students and professors at the graduate level in music education. Categories of analysis include definitions of mentorship, self esteem, "my way or the highway" instructional methods, sexuality and harassment, institutional hierarchy, and alternative configurations of the mentor/ apprentice relationship. The first study of its kind in the field, Lamb argues that we may be able to learn from the mentoring tradition in music in order to avoid a similar model for other areas of higher education and begin the examination of this embedded practice.

In the final essay of this collection, Warren Crichlow brings a critical perspective to such "glib responses to equity" as the institutionalization of cultural diversity programs, affirmative action, and multicultural curricula, and their narrow educational prescription of real or imagined role models. "While critical academic theorizing has challenged the essential unity of race, class, and gender, bureaucratic equity achievement in the university tacitly requires 'positive images' of success within these same 'naturally' binding categories. Despite recognition that identities are partial and contradictory, 'role models' are politically constituted along racial, gender and other socially and constructed lines of difference." In a dramatic refiguring of the notion of mentorship, Crichlow examines narratives of mentorship, emphasizing the "slippery contradictions of model making and model taking." The analysis of Hilton Als' memoirs opens possibilities "beyond reflexive politics of socially-inscribed identity." Contrary to the popular role model ideal of an image of achievement and socialization, Crichlow posits a mutable view of the role model process in which passion, identification, desire and love are vital categories. "Als' depictions render role models who are enigmatic, difficult, and lamentable but who nevertheless remain complexly influential through the instabilities and tragic contradictions of their identities." Crichlow suggests, therefore, that mimesis in role modeling also works through ambivalence, and that neither gender, race, nor other stable constructions of social difference can be necessary categories of role model choices: "conceptualizing radical role modeling requires an engagement with the complex ways individuals achieve such relationships," and specifically with the conscious and unconscious functioning of "self-fashioning desire." I have chosen to end this volume with Crichlow's article because of his intriguing choice of texts, his passionate and thoughtful consideration of their nuances and complexities, the scholarly and theoretical perspicacity of his argument, and the elegant satisfactions of his optimistic conclusion.

References

Carby, Hazel V. "The Multicultural Wars." *Black Popular Culture.* Ed. Gina Dent. Seattle: Bay Press, 1992. 187-199.

Mills, Nicolaus. "The Endless Autumn." *The Nation.* Apr. 16, 1990: 529-531; quoted in Carby, 191.

Readings, Bill. *The University in Ruins.* Cambridge: Harvard University Press, 1996.

1.

Equity

Another University, Now
A Practical Proposal for a New Foundation of the University

William Haver

The university, Bill Readings has recently argued, lies in ruins. Or, to follow his argument a bit more precisely, what has been ruined is a certain amalgam of commonplace assumptions about the meaning, purpose, and intellectual ground of the university in its European and North American contexts. No longer is it possible simply to assume that the university is sustained by and has its relation to reason; nor is it any longer possible to assume that the work of the university is to bring our victims to the realization of a mature cultural and national identity. And this because the university has come not merely to resemble, but to be in fact, a transnational corporation consecrated to sustaining and reproducing the metamorphoses of an inescapable postindustrial capitalism. If we are to think and teach without giving in to the seductions of either apocalyptic fantasy or nostalgia for the lost plenitude of what once the university was said to be, we must think not only about, but within, the "university in ruins"; we must thereby recognize that a new foundation of the university will have transpired only in playing out the endgame of the old rather than in a revolutionary apocalyptic conflagration. The situation is complex; I will unavoidably be schematic and reductive in my remarks. I simply want to draw attention to a few of the many aspects of the corporatization of the university I think germane to our discussions; then to take up what I see to be possibilities immanent in what I will nickname the insistence of the social; and finally to argue that a serious, existential engagement with the essential difficulty of thinking is the most practical—by which

I mean most revolutionary—of proposals.

Five aspects of the current situation seem to me to have effects simultaneously in the institutional register as well as for our substantive intellectual work. (1) As has been frequently observed, traditional hierarchies of academic rank and privilege are precipitously being reconfigured as a two-tiered system comprised of relatively few very highly paid stars on the one hand, and a large group, an academic underclass in fact, comprised of overworked and poorly paid adjuncts, graduate teaching assistants, lecturers, and untenured faculty with little chance for institutional advancement or the time to see their intellectual projects through to a rigorous and consequent conclusion. (2) Concomitantly, we are caught up in an omnivorous process of the bureaucratization of time, and of intellectual work itself. The administrative and organizational demands imposed on all of us in one way or another are so extraordinary and exhaustive that there is almost no time left for reading and thinking; thus, thought is subsumed within production. At the same time, precisely in the vague appeal to "interdisciplinarity," disciplinary boundaries become ever more sclerotic, producing intellectual technicians devoted to the bureaucratic service of the concept. Thought is thus reduced to the production of an always already commodified knowledge. As Readings argues (21–43), an endless invocation of a necessarily unspecified "excellence" obviates any substantive consideration of value. Increasingly, for example, tenure committees refuse to take up the question of whether the candidate has produced persuasive arguments (or, indeed, produced an argument at all). (3) Again, as Readings argues (89-118), the university-as-transnational-corporation is resolutely impervious to critiques of transnational capital or the university itself from cultural studies and/or the Marxist-inflected Left. And indeed, some of the most astute and articulate critics of such formations are among the best-selling commodities on offer in the academic marketplace. Institutions have always been incapable of self-reflection of course; but rarely have they devoured their most cogent critics with such appetite and apparent lack of indigestion. This means that the very category of the "enemy," without which classical political thought and classically-conceived politics are literally unthinkable, becomes entirely evacuated of any substance. To recognize this necessarily leads us to ask whether the university and the postindustrial, transnational capitalism of which it is a part, is in fact opposable. What would it take to make the university choke on its own bile? (4) For the first time in the post-Second World War period in North America, graduate students in the social sciences and humanities, certainly at public institutions and increasingly at prestigious private universities, cannot take the Ph.D. to be a virtual guarantee of academic employment. In an effort to eliminate the competition, major private graduate programs, in the U.S. at least, have begun to argue that graduate education become their private preserve and that public schools restrict themselves to undergraduate programs. But if this augers the triumph of the logic of the late capitalist corporation, it also bespeaks what might be an opportunity. Graduate programs in the period of virtually full academic employment for Ph.Ds became increasingly geared toward the production of an intellectual technocracy, populated by scholars expert in the protocols of the various putatively discrete disciplines. To get a job, the rationale has been, you must devote all your time and intellectual energy to the acquisition and deployment of disciplinary expertise; in return, the largely tacit but sometimes explicit argument has gone, you will get a job. That promise has collapsed, and with it the logic that has sustained institutional disciplinarity as such.[1]

But if the sometimes mindless mastery of disciplinary skills no longer guarantees employment, by the same token students might now be granted the freedom to undertake a labour of thought that is something other than the production of certified knowledges. I will return to this. (5) All of this, and much else of course, has been determined by, but also in turn has determined, the course of the university-as-transnational corporation. These mutual determinations are in turn part of a culture of political despair. The Left laments the disarray of the old New Left, liberals are lost in amazement at the Teflon society, the Right rails against an always unspecified "postmodernity": whatever happens, nothing happens, so to speak. Perhaps as a result, we are increasingly confronted with what Wendy Brown has recently characterized as a politics of resentment.[2] Hence the recent decision among California voters that difference itself is the enemy; hence the necessity for the right continually to reposition itself as victim; hence the institutional, intellectual, and political forgetting of the AIDS pandemic; hence, above all, the fact that what currently passes for politics in effect occludes the political as such. The most pressing demand for those who work toward a future that would be something other than a continuation of the present is to make the political appear.

The political appears only in and as what I refer to under the nickname of the "insistence of the social." Perhaps, in recent years, there has been something very like a new thought of the social, one that is essentially and necessarily irreducible to a concept of society such as would be an adequate epistemological object of and for the human and social sciences. This thought of the social has been articulated in works of political theory, in literary and philosophical texts, in film and video, in performance art, in work less readily classifiable under commonplace rubrics, as well as in concrete investigations by few social scientists. Some 12 years ago, Ernesto Laclau and Chantal Mouffe sought to theorize sociality as such as a specific resistance to objectifications of society construed according to the normative coordinates of subjectivity, identity, and community, coordinates that in their analysis in fact "suture" or "fix" the social, reducing it to an epistemological objectivity. In a not entirely dissimilar vein, Antonio Negri, in collaboration with Felix Guattari and subsequently with Michael Hardt, has sought to think, under the rubric of "communism," a sociality that is always also something other than its objectivity—a thought not without its antecedents in Marx himself (see Lefort; LaCapra; Mehlman). Thereby, Negri has sought to think a "dionysian labour" as the praxis of a poiesis that necessarily exceeds that productive poiesis most often denominated as culture by those working in the human and social sciences. If, as Jean-François Lyotard reminds us, the work of the domus (or of "culture") in all of its discrete labours is nevertheless the constitution of the community of the cultural domus itself, then a supplementary or "dionysian" poiesis will in fact be an "unworking" that reveals the putatively adequate self-identity and auto-reproduction of the cultural domus to be a nostalgic fantasy (Lyotard). This unworking is an infinite subtraction, a movement toward a radical existential destitution, toward the entropic indifference of empirical singularities bereft of the consolations of culture.

Among literary thinkers and philosophers, Maurice Blanchot sought to think that destitution that would be the existential condition of possibility for a being-in-common, or "community," that would be strictly speaking "unavowable"; similarly, Jean-Luc Nancy has sought to think what is at stake in an "inoperable" or "unworked" (*désoeuvrée*) community, a thought of community as something other than the effect of cultural production and determination, something other than the reproduction of what counts for the social and human sciences as culture (see Blanchot; Nancy) Here is a thought of an insupportable sociality, a being-in-common of the destitute grounded in no ontology, an anarchic community. And, finally, in the course of a meditation on community as the being-in-common of singularities irreducible to concepts of the individual or of subjective identity, Giorgio Agamben has given political point to such reflections when he notes, apropos of the events of the spring of 1989 at Tiananmen:

What the State cannot tolerate in any way, however, is that the singularities form a community without affirming an identity, that humans co-belong without any representable condition of belonging.... Wherever these singularities peacefully demonstrate their being in common there will be a Tiananmen, and, sooner or later, the tanks will appear. (86–87)

Here, then, we have a thought, at once more and less than a concept, of what is at stake for a thought of the heteroclite social.

What is being thought in Laclau and Mouffe, Negri, Lyotard, Blanchot, Nancy, and Agamben—as well as in work by Judith Butler, Michael Hardt, Sue Golding, Wendy Brown, among many others—in their various and discrete (indeed, often contradictory) articulations, is a thought of the social as the limit of what the social and human sciences (as such) can think, a thought of that which the social and human sciences must refuse in order to secure what has always figured as their epistemological ground. This thought of the social is not merely an event in the history of philosophical reflection or the investigations of the social and human sciences. If the thought of the social struggles toward theoretical and philosophical articulation, it is because it is first of all articulated in the existential comportments, practices, acts and arts of those who are occluded from the epistemological purview of the social and human sciences; in the lives of those whose being is situated in interstices of the "city" in the lives of the homeless, the prostitute, the injecting drug user, the queer, the person living with AIDS, the Lumpenproletariat, for example. Here, the "new" thought of the social reanimates a venerable thematics indeed, for here, as a matter of an irrecusable existential exigency, we are charged with a reflection on the possibility of founding our being-in-common. What is given to us to think is the limit as that site, locatable according to no determinate coordinates, where sociality, as the very possibility of relation, happens. And this reflection is imperative, in the strongest sense of the term, unavoidable. For what is given to us to think in this, the time of AIDS, are not simply the exigencies with which our existentiality confronts us, but that exigency which is the existential in its unbearable historicity.

I have tried to emphasize that the social is something quite other than the generality of its concept; that the social does not exist, it *happens*; that it is the very happening of relationality altogether. And it is as nothing other than its happening that it insists, that it interrupts our epistemological and political business as usual, precipitating an irrecusable stammering in the discourse of our variously constituted knowledges. Allow me to offer a concrete example of this insistence, one that I think must necessarily disturb whatever common-place assumptions we may have about the institution of the university and the disciplines that inhabit it.

I administer one of the smallest academic programs on record, the Asian and Asian American Studies Program at Binghamton University. In other words, however small the program, and however limited my authority, I am, or at least am supposed to be, a cop, responsible for maintaining the disciplinarity of a discipline. It is both as a teacher and as a cop, then, that I have had the very good luck to work with a remarkable group of students. When these students are compelled to identify themselves in the current academic rituals of what Deborah Britzman calls "identities on parade," a procedure they very much resist, they tend to refer to themselves as part of the "1.5 generation." In such situations, they tend immediately to emphasize the extremely problematic aspects of that designation. They use it, they tell me, precisely because in at least certain situations, it renders problematic naive assumptions of ethnic and cultural identity. Born in Korea under widely various economic circumstances, they typically came to the U.S., in some cases circuitously, in their early teens. Their position in the U.S. tends to be extraordinarily precarious; indeed, at least two of this group are in the country quite illegally, and thus have no existence whatsoever with respect to the government under which they have lived for as long as ten years. In any case, they tell me that in their usages of the term "1.5 generation" they intend to designate a certain "betweenness," a certain linguis-tic and cultural homelessness. Neither Asian, American, nor Asian American, but not simply *not* Asian, American, or Asian American: neither Asian nor not Asian, neither American nor not American, neither Asian American nor not Asian American, they find all of our *institutional* configurations of identity to be worse than merely inadequate to designate the existence, the "betweenness," that they have no choice but to live. Their situation cannot be construed as that of a classical cosmopolitanism, as the situation of those who, by virtue of a certain universality, are at home everywhere, cosmopolitans whose passports would presumptively authorize their transcendental subjectivity. It would be more nearly accurate to say they are "at home" nowhere than everywhere. Neither, however, can their situation be romanticized as a glorious apotheosis of non-identity; they are not the free spirits of prepredicative being. As the most practical of considerations, in fact, the problem is a surfeit, a congestion, of identities: both Asian and not Asian, both American and not American, both Asian American and not Asian American. Nor, finally, can their current situation be considered to be permanent, for to do so would be to perpetuate an unbearable structure of dependency, making of them forever refugees, eternally depending on the kindness of strangers. All this being said, I would like to focus on one aspect of the practical situation in which they find themselves, an aspect I think has institutional, epistemological, and ontological consequences.

These students are smart, no question about it; they are among the most intelligent people I have ever encountered. And they work hard; we did not spend more than one semester working together in a reading group that met on Friday nights for me not to know that. But quite consistently their grades are less than impressive, and they have not been at all successful in their graduate school applications. And all this because they are said to speak and write what is called "bad English." Now, of course, for over 30 years—at the very least— we have had innumerable astute analyses of what is at stake in the very distinction between "good" and "bad" English; we know something of the profoundly nostalgic, indeed reactionary, culturalism that in attempting to preserve the English language in the clean and proper integrity of its correct usages would preserve a certain construction of Anglo-American culture in its privilege, and thereby preserve language and thought itself from that of which it supposedly speaks. What I am trying to suggest is that in the very "badness" of the "bad English" of the so-called 1.5 generation, something essentially other than mere deviance from linguistic and cultural norms is at stake: what is at stake is the very possibility of speech and thought, the question of whether what is called communication is at all possible, the question of whether language as such is both the condition of possibility for thinking and at the same time the occlusion of the very movement of thought. It is this possibility that every invocation of "good English" cannot bear to think, for such questions expose the essential fragility, the utter contingency, of anything that might be taken to be the social bond. What if the misuse and stumbling that is the relation, non-relation, relation of non-relation, of these students to what is called the English language is something radically other than mere ineptitude? What if what is at stake in their occasional linguistic stammering and occasionally clumsy cultural comportments is something that our every invocation of language and culture serves to occlude: the fact of our non-transcendence, our non-neutrality, the fact that the ontological is the political?

In discussing these and related questions, I have asked these students how they speak to each other when they are not also speaking to me, given that they had told me they feel entirely at home neither in what is called Korean nor in what is called English. And they speak of speaking in something they call

Konglish. Konglish, they tell me, is both Korean and English, neither Korean nor English, neither the same nor different than an amalgam of Korean and English. Konglish has vocabularies, of course, but they are indeterminate; one can use a Korean word, or an English word, or construct a word out of elements of both, but in any case no protocol regulates the choice. It will never be possible, that is to say, to stabilize the incessant metamorphoses of Konglish vocabularies in a dictionary. In this respect, then, to speak Konglish is to speak the lexical instability of language. So too with syntax and grammar generally. It is not that Konglish is without syntax and grammar, without rules. Rather, those rules both pre-exist specific usages, and they exist nowhere but in their usages, and in that sense do not precede their enactments. In this sense, the grammars and syntactic structures cannot be codified: we will never be able to offer Konglish 101, for Konglish as such is a resistance to institutionalization. It is not that there are no rules in Konglish or its allotropes of cultural comportment, but that the rules have to be invented in each and every usage (as Wittgenstein by the way, noted of the rule in general).[3] And because specific rules—vocabularies, syntactic structures, grammars, cultural comportments— are necessarily incessantly reinvented, the very fact of the rule must be reinvented in every reinvention of the rules. In other words, the very possibility of language, culture, communication, and community, the very possibility of sociality, can never be taken for granted; such possibilities exist only in the act of will that is the coming into being of its very possibility. In this sense, language, culture, and sociality exist only in the act of institution, not in the fossilized forms of the institutions left in their wake.

But, of course, things are rather more complicated than this, because all this can only happen with respect to the always already there of institutions and structures. Konglish, and everything involved therein, is both an absolute instauration *ex nihilo* and the impossibility of creation *ex nihilo*. The *place* of Konglish, is the place of *signifiance*, at once the possibility and impossibility of signification, the accomplishment and unaccomplishment of communication, the making and unmaking of sense. This is the place of an ontological stammering, where to speak is always to speak of the impossibility of speaking, a communication of the impossibility of communication. It is this pure interruption that is nothing other than the very movement of thinking. What we call existence is nothing but this pure interruption. These students know very well that subjectivity is no chimera, but they know equally well that subjectivity exists only in and as its unaccomplishment. There is that which, as a matter of inexorable necessity, calls subjects and subjectivity into being, but it is also that which interrupts the consummation of the subject in subjectivity.

What is given to us to think here under the entirely insufficient and misleading rubric of the "1.5 generation," as pure interruption, confounds not only the enabling categories of the discrete disciplines, but also the epistemological work of category maintenance that sustains disciplinarity *per se*—the epistemological police work of the disciplines altogether. It is not most seriously a matter, than it seems to me, of providing, or even of inventing, a disciplinary home for the "1.5 generation," Asian American studies, ethnic studies, queer studies, women's studies, or cultural studies altogether. To do so would be complicit with the institutional betrayal of the animating impulse and intellectual substance of much of the work that goes on under, but always also in spite of, such rubrics.

In their institutionalization, cultural studies become nothing but the bureaucratic expression of the crudest forms of what is called "identity politics." Substantively, that is to say intellectually, existentially, and politically, much of the work that is now categorized as cultural studies has always taken its enabling categories to be questions rather than answers. Race, ethnicity, gender, class, sexuality, language, culture: such categories have not been merely self-evident for those who have been thinking for many years about the questions of cultural studies. After all, it is not those working in cultural studies who have brought us the notion of identity politics; we have the reactionary backlash against the work of cultural studies to thank for that. But in any case, it is in their institutionalization, in their bureaucratic expression, that the work of cultural studies is reduced to answers rather than its questions. For "cultural studies" are the institutional index of the insistence of the social, construed as the infinite proliferation of a difference that can never be reduced to its concept. And it is precisely in that reduction that the questions of cultural studies have become categories, categories that are entirely consonant with the managerial techniques and style of the late capitalist transnational corporation that calls itself the University.

Apparently we, or at least those of us who are interested in pursuing the various questions of cultural studies, are caught in a contradiction. We are persuaded of the intellectual and political importance and practical necessity of providing some institutional shelter where it might be possible to pursue such questions. And yet the very institutionalization that would provide shelter for such a questioning, that would enable the various and often discrete inquiries of cultural studies, not only results, as we know very well, in the creation of intellectual and political ghettos, but also (and thereby) constitutes a specifically bureaucratic resolution of essentially disturbing epistemological and existential questions; and this precisely in the category maintenance of disciplinarity altogether. I have no answer to this dilemma. In the most immediate practical terms, it seems to me that the necessary negotiations are historically specific to such an extent that there can be no general program that would effectively address the practical considerations involved. In other words, any negotiations that would acknowledge the insistence of heteroclite sociality are necessarily contingent. And the fact of that contingency means that the relations in question, relations between the institution as such and the heteroclite sociality that insists—and thereby interrupts institutionality as such—are relations of power, indeed, the fact of relationality as power. Power is relationality, the ontological is the political.

Let me be blunt. I do not think there has been, is, or can ever be, an equitable institution. Institutions do not, cannot, by virtue of their very institutionality, be equitable, if by equity we mean a certain symmetry, a certain equality, and therefore a certain outside of power. And this because the institution of institutionality—that is, the act of foundation that establishes the institution as such—is always the instauration of a certain power relation that it is the task of the institution as such to reproduce.[4] If equity means equality, the absence of power, then the university, as both political and epistemological construct, is necessarily and essentially the betrayal of its inaugural impulse; and this includes every call for another university, a new act of foundation. I would rather say that what is at stake in the demand for equity, for a new foundation, is the demand, not to dream of an outside of power, that would exist within and be protected by the power of the institution (as the liberal state writ small), but to reveal the contingency of power, to disrupt the presumptive connaturality of the current situation: in short, to make power negotiable. And this is possible, it seems to me, only in the practical revelation of the essential instability of being altogether, the exposure in practice of being as instability, as non-transcendence, as non-neutrality.

This possibility has been pursued in work by Gerard Granel and Christopher Fynsk, who have argued that guerrilla tactics constitute the only possible strategy for a new foundation of the university in the current situation; by Peggy Kamuf, who argues that what is called "literature" is the site at which the institution of the university must confront that which it has excluded in its act of foundation; by Joan Scott in considering the contradictory possibilities of gender studies at a time when the legal protection that enabled such inquiries is being eroded; and by Bill Readings in his attempt to rethink the university as a "community of dissensus" (see Fynsk; Kamuf; Readings). It might be objected that such proposals are too abstract when it is a matter of what to say or what to do when we walk into the classroom; but Deborah Britzman has suggested three pedagogical "methods," three ways of reading: "the study of limits, the study of ignorance, and the study of reading practices." These might provoke further reflections upon the thoroughly practical task of "thinking the unthought of education."[5]

Finally, it might be further objected that such projects which take up as the most serious of questions the very possibility of thought are at once too utopian, insofar as they disrupt the constraints of professionalization to which contemporary graduate education is consecrated, and thus have no chance for practical implementation; and at the same time that such projects are not utopian enough, that they fail to project a politics that would, on the authority of a better understanding and explanation of the world, work to create a better, more equitable world. But it is necessary in the first instance to acknowledge that graduate education must now be something other than mere professionalization if it is to be germane to the intellectual lives and existential difficulties of any except those few who will in fact have the privilege of an academic career. It is only a fundamental questioning that can engage the passion of those for whom the university as currently constituted is nothing but yet one more exclusion. In the second instance, I think the only possibility for a seriously political engagement lies in the explicit refusal to transcend the limits of our histories; the only possibility for a future that might be attentive to the demands for justice and freedom lies in a discipline, irreducible to disciplinarity, of refusing to conceive of that future as a reproduction of the present, in the practical realization that what currently passes for politics serves only to obscure the political. We belong, as Marx said long ago, to the prehistory of the political; our task is to actualize the political as such.

[1] I am aware, of course, that disciplines are constituted according to epistemological protocols that are not in the first instance institutional. But I would argue that what has happened in recent years is that epistemology has given way to institutionality, that the various disciplines of the social and human sciences have long since acknowledged their essential epistemological ambiguities, but are nonetheless sustained in their autonomy by nothing except the habit of institutionality.

[2] I have learned much in this respect from Wendy Brown, "Toward a Genealogy

of Contemporary Political Moralism" (forthcoming). See also her *States of Injury: Power and Freedom in Late Modernity.*

[3] For a germane reading of Wittgenstein on the rule, see Sue Golding, "Sexual Manners" in Victoria Harwood, D. Oswell, K. Parkinson, and A. Ward, eds., *Pleasure Principles: Politics, Sexuality and Ethics* (London: Routledge, 1993), 80-89.

[4] Following certain indications of Jacques Derrida's texts, Peggy Kamuf has explored this question with regard to the university and its disciplines in *The Division of Literature: Or the University in Deconstruction* (41–55 and 133–161).

[5] See Deborah P. Britzman (1995). I have attempted a reading of this essay in "Queer Research: How to Practice Invention to the Brink of Intelligibility." Britzman's *Lost Subjects, Contested Objects: Towards a Psychoanalytic Inquiry of Learning* is more than pertinent to these questions.

This essay was written whilst a member of the School of Social Science at the Institute for Advanced Study in Princeton, New Jersey in 1996-97, supported by a fellowship from the National Endowment for the Humanities and a sabbatical leave from Binghamton University. I am grateful to the Institute for its hospitality.

References

Agamben, Giorgio. *The Coming Community.* Trans. Michael Hardt. Minneapolis: University of Minnesota Press, 1993.

Blanchot, Maurice. *The Unavowable Community.* Trans. Pierre Joris. Barrytown, NY: Station Hill Press, 1988.

Britzman, Deborah P. *Lost Subjects, Contested Objects: Towards a Psychoanalytic Inquiry of Learning.* Albany: State University of New York Press, 1998.

Britzman, Deborah P. "Is There a Queer Pedagogy? Or, Stop Reading Straight." *Educational Theory* 45.2 (Spring 1995): 151–165.

Brown, Wendy. "Toward a Genealogy of Contemporary Political Moralism." 1998.

Brown, Wendy. *States of Injury: Power and Freedom in Late Modernity* (Princeton: Princeton University Press, 1995).

Fynsk, Christopher. "But Suppose We Were to Take the Rectorial Address Seriously ... Gérard Granel's De l'université." *Graduate Faculty Philosophy Journal* 14.2–15.1 (1991): 335–362.

Golding, Sue. "Sexual Manners." *Pleasure Principles: Politics, Sexuality and Ethics.* Eds. Victoria Harwood, D. Oswell, K. Parkinson, and A. Ward.

London: Routledge, 1991. 80-89

Guattari, Felix, and Toni Negri. *Communists Like Us: New Spaces of Liberty, New Lines of Alliance.* Trans. Michael Ryan. New York: Semiotext[e], 1990.

Hardt, Michael, and Antonio Negri. *Labor of Dionysus: A Critique of State-Form.* Minneapolis: University of Minnesota Press, 1994.

Haver, William. "Queer Research: How to Practice Invention to the Brink of Intelligibility." *The Eight Technologies of Otherness.* Ed. Sue Golding. London: Routledge, 1997.

Kamuf, Peggy. *The Division of Literature: Or the University in Deconstruction.* Chicago: University of Chicago Press, 1997.

LaCapra, Dominick. "Reading Marx: The Case of The Eighteenth Brumaire." *Rethinking Intellectual History: Texts, Contexts, Language.* Ed. D. La Capra. Ithaca, NY: Cornell University Press, 1983. 268–290.

Laclau, Ernesto, and Chantal Mouffe. *Hegemony and Socialist Strategy: Toward a Radical Democratic Politics.* Trans. Winston Moore and Paul Cammack. London: Verso, 1985.

Lefort, Claude. "Marx: From One Vision of History to Another." Trans. Terry Kartel. *The Political Forms of Modern Society: Bureaucracy Democracy and Totalitarianism.* Ed. John B. Thompson. Cambridge, MA: MIT Press, 1986. 139-180.

Lyotard, Jean-François. *The Inhuman: Reflections on Time.* Trans. Geoffrey Bennington and Rachel Bowlby. Stanford: Stanford University Press, 1991.

Mehlman, Jeffrey. *Revolution and Repetition: Marx/Hugo/Balzac.* Berkeley: University of California Press, 1977.

Nancy, Jean-Luc. *The Inoperative Community.* Ed. Peter Connor. Trans. Peter Connor *et al.* Minneapolis: University of Minnesota Press, 1991.

Readings, Bill. *The University in Ruins.* Cambridge, MA: Harvard University Press, 1996.

Scott, Joan W. "Inaugural Lecture at the Center for Gender Studies." University of Chicago, 18 October 1996.

Educational Equity
"No Turning Back"

Juanita Westmoreland-Traoré

Today, more than ever, we need to return to basics when discussing equity. We seek equity to make this world a better place for all—not for some, but for all. If we are sincere in our quest for equity, we will work for it both within and beyond our borders. The struggle to advance meaningful concepts of equity and the programs that promote it must not be restricted to the narrow spheres that define our everyday lives. These themes are relevant around the world, and we must share ideas and experiences with others who share our common objectives.

Structural adjustment and its effects on equity

Many of us remained oblivious to the suffering created by structural adjustment programs administered in developing countries during the 1980s and 1990s. Today, we are undergoing similar structural adjustment here in Canada. We see the gap between rich and poor in our communities continue to widen as jobless economic recovery continues to erode the middle class. With ever-decreasing social safety nets, women as a group become more vulnerable and poor. They, along with members of other traditionally disadvantaged groups—Aboriginal peoples and racial minorities, people with disabilities, lesbians and gay men, and the working poor—are now experiencing hardened social attitudes by those whose position in society has been left intact.

Early in its initiative to bring major structural changes to the public and broader public sector, the Conservative Government of Ontario repealed the province's employment equity legislation.[1] By doing so it also eliminated the regulations that accompanied the legislation and dismantled the Commission that administered it, along with that Commission's policy guidelines, data base, and resources. The Government is presently restructuring its ministries, agencies, boards, and commissions. Unfortunately, it is precisely during periods of restructuring that equity protections are important and that the educational and monitoring functions of commissions and tribunals are most needed.

However, all is not lost. Some of the Employment Equity Commission's work has found its way into other legislation. For example, the Federal *Employment Equity Act*, adopted in 1995, incorporates the obligation for the employer "to make all reasonable efforts to implement its employment equity plan;"[2] and perhaps most importantly it calls for monitoring and enforcement by the Canadian Human Rights Commission.[3] In addition, other important Canadian laws which support equity principles still exist. Despite legislative setbacks such as we have experienced in Ontario with the repeal of the *Employment Equity Act*, our Constitution and "quasi-constitutional" laws remain in force. These, along with the jurisprudence flowing from them, support equity initiatives.

This paper will examine the existing support for equity initiatives. Secondly, it will assert that the shift in terminology from "affirmative action" or "employment equity" to "equal opportunity" is significant and reflects a fundamental change in the government's approach to these issues. Thirdly, it will be useful to review briefly the current status of the effort to remove historical and ongoing disadvantage experienced by equity-seeking groups within the university. Finally, this paper will highlight some of the tenets of inclusive teaching and learning environments.

The constitutional protection of equality

With the 1982 entrenchment of the *Canadian Charter of Rights and Freedoms*,[4] equity rights have become a central concern in Canadian society. The *Charter*, the supreme law in Canada, along with related case law, explicitly and consistently promotes the underlying principles of employment equity. Let us examine the key provisions of the *Charter* which offer substantial support for equity programs.

Section 15(1) guarantees "equality before and under the law and the right to equal protection and equal benefit of the law to every individual without discrimination, in particular, discrimination based on race, national or ethnic origin, colour, religion, sex, age, or mental or physical disability." This expanded definition of equality was drafted specifically to overcome weaknesses in the *Canadian Bill of Rights*, which by 1982 appeared to be nothing more than a hollow shell.

Section 15(2) recognizes the constitutionality of laws, programs, or activities that endeavour to ameliorate conditions for individuals or groups who are disadvantaged based on the grounds listed in section 15(1). In a recent decision, the Ontario Court of Appeal determined that section 15(2) is substantive law, and

> ... because special programs for the disadvantaged further the guarantee of equality, government action under section 15(2) should be *generously and liberally assessed*, consistent with the court's approach to the interpretation of the rights and freedoms in the rest of the *Charter*. (*Lovelace* v. *Ontario* (1997), 33 O.R. (3d) 735 at 754 (C.A.).) [emphasis added]

In the area of equality rights and affirmative action, more commonly called special programs, Canadian constitutional law differs fundamentally from American law. Section 15(2) is new law, unique to Canada. It was adopted following the recommendation of the Canadian Human Rights Commission and the Canadian Advisory Council on the Status of Women, to provide explicit constitutional authority for special programs.[5] To date, very few cases have been litigated under section 15(2).[6]

Section 1 of the *Charter*, however, can be raised by government to restrict section 15 guarantees by subjecting these protections "to such reasonable limits prescribed by law as can be demonstrably justified in a free and democratic society" (*Charter* s. 1). In applying section 1, the courts are called upon to define the basic values in Canadian society which can be invoked to restrict the equality rights guarantees. The application of section 1 in several recent cases has heightened public awareness of the role of the courts in defining prevailing Canadian standards.[7]

Despite arguments alleging reverse discrimination, Canadian courts have recognized affirmative action programs as valid, even before the *Charter*. In 1981, the Supreme Court of Canada considered the Athabaska Tribal Council's request that the Alberta Energy Resources Conservation Board impose affirmative action measures for Aboriginal workers as part of its approval of a tar sands plant. The Court held that such measures exceeded the power of the Board and for that reason could not be ordered, a minority of the judges expressed the opinion that an affirmative action program in itself would not constitute reverse discrimination. Considering the disinheritance of the Aboriginal people since the arrival of white colonial settlers in Athabaska, and level of poverty as well as the dramatic changes which would result from the projected petroleum development, affirmative action was not discriminatory. In the words of Mr. Justice Ritchie, writing for himself and three other members of the court,

> With all respect, I can see no reason why the measures proposed by the "affirmative action" programs for the betterment of the lot of the native peoples in the area in question should be construed as "discriminating against" other inhabitants. The purpose of the plan as I understand it is not to displace non-Indians from their employment, but rather to advance the lot of the Indians so that they may be in a competitive position to obtain employment without regard to the handicaps which their race has inherited.... I am of the opinion that the Court of Appeal was in error in holding that an affirmative action programme based on racial criteria would be in breach of the *Individual's Rights Protection Act*. (*Athabasca Tribal Council* v. *Amoco Canada Petroleum Co. Ltd.*, [1981] 1 S.C.R. 699 at 711)

Most human rights legislation, recognized by the courts as quasi-constitutional in nature,[8] also protects the right to implement "special programs" designed specifically to alleviate disadvantage.[9] Furthermore, human rights legislation is more general in its application than the *Charter*. Such legislation applies to discrimination in private interactions, for example in employment or in services such as education and housing, whereas the *Charter* applies only to legislation and to government action.

In the landmark human rights case, *Action Travail des Femmes* v. *Canadian National Railway Co.* (1987) 40 D.L.R. (4th) 193 (S.C.C.), the Supreme Court of Canada upheld an order by the Human Rights Tribunal which included measures as an appropriate remedy for systemic discrimination. Chief Justice Dickson concluded,

> To render future discrimination pointless, to destroy discriminatory

stereotyping and to create the required "critical mass" of target group participation in the workforce, it is essential to combat the effects of past systemic discrimination. In so doing, possibilities are created for the continuing amelioration of employment opportunities for the previously excluded group. The dominant purpose of employment equity programs is always to improve the situation of the target group in the future. (215)

This case illustrates the characteristic disadvantage faced by women and minorities in non-traditional employment. Ingrained negative attitudes and practices prevented the hiring and promotion of women at CN.[10] The Tribunal concluded this under-utilization of women was not "fortuitous," but the result of the recruitment, hiring, and promotion practices of the company. To end these discriminatory practices, the Tribunal ordered both permanent measures for "Neutralization" or barrier removal, and temporary positive measures to attract and hire women candidates into the non-traditional positions, thus creating a critical mass which would help to end the chilly climate and harassment of women in the workplace. Included in the Temporary Order were numerical hiring and composition measures to take effect after recall requirements had been fulfilled. Finally, the Commission established a reporting process for the company. Similar positive rulings from other jurisdictions have since followed.

The evolution of equality rights guarantees

In interpreting the *Charter*, the courts have adopted a large and liberal interpretation of equality rights, relating them to the alleviation of disadvantage and recognizing the need to consider the social context when deciding whether an equality right has been breached. Courts have repeatedly held that equality may mean treating people the same despite their differences or treating people differently because of their differences. These and other significant principles form a valuable body of law, upon which equality seekers can base their arguments in new cases that come before the courts (see generally Black and Smith).

Beginning with *Andrews* v. *The Law Society of B.C.* (1989), 56 D.L.R. (4th) 1 (S.C.C.), the courts have broadened the guarantees. Mr. Justice McIntyre rejects the theories of formal equality in favour of a substantive definition of equality. In his words, the "similarly situated test" is seriously deficient in that it excludes any consideration of the nature of the law. If it were applied literally, it could be used to justify the Nuremberg laws of Adolf Hitler.... Consideration must be given to the content of the law, to its purpose, and its impact upon those whom it excludes from its application. (13)

He explicitly recognizes that the reformulated definition of equality in the *Charter* "reflected the expanded concept of discrimination being developed under various *Human Rights Codes since* the enactment of the *Canadian Bill of Rights*" (14). Madame Justice Wilson adds,

[i]t can be anticipated that the discrete and insular minorities of tomorrow will include groups not recognized as such today. It is consistent with the constitutional status of section 15 that it be interpreted with sufficient flexibility to ensure the "unremitting protection" of equality rights in the years to come. (33)

While the protection of equity programs is constitutionally entrenched and the leading cases have given effective recognition of their validity, current decisions interpreting equality rights may indicate that after a period of judicial activism the courts have begun to retrench. This apprehension arises from the observation of the divided decisions of the courts on whether or not to recognize equality protection to same sex couples and from the renewed expression of judicial deference to the legislature. The study of the decisions on the rights of same sex couples reveals a new and troubling divergence of opinion on the requisite elements for proving a breach of equality rights.

The extent of Charter protection

While it is now well established that section 15 of the *Charter* prohibits discrimination on both enumerated and analogous grounds, two appeals recently heard by the Supreme Court of Canada raise the important issue of whether the *Charter* requires specific legislative protection of a protected group where a provincial legislature has explicitly refused to enact such legislation. In *Vriend* v. *Alberta* [1998] S.C.J. No. 29 Q.L. para. 50–64 the Supreme Court of Canada rejected the Alberta Court of Appeal's reasoning that governmental inaction was not subject to *Charter* scrutiny; the Supreme Court rendered a decision requiring the reading in of sexual orientation as a prohibited ground of discrimination in the *Individual's Rights Protection Act.*

Similarly, in *M.* v. *H.* (1997) 31 O.R. (3d) 417 (C.A.) the Ontario Court of Appeal held that a section of the *Family Law Act* of Ontario which defined spouse as a person of the opposite sex was unconstitutional because it discriminated against same sex couples. Madam Justice Charron cites a passage from the judgment of Mr. Justice Cory in the *Egan* decision, to the effect that,

> ... the legislation denies homosexual couples equal benefit of the law. The Act does this not on the basis of merit or need, but solely on the basis of sexual orientation. The definition of "spouse" as someone of the opposite sex reinforces the stereotype that homosexuals cannot and do not form lasting, caring, mutually supportive relationships with economic interdependence in the same manner as heterosexual couples. The appellants' relationship vividly demonstrates the error of that approach. The discriminatory impact can hardly be deemed to be trivial when the legislation reinforces prejudicial attitudes based on such faulty stereotypes. The effect of the impugned provision is clearly contrary to s. 15's aim of protecting human dignity, and therefore the distinction amounts to discrimination on the basis of sexual orientation. (444)

Recalling that the *Equality Rights Statute Law Amendment Act*, 1994 had been defeated on a free vote, Mr. Justice Finlayson, speaking for the minority, remarked that the appellant was asking the Court "to do specifically what the legi-slature refused to do" (424). Nevertheless, the majority held that the words, "two persons" should be read into the statute but suspended the effect of their decision for one year to allow the Legislature to fashion an appropriate and just remedy.

While awaiting the Supreme Court's response to the *M.* v. *H.* appeal, many are questioning whether the Court will distinguish the two cases by either seeing the first as a failure to legislate and the second as a legislative section which is discriminatory, or by reopening the question of judicial deference to the legislature. At the same time, the effective remedy sought by the appellants is identical: extending equal protection to same-sex couples. Besides the importance of the immediate issue, these appeals also directly raise the question of judicial deference to political will, an issue which has emerged more centrally in the renewed debate among justices concerning the relevant factors to be considered on a finding of discrimination and the sequencing of the consideration of relevancy criteria.

Increasing judicial deference

The re-emerging deference to parliamentary sovereignty both through the introduction of the relevancy criteria and the more restrained approach to limiting legislative or executive action under section 1 of the *Charter* is disquieting because it evokes the all too recent history of the *Canadian Bill of Rights*. Despite the initial promise of the *Canadian Bill of Rights*, it soon became synonymous with a noble but ineffective document. The newly formulated relevancy test is strikingly similar to the "legitimate federal objective" criterion used as a standard of justification under the *Canadian Bill of Rights* (see Smith). While the separation of powers is a fundamental protection of civil liberties and human rights, the Courts must continue to fulfill their mandate under the *Charter*, a mandate conferred on them by Parliament and the Legislatures when the constitution was repatriated and the *Charter* entrenched.

As an American Justice of the Supreme Court and former professor and equality rights activist, Madam Justice Ruth Bader-Ginsburg reminds us, through the question of her colleague, Judge Scalia,

> Do conservatives "really believe, as they have been saying, that the courts are doing too much, or (are they) actually nursing only the less principled grievance that the courts have not been doing what they want?" (Ginsburg at 44)

The most striking illustration of judicial deference is the case concerning the repeal of the Ontario employment equity legislation, *Ferrel et al.* v. *Ontario (A.G.)* (1997), 149 D.L.R. (4th) 335 (Ont. Gen. Div.), in which the Court held that the authority of the legislature to repeal an act was not governed by the *Charter*. Distinguishing the recent decision on the repeal of the Ontario pay equity legislation as a case of partial legislative repeal, as opposed to the case of repeal of an entire act as in the case of the *Ontario Employment Equity Act*, the Court declared that the complete repeal of legislation was not amenable to judicial review. The Ontario Court of Appeal in *Ferrel* upheld the lower court's decision stating "the legislature is free to return the state of the statute book to what it was before the 1993 Act, without being obligated to justify the repealing statute under section 1 of the *Charter*" ([1998] O.J. No. 5074, para. 36).[11] Based on this case, and others, future advances in equity issues through the courts may prove to be more difficult. Indeed, as in other areas, the true challenge may become one of maintaining and consolidating gains as opposed to making significant new advances.

Two recent decisions of the Supreme Court of Canada may allay fears that judicial deference will stunt equity advancement. In *Eldridge* v. *B.C. (A.G.)* (1997), 151 D.L.R. (4th) 577 (S.C.C.) the court found that refusing to fund sign language interpreters for the deaf was a section 15 violation that could not be saved by section 1 of the *Charter*. Honourable Justice La Forest, rejecting the argument that the court should show judicial deference to the legislature, stated that "the leeway to be granted to the state is not infinite. Governments must demonstrate that their actions infringe the rights in question no more than is reasonably necessary to achieve their goals" (627). In addition Mr. Justice Cory in *Vriend* v. *Alberta* quoted Madae Justice McLachlin, with approval, when he reiterated,

> To carry judicial deference to the point of accepting Parliament's view simply on the basis that the problem is serious and the solution is difficult would be to diminish the role of the courts in the constitutional process and to weaken the structure of rights upon which our constitution and our nation is founded. (para. 126)

As Mr. Justice Cory wrote, "[q]uite simply, it is not the courts which limit the legislatures. Rather, it is the constitution, which must be interpreted by the courts, that limits the legislatures" (para. 56).

The significance of changing terminology

One of the key roles of equity advocates will be to deconstruct and decipher the reality behind the words, the practice behind the policies. The terminology associated with efforts to achieve full and representative participation in our workplaces and educational institutions has changed throughout the years. These changes in language are significant. Upon examination, one can see that the terms used to describe legislative or programmatic initiatives reflect underlying political ideology and hence, from time to time, reveal significant shifts in the overall commitment to achieving equality.

In 1984, the change in terminology from "affirmative action" to "employment equity" was proposed and adopted in order to avoid an emotionally charged debate (Abella 6–7). However, the purpose and substance of the programs remained unchanged. Although employment equity programs place

greater importance on qualitative measures such as barrier elimination measures, positive measures, supportive measures and accommodation, both employment equity and affirmative action programs involve working to eliminate
barriers to full participation in education or employment, using quantitative
measures to gage the results. Both include remedial measures to accelerate the
pace of change. Under both affirmative action and employment equity programs, training is a priority. Both are results-oriented approaches, consistent
with the interpretation that Canadian courts have given to the section 15
equality guarantees and based on the hypothesis that,

> ... the important and accumulated disadvantage experienced by target
> group members in employment and in certain other sectors maintains
> them in a vicious circle; the simple elimination of barriers is of limited
> effect in the face of the magnitude and persistence of inequality.
> (Chicha-Pontbriand 4)

In a recent successful constitutional challenge to the repeal of pay equity
provisions in Ontario which had introduced the proxy method of evaluation of
the work of women in the broader public sector, the court restates and applies
the law applicable to affirmative action programs in Canada (*Service Employees
International Union, Local 204* v. *Ontario (A.G.)* (1997), 35 O.R. (3d) 508 (Gen.
Div.) Section 15(2) was included in the *Charter*

> to make it clear that s. 15(1) does not preclude affirmative action
> programmes in favour of disadvantaged individuals or groups even
> though such programmes inevitably involve some element of reverse
> discrimination against those not belonging to the disadvantaged
> group. (525)

At the same time, section 15(1) continues to afford members of disadvantaged groups protection against discrimination in the design of these special
programs (see also *Roberts* v. *Ontario* (1994), 117 D.L.R. (4th) 297 (Ont.
C.A.)).

Pay equity legislation was found to be a remedy for gender-based systemic
wage discrimination. The repeal legislation created an unjustifiable prejudicial
distinction between groups of women segregated in female-dominated and
undervalued workplaces and other women in workplaces which continued to
be covered by the legislation. In interpreting the *Pay Equity Act*, the Court held

that women in exclusively female workplaces were also intended to be among the beneficiaries of legislation and that although section 15(2) protects special programs, "[s]ection 15(2) does not protect affirmative action legislation from attacks by members of the disadvantaged groups it was designed to benefit" (525).

The courts have confirmed the discretionary power of the government to designate the class of beneficiaries under a special program; the courts distinguish between those intended to be included and those not intended to be included according to the purpose or object of the program.[12] Furthermore, neither essentially budgetary considerations nor pretextual reasons would satisfy the requirements for justification of restrictions to equality under section 1 of the *Charter*.

Unfortunately, the "simple elimination of barriers" is the cornerstone of the reborn "equal opportunity" programs. In theory and practice, therefore, critical differences in expectations and outcomes distinguish affirmative action/employment equity programs from equal opportunity programs. Care should be taken to avoid classifying programs solely according to the in nomenelature;; rather, classifications should determined by context. Effective programs to reduce or eliminate disadvantage necessarily include positive measures. Special programs must include barrier removal or anti-discrimination measures but must go beyond these in order to eliminate cumulative disadvantage. Measures such as posting job openings, eliminating irrelevant criteria, and providing systems for evaluating foreign qualifications are all barrier elimination measures. They are the first step in eliminating disadvantage.

Accommodation may be seen as a barrier-elimination measure; essentially accommodation adapts a service or facility so that it becomes equally accessible to persons who are differently-abled; accommodation takes differences into account. It may be that analyzing equality in terms of sameness and difference is itself conceptually flawed. Emphasis should be placed on providing equal access to employment and services according to the needs of each candidate (Phillips; see also Day and Brodsky).

These equal opportunity measures do not, however, address the uneven playing field. They do not address the obstacles that have stymied employment and advancement for decades. People from the disadvantaged groups have usually not had access to on-the-job training; have usually not been mentored; and have certainly not enjoyed the same degree of job mobility. Simply to remove barriers does not place them at the same starting gate. Appropriate positive measures are required to reduce or eliminate the disadvantage; these measures may consist of training, bridging opportunities, mentoring, or support groups. Existing systems and informal networks within the institution will tend to perpetuate themselves. Without these measures, access to equality will be limited or denied.

Economist Monica Townson articulated these differences clearly over a decade ago when she and others urged governments to move *from* equal opportunity models *to* affirmative action/equality models:

> *Equal opportunity programs have failed.* For the past ten years, the federal public service has operated equal opportunity programs for the four target groups. The programs appear to have had very little impact. Data show increased occupational segregation of women in the public service; very little progress in moving women or other target groups into the officer categories; appointments of blacks in Nova Scotia at a rate below that which their representation in the general population would suggest; and very limited hiring of disabled peoples, mostly to term positions.
>
> By contrast, a comprehensive affirmative action program for francophones, under the Official Language Program, proved extremely effective and was able to achieve dramatic results in less than three years.
>
> This experience confirms the conclusion reached in the United States more than a decade ago. *Anti-discrimination and equal opportunity programs may fail not because the programs themselves are failures, but because they do not address the true nature of discrimination. Biased systems, and not necessarily deliberate discrimination, may result in unequal outcomes, and it is this systemic discrimination that affirmative action is designed to correct.* (341 at 351) [emphasis added]

Equal opportunity programs are at best short-sighted or partial remedies. They may even be considered dangerous as they allow governments to appear to be taking steps to correct the under-representation of certain segments of the population in the workforce. When the lack of representation continues unabated, the fault then appears to lie with those who remain on the outside.

Over ten years later, Monica Townson's economic analysis remains remarkably timely. Her study also reports on shifting demographic trends, in particular, a significant increase in the population of young Aboriginal people. Recent reports published by Statistics Canada point to other important

demographic trends, such as an increase in single-headed households, especially those headed by women (Kerr and Kopustas). They also note a projected
increase of the racial minority population in Canada, increasing from nine
percent to nineteen percent by the year 2016. Townson discusses the risks
inherent in failing to implement the social and employment policies necessary
to address these changes.

Townson's approach is pragmatic as well. She suggests increasing public
education initiatives to reduce the controversy surrounding affirmative action
programs. She also notes that although employers may have some awareness
that employment barriers deprive them of the full potential and talents of the
work force, projections about a labour surplus may in certain sectors override
that awareness. Particularly in difficult economic times, demonstrating the
relationship between employment equity and good human resources management, and even good customer relations, may be more effective.

Indeed, through such public education initiatives, and through experience, some employers now see equity as not only the right thing to do, but
also the smart thing to do. Our society has changed. Banks and other
institutions have seen the need to examine their practices and to incorporate
equity measures in response to the changes. They have reexamined the skills
required for successful communication in a diversified working environment
and also examined their testing to make sure it is culturally sensitive. A
diversified workplace is an asset in the marketing of services or products to
expanded groups of consumers. The Association of Canadian Bankers' publication, entitled *Banking on Employment Equity*, outlines a number of programs instituted by banks to promote equity and explains why banks have
benefitted from them.[13]

The current context for equity in universities

As federal contractors or beneficiaries of government grants, universities,
like banks, have had to establish or expand employment equity programs. They
have, in addition, set up educational equity initiatives. In many respects, there
have been important accomplishments over the years, yet serious limitations
remain for us to overcome. A recent report in Statistics Canada's publication
Canadian Social Trends (Normand), reviews women's position in the field of
education, highlighting the fact that the proportion of women students in post-
secondary institutions has increased dramatically. My own experience illustrates this point quite well. In the 1960s, approximately ten percent of my law

school class was made up of women. Today, women comprise 50 percent or more of law school enrolment.

This trend is not restricted to law schools; it applies more generally. For example, in 1997, for the first time ever female medical school graduates slightly outnumbered male graduates (Buske). The changes that have occurred over time are reflected in the variation of statistics between age groups. Between 1981 and 1996, the proportion of women age 20–29 with a university degree increased from 11 percent to 21 percent compared with an increase from 12 percent to 16 percent for men (Statistics Canada 1998). Moreover, according to the results of the 1996 Census, for the first time in history more than half the females in this age group have completed higher education. Indeed, women now form a majority of students at the undergraduate level. They also form the majority of part-time students as many working women attend university to upgrade their job qualifications (Statistics Canada 1998).

At the graduate level, women do not generally form a majority of students. Nevertheless, the proportion of women at the graduate level has increased substantially in the last two decades. In 1972–73, women constituted 27 percent of full-time Masters students and 19 percent of full-time doctoral students. By 1992–93, these figures had changed to 46 percent and 35 percent respectively (Statistics Canada 1998).

While this increase in female representation is encouraging, a further examination of the data reveals the persistence of many historic trends. Women remain concentrated in certain areas of study. Far fewer women than men are enrolled in mathematics or engineering. At the Master's level, women still account for a majority of full-time enrolment in four major fields of study: education, health, fine and applied arts, and humanities (Statistics Canada, University degrees granted by field of study, by Sex). Women's employment has also traditionally fallen into these sectors. These patterns of student concentration strongly suggest that traditional employment patterns will remain the norm for some time to come.

The data tells us that with respect to graduate studies, there is also a fair representation of visible minorities in universities. Indeed, visible minorities form ten percent of the student population at the undergraduate level, 13 percent at the master's level, and approximately 20 percent at the doctorate level. This is compared to their approximately eleven percent representation in the general population (Statistics Canada 1998).

The 1996 census data indicate that racial minority groups are more concentrated in major urban centres, such as Toronto census region, where minorities constitute 32 percent of the total city population; Vancouver, where they constitute 31 percent; Calgary, 16 percent; Ottawa/Hull, 12 percent; and Montreal, 12 percent (Statistics Canada 1998). Of even greater significance for the educational system is the differential age distribution between the racial minority population and the total population. For example, the African-Canadian population is considerably younger. In 1996, 29.8 percent or 30 percent of Blacks were under 15 years of age as compared to 20.7 percent of the total Canadian population (Statistics Canada 1998). These data are reflected in the school population and already, to a large extent, in university student enrolment. This rapidly changing cultural milieu presents benefits and challenges. The increasing diversity of the student body brings the potential for increased cross-fertilization of knowledge, ideas, and cultural values; the diversity also places stress on public and private institutions where individuals or systems have not reasonably adapted their policies and practices to their new reality. With few exceptions, most educational institutions have policies and officers responsible for multiculturalism, educational equity, or anti-racism; in practice, however, there is a growing gap between the policy and the practice.

There are, as well, major differences in the representation of different racial minority groups. Nonetheless, for racial minority groups as a whole, equity concerns do not arise with respect to access to education, although some groups, such as candidates who are native born, or permanent residents of Canada, may be under-represented. Generally, the issues for racial minority groups concern conditions of study and access to employment, to faculty and teaching positions, and to required internships, such as articling positions for law school graduates. In these areas, unfortunately, barriers continue to exist.

For persons with disabilities, both access to university studies as well as access to employment remain critical issues. True achievements in the area of employment equity for this group remain virtually nonexistent. The 1996 *Report, Employment Equity Act*, indicates increased hiring of people with disabilities (27). Closer reading discloses, however, that the advances are largely due to improved reporting, i.e. employees choosing to change their status and to self-identify as people with disabilities.

Access to university studies is conditioned by the existence of barriers throughout the educational system. The few students with disabilities who do succeed in accessing university studies are confronted with continuing physical barriers both inside and outside university buildings, as well as lengthy delays in obtaining accommodation; the continuous effort required to obtain ongoing accommodation, sometimes in spite of the best intentions of the institution, combined with the normal pressures of university studies, is extremely demanding.

Serious attitudinal barriers remain. Many universities receive complaints from other students about the accommodations provided to students with disabilities. Universities must create positive conditions for discussion of equality issues in the general student body and encourage, to the extent feasible, the participation of other students in supportive programs for equity-seeking students. Special attention is required to avoid further negative stereotyping.

Creating inclusive teaching and learning environments

Indeed, to make genuine progress toward achieving equity, universities must design and implement appropriate programs to "level the playing field" for students and faculty members of different gender, abilities, and background. Working towards equity requires periodically reviewing curriculum offerings and teaching methodologies, including evaluation methods; broadening the definition of research; and reviewing policy and bylaws on academic and administrative issues such as admissions, search committees, and hiring committees. Such reviews cannot be superficial; they must be undertaken systematically, with channels of reciprocal communication, and wide participation that provides a level of comfort conducive to candor, confidence, and ongoing commitment. Participation of equity-seeking groups and unions, where they exist, is a key to revealing the potentially discriminatory impact of employment or educational practices which appear neutral, but which have a disproportionately negative effect on these groups. The process must be carefully planned and appropriately resourced to avoid generating cynicism, tokenism, and hostility. Response to consultations should present findings and comments on how recommendations were dealt with; consultations which are not seen to contribute to decision-making are counterproductive.

Turning to the concerns of students, equity advocates must think in terms of the curriculum being offered—to all the students. The education we provide young people will, of course, shape their attitudes and consequently affect the way they perceive and react to situations which arise during their working lives (James 48). Positive role models of both genders and of differing backgrounds, abilities, and lifestyles will involve, support, and challenge all students.

Professor Paul Chartrand, associate professor of Native Studies at the University of Manitoba and a commissioner of the Royal Commission on Aboriginal Peoples, suggests ways to make a curriculum inclusive and relevant to native people in Canada. His comprehensive approach includes learning about the living conditions of First Nations people; the cultural differences which are often ignored by government officials and other non-native professionals; the loss of language and cultural identity; and the exposure to racial taunts based on appearance. He introduces this information to help others understand the factors that have led to the disempowerment of First Nations peoples and subsequently to the renewed claim for self-determination—a concept which includes a meaningful degree of control over First Nations lands and First Nations affairs accompanied by the right to participate in the affairs of the larger State.

Undoubtedly, universities face tough challenges and decisions with respect to ensuring curricula that will promote equity. First, university courses which specifically and actively encourage inclusive perspectives have traditionally fallen outside the core curriculum. Add to that the declining number of optional courses as a result of funding shortages. Add further the declining demand for such courses by students who, worried about competing for scarce employment opportunities, focus their studies almost entirely on market-oriented courses. The result is that in an age of increasing awareness of the need for an inclusive curriculum, fewer and fewer students are being exposed to such a curriculum.

University administrators are hesitant to incorporate more such courses into the core curriculum. Years ago, it was recommended to the Council of Canadian Universities that students, particularly at the graduate level, be required to develop a certain level of fluency in, or at least competency with, a second language as part of the educational process. The response was tepid, as it probably would be today. Such a requirement would not only encourage a valuable skill but would promote a greater understanding of cultural differences and a better appreciation of diversity—a simple and positive tool to advancing equity. In an era of information and rapid internationalization, multilingualism and cross-cultural competencies will find their place in programs geared for the twenty-first century.

Issues concerning curriculum are rarely considered simple. In fact, they often become extremely controversial and contentious. For example, the Ministry of Education disseminated a report entitled, "Creating an Inclusive Post-Secondary Learning Environment."[14] This excellent document is essentially a compendium of measures that can be taken to improve equity at college and university levels. It offers substantive information and models for process. However, opposition and criticism of the report soon hampered its dissemination. Some post-secondary educators voiced strong opposition on the grounds that the approach and measures proposed would violate academic freedom.

We cherish academic freedom as fundamental to scholarship. It ensures the integrity and originality of both research and teaching. There is no conceptual opposition between academic freedom and policies and practices of inclusivity. Certainly, issues may arise because of the way such policies are administered; however, one expects that these instances can be addressed and corrected. Imperfections with a policy do not erase the underlying need for one. And programs designed to increase equity are needed. Like academic freedom, these too constitute essential ingredients for a healthy university. In fact, one could argue rather forcefully that when diversity and inclusiveness are stifled rather than promoted, academic freedom suffers.

Finally, the inextricable relationship between educational equity and employment equity becomes all the more apparent when working towards an inclusive learning and teaching environment. The equitable participation of women and other groups can contribute to greater diversity in teaching methods, areas of research and scholarship, and in contributions to the community. An inclusive climate can more easily be fostered by the presence of many role models from different backgrounds, cultures, and lifestyles; the presence of professors, sessionals, professionals, and staff from different milieu, including persons with disabilities, increases the sense of belonging and self-worth in students who then see themselves reflected in the teaching body. Very often, it also broadens their horizons and encourages them to aspire to previously unattainable goals. Put succinctly, "the influence of role models is subtle but often decisive" (Abella 133).

The presence of women faculty members and faculty members from other groups does not automatically create an inclusive environment, but it helps create an atmosphere which is conducive to creating that environment. The participation of all members of faculty is a crucial factor. It is still not rare today for racial minority students, students with disabilities or other minority groups to complete all their studies without once having had a teacher, principal, or director with whom they could readily identify.

Many women and minority faculty members continue to run into unforeseen barriers when they apply for renewal or for tenure. For example, Aboriginal professors often remain as sessional instructors. Although statistics show an increase in the proportion of professors who fall into the tenured category in Canada, many Aboriginal professors find themselves unable to attain tenure-track, permanent positions.

Twenty years ago, I was involved in the case of a woman professor applying for contract renewal. Her contract had already been renewed once, and no one had raised any concerns regarding the quality of her publications. During the second renewal process, however, those reviewing her standing noted that she had taken two leaves of absence for maternity reasons; these had naturally affected the number of articles she had published. In discussing the renewal application, some colleagues commented on their perception that women teachers tend not to give birth during holidays but only during the school year(!). We were shocked even then, but unfortunately these issues still arise today. Once again, we must educate if we are to change attitudes; non-discriminatory practice will also, over time, change attitudes and culture. Employment equity planning and implementation can help remove, in a systematic way, the barriers that stand in the way of equality. Equally important, equity practices can help introduce a critical mass of women and minority people and contribute to the creation of a new and hopefully more equitable culture within the institution.

Conclusion

A tremendous amount of valuable work has been accomplished by people associated with universities. Research studies, scholarly papers, new curriculum models, analytical work, and conferences all contribute to our understanding of equity issues and give us new ideas and impetus for resolving them. At the same time, we realize the distance that has yet to be travelled. Vision and openness are essential to the task of ensuring that our universities keep pace with changes in our global society. Determination and courage are always required when confronting these issues.

Harriet Tubman, leader of the Underground Railroad, practiced her motto "No turning back." She used it to forcefully keep people moving ahead often in daunting circumstances when they wanted to quit. With unswerving determination, skill, and strategy, she managed, over a 16-year period, to lead more than 300 slaves and freed men and women into Canada without losing a single "passenger." We need the same steadfast determination to face the work on equity issues and social change that lies ahead of us. We are, after all, on sound legal and moral ground, headed in the right direction, with "no turning back."

I gratefully acknowledge the research assistance of Kyla Mahar, and the editorial assistance of Susan Joanis. I thank the Law Foundation of Ontario for their financial contribution. I am solely responsible for opinions expressed in this article.

[1]*Employment Equity Act*, R.S.O., 1993, c.35, repealed by *An Act to Repeal Job Quotas and to Restore Merit-Based Employment Practices in Ontario*, R.S.O., 1995, c.4.

[2]*Employment Equity Act*, R.S.C., 1993, c.44, s.12(1). Section 14 of the Ontario legislation had required employers to make all reasonable efforts to implement their employment equity programs and to achieve their objectives within the time lines set out in the plan. Employers, along with unions where applicable, were to set goals that, when met, would constitute reasonable progress towards achieving employment equity. The "all reasonable efforts" removes the basis for any allegation that either legislation requires quotas.

[3]One of the objectives of the former Ontario Government was harmonization of legislative requirements. Ontario workplaces needed to be spared conflicting or differing requirements, and wherever possible, duplication of efforts.

[4]*Canadian Charter of Rights and Freedom, Part 1 of the Constitution Act*, 1982, being Schedule B to the Canada Act, 1982 (U.K.), 1982, c.11 [hereinafter *Charter*]. These grounds have been held to include other "analogous" grounds as well.

[5]See Record of Hearings of the Special Joint Committee of the Senate and House of Commons on the Constitution of Canada Appointed to Report on the October 6, 1980 Resolution, November 1980, *The Canadian Charter of Rights and Freedoms*, paragraphs 1.5.3 and 1.5.4 and *Minutes of the Proceedings and Evidence for the Committee's Report to Parliament Submitted on February 13, 1981. Minutes 20-11-1980 9:128*. The Canadian Advisory Council on the Status of Women argued for a permissive clause, authorizing affirmative action programs for disadvantaged groups providing that the programs are developed according to a legislative framework.

[6]Early cases have been analyzed by Professor Colleen Sheppard in *Litigating the Relationship Between Equity and Equality*, Ontario Law Reform Commission, 1993, pp. 25 and following.

[7]See *e.g. Egan* v. *Canada*, [1995] 2 S.C.R. 513, where the majority of the

Supreme Court of Canada upheld an infringement of the section 15 *Charter* rights of same sex couples by finding that the *Old Age Security Act* was intended to provide income securities to families, an institution premised upon child-bearing and implying heterosexuality. More recently, see *Vriend* v. *Alberta*, [1998] S.C.J. No. 29 Q.L., wherethe failure to include sexual orientation as a prohibited ground of discrimination in Alberta's *Individual's Rights Protection Act*, was not saved by section 1 of the *Charter*.

[8]See *R.* v. *Brownridge*, [1972] S.C.R. 926 and *R.* v. *Curr*, [1972] S.C.R. 889. This status was initially recognized to the *Canadian Bill of Rights* and subsequently to Human Rights codes. See *Insurance Corporation of British Columbia* v. *Heerspink*, [1982] 2 S.C.R. 145 at pp. 157–158.

[9]See *Human Rights Code*, R.S.O., 1990, c.19, s.14.3; *Canadian Human Rights Act*, R.S.C., 1985, c.6, s.15.

[10]The employment figures at CN compared to the general population were staggering. As is noted in the decision at p.199:

> By the end of 1981, there were only 57 women in "blue collar" posts in the St. Lawrence region of CN, being a mere 0.7 percent of the blue collar labour force in the region. There are 276 women occupying unskilled jobs in all the regions where CN operated, again amounting to only 0.7 percent of the unskilled workforce. By contrast, women represented, in 1981, 40.7 percent of the total Canadian labour force. At the time, women constituted only 6.11 percent of the total workforce at CN. Among blue-collar workers in Canada, 13 percent were women during the period January to May, 1982, yet female applicant for blue-collar jobs at CN constituted only five percent of the total applicant pool.

[11]The appeal court also considered the special programs authorized by the Human Rights Code of Ontario. Application for leave to appeal has been filed in the Supreme Court of Canada.

[12]See *Lovelace* v. *Ontario* (1997), 33 O.R. (3d) 735 at 754 (C.A.), where the Ontario Court of Appeal determined that the Government could, as an affirmative action program authorized by section 15(2) of the *Charter*, desig-nate status Indians as beneficiaries of funds procured from casino gambling to the exclusion of non-status Indians and Metis. This judgment is questionable since the decision excluded disadvantaged non-status Indians and Metis who should arguably fall within the intent of those who framed the program.

[13]See Canadian Bankers' Association, *Banking on Employment Equity*, where it is stated:

> All of the banks see a direct relationship between employment equity objectives and their other business objectives. They recognize that a fair and equitable workplace supports high employee productivity and individual initiative and creativity. By addressing the needs of a changing workplace, the banks believe they will be better positioned to satisfy the needs of a diverse customer base. (13)

[14]Edited by Gail Benick and Anver Saloojee, a resource funded by the Post-Secondary Anti-Harassment and Discrimination Project Coordination Committee under the Auspices of the Ontario Council of Regents and the Ontario Council on University Affairs, 1996.

References

Abella, Rosalie. *Report of the Commission on Equality in Employment*. Ottawa: Supply and Services Canada, 1984.

Action Travail des Femmes v. *Canadian National Railway Co.*, (1987) 40 D.L.R. (4th) 193 (S.C.C.); (1985) 20 D.L.R. (4th) 668 (Fed. C.A.).

An Act to Repeal Job Quotas and to Restore Merit-Based Employment Practices in Ontario, R.S.O., 1995, c.4.

Andrews v. *The Law Society of B.C.*, (1989) 56 D.L.R. (4th) 1 (S.C.C.).

Athabasca Tribal Council v. *Amoco Canada Petroleum Co. Ltd.*, [1981] 1 S.C.R. 699 at 711.

Black, William, and Lynn Smith. "The Equality Rights." *The Canadian Charter of Rights and Freedoms. 3rd Edition*. Ed. Gerald A. Beaudoin and Errol Mendes. Toronto: Carswell, 1996. 14.1–14.75.

Buske, L. "For First Time, Men a Minority in Graduating Class." *C.M.A.C.* 158.4 24 Feb. 1998.

Canadian Bankers' Association. *Banking on Employment Equity*. Toronto: Canadian Bankers' Association, 1994.

Canadian Bill of Rights, S.C. 1960, c.44.

Canadian Charter of Rights and Freedom, Part 1 of the Constitution Act, 1982, being Schedule B to the Canada Act, 1982 (U.K.), 1982, c.11.

Canadian Human Rights Act, R.S.C., 1985, c.6.

Chicha-Pontbriand, Marie-Therese. *Discrimination Systematique, fondement et methodologie des programmes d'access à l'égalité en emploi.* Cowansville: Les editions Yvon Blais Inc., 1989.

Day, S., and G. Brodsky. "The Duty to Accommodate: Who Will Benefit?" (1996) 75 Can B Rev 433.

Egan v. *Canada*, [1995] 2 R.C.S. 513.

Eldridge v. *B.C. (A.G.)*, 151 D.L.R. (4th) 577 (S.C.C.).

Employment Equity Act, R.S.O., 1993, c.35.

Employment Equity Act. Annual Report, 1996.

Family Law Act, R.S.O. 1990, c. F.3.

Ferrel et al. v. *Ontario (A.G.)*, (1997), 149 D.L.R. (4th) 335 (Ont. Gen. Div.); [1998] O.J. No. 5074 (Ont. C.A.).

Ginsburg, R. Bader. "Interpretation of the Equal Protection Clause." *Harvard Journal of Law and Public Policy* 9 (1986): 41 at p.44.

Human Rights Code, R.S.O., 1990, c.19, s.14.3.

Individual's Rights Protection Act, R.S.A. 1980, c.I-2, preamble, ss. 2(1), 3, 4, 7(1), 8(1), 10, 16(1).

Insurance Corporation of British Columbia v. *Heerspink*, [1982] 2 S.C.R. 145 at pp. 157–158.

James, C. "Reverse Racism: Students' Response to Equity Programs." *Journal of Professional Studies* 3.1 (1995): 48–54.

Kerr, D. and N. Kopustas. "Projections on Households and Families for Canada, Provinces, and Territories 1994–2016." Ottawa: Statistics Canada, No. 91–522.

Lovelace v. *Ontario* (1997), 33 O.R. (3d) 735 at 754 (C.A.)

M. v. *H.*, (1997) 31 O.R. (3d) 417 (C.A.).

Normand, J. "Education of Women in Canada." *Canadian Social Trends* (Winter 1995) Ottawa: Statistics Canada.

Phillips, R.D. *Affirmative Action as an Effective Labour Market Planning Tool of the 1980's.* Technical Study 29, Labour Market Development Task Force, Employment and Immigration Canada. Ottawa: Ministry of Supply and Services, 1981.

R. v. *Brownridge*, [1972] S.C.R. 926.

R. v. *Curr*, [1972] S.C.R. 889.

Roberts v. *Ontario* (1994), 117 D.L.R. (4th) 297 (Ont. C.A.).

Service Employees International Union, Local 204 v. *Ontario (A.G.)* (1997), 35 O.R. (3d) 508 (Gen. Div.). O'Leary, J.

Sheppard, Colleen. *Litigating the Relationship Between Equity and Equality.* Toronto: Ontario Law Reform Commission, 1993.

Smith, Dean L. "Does Section 15 Have a Future?" *Human Rights in the 21st Century: Prospects, Institutions, and Processes*. Montreal: Canadian Institute for the Administration of Justice and Les Editions Thémis, 1996. 101–128.

Special Joint Committee of the Senate and House of Commons on the Constitution of Canada Appointed to Report on the October 6, 1980 Resolution. *Minutes of the Proceedings and Evidence for the Committee's Report to Parliament Submitted on February 13, 1981. Minutes 20-11-1980 9: 128.*

Statistics Canada. "1996 Census: Education, Mobility, and Migration." Daily Bulletin of the Dominion Bureau of Statistics, 14 Apr. 1998.

Statistics Canada. "University Degrees Granted by Field of Study, by Sex." CAN SIM cross-classified table 00580602.

Townson, M. "The Socio-Economic Costs of Affirmative Action." *Research Studies*. Royal Commission on Equality in Employment. Ottawa, 1985.

Vriend v. *Alberta*, [1998] S.C.J. No. 29 Q.L.

Linking Employment and Educational Equity

Allison Young

The term equity is a very broad concept. In order to develop effective strategies of "how to get it" in the graduate education environment, it is very important to define our approach to equity. That is, in what area of graduate education are we talking about equity? Does achieving equity in the entire graduate education experience mean different things in different areas? Can strategies to achieve equity in the graduate education environment be productively linked? Are we referring to equity as an ideal we would like to realize in an environment where there are limited avenues to pursue it, or as some form of established institutionalized equity process that needs to be better utilized? Does achieving equity within graduate education require well defined institutional structures, or is it adequate to rely on the goodwill of liberal minded actors who acknowledge that we can and should pursue equity but do not need additional bureaucratic structures to do it? This paper will explore these questions by looking at how we can use the process required to achieve employment equity at universities as a way to secure educational equity in the graduate education environment.

Employment equity

Employment Equity is about removing arbitrary barriers to employment so that no one is denied opportunities for employment if they are willing and able to do the job. In Canada, employment equity legislation is contained within Bill C-64. The purpose of the act is

> to achieve equality in the workplace so that no person shall be denied
> employment opportunities or benefits for reasons unrelated to ability
> and, in the fulfilment of that goal, to correct the conditions of
> disadvantage in employment experienced by women, aboriginal peo-
> ples, persons with disabilities and members of visible minorities by
> giving effect to the principle that employment equity means more
> than treating persons in the same way but also requires special
> measures and the accommodation of differences. (Section 2)

Private employers and portions of the public service employing more than
100 employees are bound to implement the legislation on pain of monetary
penalty or loss of a government contract. In the university context, employment
equity applies to the university as employer, employing people working more
than 30 per cent of the full time equivalent. Accordingly, this legislation will
not cover the many students (graduate students included) employed by the
university who are working less than 30 per cent of the full-time equivalent.
However, this does not prevent the employer from including these employees
in its employment equity program if it so desires.

This legislation only covers those employees whose employers are part of
the Federal Contractors Programme. People working for other employers on
campus, such as contracted-out food services, student unions, and faculty who
hire students and pay them out of their research grants, are not covered.

Essentially, employment equity requires employers who are part of the
Federal Contractors Programme to identify and eliminate employment barriers against persons in the designated groups (women, people with disabilities, visible minorities, and Aboriginal peoples) that result from the employer's employment systems, policies, and practices that are not authorized by
law. Accordingly, universities which are part of this program must create a
plan to identify and eliminate employment barriers and demonstrate to the
federal government, through Employment Systems Reviews (ESR) conducted
every two years, that they are following through on the plan in a timely and
effective manner. The monitoring of the plan in this manner encourages
institutions, over time, to delve deeply into their employment systems, policies, and practices at all levels. For universities, this means implementation
not only at the institutional level, but also at the faculty and unit levels
including departments.

Educational equity

Unlike Employment Equity, there is no specific federal legislation to define educational equity. Instead, we may find broad applications in the *Canadian Charter of Rights and Freedoms* which refer in Section 15, for example, to equality rights, or we may garner a definition from academic sources and institutional statements. For example, educational equity can be defined as a) respect for diversity as a positive value to be developed through academic programs, policies, and structures, and assertive institutional policies to address systemic deficiencies and encourage access, support, and opportunity (adapted from The Report of the Senate Advisory Committee on Affirmative Action in Education; see also, Educational Equity at Dalhousie: A Discussion Paper: 4); and as b) the ability, as stated in Goal #10 of Dalhousie University's Statement, "to ensure the intellectual, professional and personal development of faculty, staff and students within a fair, progressive and caring environment that stimulates open-mindedness, adaptability, creativity and imaginative thinking and is committed to equity and affirmative action."

It is widely acknowledged that people in the designated groups face multiple barriers to learning at all levels in Canadian educational environments (see Mohanty; Ng; Pothier; Willis.) In securing a supportive and bias-free environment for all graduate students as well as one which encourages diversity and exchange on campus, educational equity must be pursued in at least four specific areas.

Climate

The relationship between the student and the university is a partnership of intellectual and personal development. For graduate students who are also employed at the university as teaching assistants or sessional lecturers (or some other equivalent), this partnership is overlaid with an apprenticeship-like relationship whereby the student/employee is being trained to become a qualified member of the academy at a professional level. However, though there appears to be a commitment by both the student/employee and the university to pursue intellectual and professional training, there are very few explicit rules which exist to govern this training, especially where professional development is concerned.

For example, few rules exist across departments about the involvement of graduate students/employees in departmental meetings, hirings, student rankings, scholarship selection, and so on. Indeed, there seem to be few formal mechanisms which exist, for example, to rank or hire students for teaching assistantships and scholarships. This is especially the case at universities where teaching assistants and sessional lecturers are not unionized. Consequently, it makes it very difficult for students to take steps to improve their record once rejected for hirings or scholarships since there is little information available about how decisions concerning their records were made. The same is often true at the university level. For example, though the Social Sciences and Humanities Research Council (SSHRC) makes it possible for students to inspect files they have submitted for federally-funded scholarships (SSHRC 16), students whose files are not forwarded on to SSHRC by their universities but who still want access to their files are subject to university-specific regulations which often do not provide students with clear avenues to access their files.

Without this information and without rules governing these decisions, access is impeded because it becomes incumbent upon the student/employee to somehow penetrate established academic culture (often dominated by older white males) in order to obtain a favourable ranking, scholarship information, teaching contracts, publishing information, employment, and so on. It is here that the designated groups (Aboriginal peoples, persons with disabilities, racially visible people, and women) often fall through the cracks since there are no established mechanisms to teach these students/employees about the academic culture, how to shape or change it, or how to improve one's chances of success while immersed in it.

Access to universities also represents a climate issue for the designated groups. That is, what policies and practices does the university pursue in order to recruit and admit students from these groups into the institution? In addition to academic background, does the university consider life experience in its admission procedures in order to account for the barriers people in the designated groups face at other levels of the education system? For students with disabilities, does the university attend to all physical barriers which may prevent access and, therefore, hinder learning and academic success?

Ultimately, the inability of students from the designated groups to penetrate established academic institutional culture reduces the pool of people available to make programs like employment equity a success.

Cost

The cost of pursuing graduate level education in Canada is becoming increasingly prohibitive. Since the ability of the designated groups to pay for graduate education is limited by lower socio-economic status across the board, and since the graduate degrees attained by these groups will not cause them to earn as much as dominant members of the population, it is difficult to convince students from the designated groups to go on to graduate studies and to incur the enormous expense associated with completing graduate programs. Consequently, realistic financial support mechanisms are needed to recruit, retain, and support graduate students from the designated groups as they make their way through graduate programs. Without these supports, the pool of people in the designated groups available to be hired for academic appointments will be reduced.

This problem has recently been acknowledged by Human Resources Development Canada. This Ministry has now created special opportunity grants for female doctoral students in fields of study with less than (on a national average) 30 per cent female enrolment and for all students with permanent disabilities (see Human Resources Development Canada). Interestingly, the eligible fields of study where there are less than 30 per cent female enrolment are not just confined to science-related areas such as engineering and applied sciences, agriculture and biological science, and mathematics and physics where it is commonly known that women are under-represented, but also includes economics, philosophy, political science, physical education, religious studies, law and jurisprudence, music, and so on.

Pedagogy

The impact of pedagogical practices in the university classroom[1] differs depending on who is being exposed to them. Here, it must be acknowledged that different groups in society have been socialized differently and, therefore, learn differently. It is not uncommon now, at the elementary and secondary school level, to encounter pedagogical styles which take this reality into account by striving to accommodate the culture and learning styles of girls, Aboriginal students, African-Canadian students, and so on. It is, therefore, necessary to begin to employ different pedagogical practices in the university classroom in order to ensure that all students have an equal chance to learn and to develop intellectually and emotionally. Such an undertaking requires communication and training programs for faculty in order to enhance awareness of the impact of their pedagogical practices and to expose them to alternative ways of teaching.

Curriculum

The curriculum is an important aspect of educational equity because it reflects the forms of knowledge and approaches used which lend meaning to the way we understand the world and the way power relations are shaped. Curriculums may be inclusive or exclusive of different forms of knowledge and approaches. In an educational environment such as the university classroom, a curriculum should strive to be inclusive in order to cultivate as comprehensive and rich an understanding of our society as possible.

Some universities have attempted to take account of less dominant forms of knowledge by setting up separate curriculums in such areas as women's studies, encouraging the creation of courses within departments devoted to, for example, Aboriginal issues, and also encouraging faculty to include in their courses lectures on less dominant approaches to the world such as feminism. Some faculty even take the much-needed step of incorporating diverse forms of knowledge and perspectives into all of their teaching material. All of these initiatives require training programs for existing faculty and the hiring of people (often from the designated groups) who are willing to make subordinated forms of knowledge and approaches a priority in the university classroom.

In addition, programming for curriculum is not just about what goes on in the classroom, but it is also about how programs are organized. For example, an inclusive curriculum might make provisions for part-time graduate programs, part-time tenure track positions, interdisciplinary studies, and so on. In the Winter 1996 issue of the *Dalhousie Alumni Magazine*, the cover story addressed why so few women are becoming career scientists (Tutton). In addition to identifying problems such as the lack of supervisors and role models for young female science students, female science students observed that a career in science penalizes women with families since scholarships and jobs are always offered on a full-time basis and programs like "post-docs" encourage the student to move to a different university for their research work. Since women are almost always the primary caregivers of children, establishing careers in science-related fields under these conditions is extremely difficult. These students are aware, however, that the system can and must change to accommodate the needs of different people. As one female science student in the article put it, "science is a social construct. It's the way we made it" (Tutton 15).

Inclusive curriculums, then, account not only for diverse forms of knowledge but also for the varied life realities of a diverse student body. It is these varied life realities which, ultimately, make the development of different perspectives and rich bodies of knowledge possible.

Interestingly, ignoring educational equity issues with regard to curriculum can lead to resentment among students (and faculty) that there exists a lack of respect in the university environment for diverse forms of knowledge. Certainly, this has been one of the (many) complaints made by graduate students in the Department of Political Science at the University of British Columbia about their department (McEwen).

Linking employment and educational equity

The approach taken by employment equity legislation to deal with inequality in the workplace is systemic in nature. This legislation attempts to deal with how a workplace system produces inequality rather than making any one group or individual responsible for it. Similarly, the problem of educational equity requires a systemic approach because it, too, is a systemic problem.

That is, the problem of educational inequality is more widespread than any one individual or activity, but all individuals and activities, as part of a social structure or system, are involved in it. Consequently, responsibility for systemic inequality, whether in the workplace or in educational settings, lies with everyone because we are all part of the system.

The Supreme Court of Canada has defined systemic discrimination as

> practices or attitudes that have, whether by design or impact, the effect of limiting an individual's or a group's right to the opportunities generally available because of attributed rather than actual characteristics.... It is not a question of whether this discrimination is motivated by an intentional desire to obstruct someone's potential, or whether it is the accidental by-product of innocently motivated practices or systems. If the barrier is affecting certain groups in a disproportionately negative way, it is a signal that the practices that lead to this adverse impact may be discriminatory. This is why it is important to look at the results of a system. (*Action Travail des Femmes* vs. *C.N.R.* Co.: 210).

By looking at the results of employment and education practices at Canadian universities, we can see that systemic discrimination does exist. We can also see that the achievement of employment and educational equity is co-dependent. That is, for a university to achieve the goals of employment equity, there must be an available population of potential employees from the designated groups who would be able to fill available positions. However, without educational equity programs in place, it will be difficult to build the pool of qualified candidates needed to achieve employment equity.

For example, there are few Aboriginal people in Canada who hold Ph.Ds. This reality makes it difficult to implement employment equity successfully. We must, therefore, question whether or not there is something in university programs that prohibits Aboriginal people from obtaining doctoral degrees. If we do not ask these questions and do not move to implement educational equity, we will never have an adequate pool of qualified Aboriginal people to achieve employment equity. A similar approach is needed for other designated groups. At the same time, without employees from the designated groups in place, educational equity will be difficult to achieve (particularly in the university classroom) since there will be few role models available to promote designated group advancement through climate, curriculum, pedagogy, or funding changes. Ultimately, this situation constitutes a vicious cycle which is very difficult to break by any one person or sector of the university community.

Indeed, this vicious cycle is a characteristic of the systemic nature of discrimination in which the voices and agency of marginalized groups, in this case the designated groups, are impeded or oppressed. Systemic problems are difficult to identify because they are so pervasive.

There exists a variety of theoretical approaches to systemic discrimination ranging from modern liberal philosophers like Charles Taylor, to feminists like Catherine MacKinnon, postmodernists like Michel Foucault, and postmodern feminists like Gayatri Chakravorty Spivak. Certainly, these examples only begin to display the complex and varied approaches to systemic discrimination which exist in the literature. It is not the purpose of this paper to review or even summarise this literature. Suffice to say that the debate surrounding systemic discrimination serves to establish systemic discrimination as a legitimate point of inquiry and to open up new ways of being critical, of naming power structures, of uncovering hitherto silent and silenced voices. Fundamentally, it begins to position society as a complex and heterogeneous site consisting of multiple actors with a variety of legitimate needs.

However, being aware of systemic discrimination as it may manifest itself through educational inequity does not mean an effective strategy exists for dealing with the problem. Indeed, the manner in which graduate education is configured discourages effective strategies from being developed. Wholly dependent on supervisors, graduate coordinators, and chairs of departments for information, recommendations, and affirmation, graduate students possess few, if any, formal or informal avenues for pursuing educational equity. It is, therefore, important to ask what practical strategies exist for achieving educational equity at institutions like universities? Since graduate students are very often employees of universities and since these employment experiences are closely linked to their educational success, one possible strategy is to formally link educational equity with employment equity. This would require educational equity to be placed onto the agenda of university Employment Equity Programs as they develop via the Federal Contractors Programme and its monitoring mechanism, the Employment Systems Review.

Since most universities in Canada are part of the Federal Contractors Programme, they possess some structure for implementing employment equity. These structures vary widely and some universities have more developed employment equity structures than others. At Dalhousie University in Halifax, Nova Scotia, there is an Employment Equity Officer (EEO) and an Employment Equity Council (EEC). Generally, the EEO is responsible for "the implementation and effective maintenance of Dalhousie's policy on affirmative action and equal opportunity"; "compil(ing) and monitor(ing) inventories of designated group members employed at Dalhousie"; "collect(ing) and analyz(ing) external workforce data"; "prepar(ing) and recommend(ing) to the EEC measurable goals and timetable for the recruitment, advancement and work environment of members of the designated groups," and "monitor(ing) the University's performance under this policy, receiv(ing) complaints, and, with the EEC, recommend(ing) strategies for improvement to the President and other levels of administration" (Employment Equity Through Affirmative Action at Dalhousie University 3–5).

The EEC, in consultation with the EEO, "determine(s) and propose(s) to the President measurable goals and timetables for the recruitment, advancement and work environment of the designated groups, and devise(s) and recommend(s) recruitment, outreach, training and sensitization strategies relating to affirmative action for members of the designated groups" (Employment Equity Through Affirmative Action at Dalhousie University 3–5).

The composition of the EEC includes one representative from each employee group, two women, one Miq'mac person, one person with a disability, one African Canadian, one student, three vice-presidents, the director of Personnel Services, and the EEO. Without being members of an employee group, such as the Canadian Union of Public Employees (CUPE) Local 3912, teaching assistants and sessional lecturers would not have a direct voice on the

EEC. Instead, their voices would be diffused through the student representative (representing all students on campus) and the designated group representatives. Without this voice, it would be difficult to speak solely about the unique position of graduate students as both employees and students whose desire to achieve employment equity is so closely linked to the achievement of educational equity (and vice versa) and their future success (see Young). In addition, there would be no opportunity to hear the opinions of other council members, participate in discussions about employment equity programming, or to understand why employment equity is an important process for all employees and students at Dalhousie, or any other university. Moreover, without a presence on the EEC, teaching assistants and sessional lecturers would not be as well integrated into the ESR as they are given that many (though not all) of its members fall below 30 per cent of the full-time equivalent work minimum required to be included in the ESR.

Despite this representation, efforts to bring educational equity onto the EEC's agenda have not been successful. Some members of the EEC contend that educational issues should be dealt with elsewhere in the university environment such as in the Senate. However, because the representation exists, this view does not prevent conceptual links about employment and educational equity from being made. It also does not prevent CUPE Local 3912 (Teaching Assistants and Sessional Lecturers) from focusing some attention on educational equity issues as employment equity is implemented and as the ESR is carried out. For example, when Dalhousie University administered an organizational level ESR Questionnaire concerning employment practices to all Dalhousie employees, it discovered that there were areas of concern about inequitable employment practices concerning teaching assistants and sessional lecturers which needed further investigation at the unit level (see Employment Systems Review Questionnaire). Respondants voiced concerns about the absence of policies for affirmative action hirings for sessional lecturers, a general lack of training programs, and so on. Evidence of these concerns allows CUPE 3912 to make links at the EEC with educational equity issues insofar as they impede academic success by limiting student experiences and preventing them from garnering the training they need for future employment and scholarship opportunities.

As teaching assistants and sessional lecturers draw attention to these issues at the EEC and elsewhere, the possibility of placing educational equity onto the employment equity agenda is increased. By linking educational issues to information gathered through the organizational level ESR, these issues begin to be seen as legitimate areas of concern for the entire university community. This reinforces the need for a systemic approach to educational equity issues and simultaneously provides a forum for such an approach which has the backing of actual federal legislation.

Implementing employment equity: connections to educational equity

Dalhousie University is one of the first universities in Canada to be gathering information for its third ESR. At this point, the ESR is still focusing on the organizational level of comparing policies and practices concerning employment equity. The next step is to move toward unit reviews concerning policies and practices. Under the Federal Contractor's Programme and Dalhousie's institutional plan for achieving employment equity, all units are supposed to be moving forward on their own with implementing employment equity. Generally, there is a great deal of institutional inertia at the unit level for implementing employment equity. This does not bode well for educational equity. Units at Dalhousie which are actually going ahead with employment equity implementation include the School of Nursing, the Maritime School of Social Work, some areas of Medicine, and the Killam Library.

The latter is particularly interesting because it has established an Employment Equity/Race Relations Committee charged with implementing employment equity within the unit (Employment Equity Council, Dalhousie University). This committee has taken upon itself the job of looking not only at recruitment, hiring, and mobility for full-time positions, but also those part-time positions designated as less than 30 per cent of the full-time equivalent. Most of these part-time positions are filled by students (graduate and undergraduate) and, as such, they are being fully included in employment equity programming and will likely become part of the future unit ESR. The committee decided to proceed in this way because it regularly draws from its pool of part-time employees to fill full-time openings. Since so many part-time employees at the library are members of the designated groups, they provide an excellent pool of experienced people which the library can draw on to fulfill its employment equity obligations regarding positions which are over 30 per cent of full-time equivalent. In addition, the committee decided to enforce the minimum qualifications hiring standards established for all positions. Though somewhat controversial, the committee proceeded in this manner in order to avoid the trap of reducing their pool of applicants solely because they were hiring people with qualifications way beyond the minimum required. Such a move serves to focus attention on what are legitimate minimum qualifications needed for a job and away from the criticism that employment equity is about hiring unqualified people in order to fill quotas.

While not an academic unit, the move by the Killam Library at Dalhousie to include those employees working less than 30 per cent of the full-time equivalent (mainly students) in its employment equity programming is significant because it means that students from the designated groups are better able to earn the money needed to pursue higher education and can begin to access the training necessary to advance upward through available positions. This is particularly significant for students of library science whose academic and employment success depends on relevant employment experience. In addition, their inclusion solidifies the view that all employees should be included in employment equity programming regardless of their work-time status and it works toward comprehensively incorporating student realities into the work environment.

The problem of co-optation

Generally, this paper assumes that employment equity is a good thing and that incorporating educational equity into employment equity programming will be a productive way to advance educational equity. There are, however, valid criticisms of employment equity programming which need to be addressed. First, employment equity is a long and drawn out process that can, because of its complexity, be opposed in many different ways by many different groups both internal and external to the institutional environment. This opposition can potentially locate itself in at least three different places: the ESR, the institution's employment equity plan, and individual complaints directed at the EEC by employees who believe they have experienced discriminatory harassment in their work environment. Although not the case at Dalhousie University, some universities also locate the responsibility of sexual harassment complaints under the auspices of their employment equity offices. Since the EEO is at the centre of all of these locations, it is possible that this person and his/her office could be coopted by opposition forces within the university thereby subverting the whole employment equity process. According to those at the University of Victoria in British Columbia who sought to have their equity complaints about the Department of Political Science addressed by the university's equity office,

Equity professionals are encouraged by the university to show leadership to women on campus and be examples of allegiance to adminis-
trated equity and administrative "protection." In this con, the function
of the equity office is to silence women by convincing them to trust the
process: The Problem is being handled by The Process. Trust is the
trick, and most are prepared to trust the equity office because it is a
"process" and because faith and trust must be declared if complaints
are to be taken up. The strategy of sexist interests has been to make
women's grievances the property and copyright of the equity office. In
our situation, there has been a move to franchise equity and make the
administration's equity office the professional authority and copyright
holder to all rights and speech that protest power and dissent from
discrimination. With the delegitimization and dis-crediting of the
speech of unauthorized women and minorities, there has been a
reaffirmation of men's rights to sue and be protected from women's
speech. The message to dissenting and harassed women is: Report to
the Equity Office; go to where we control what you have said, go and
tell it in confidence to those we have authorized. The disenfranchised
are opened up to civil liability if they speak out, and the only
"protection" seems to be at the equity office, the University owned and
operated rallying point for praise of white and male power. In fighting
this, we realize and remember how systemic, organized and sustained
discrimination really is. (See Brodribb *et al.* 20).

Certainly it is to be acknowledged that the main purpose of channeling
equity complaints through an EEO is to avoid the expense (incurred by the
university and the complainant) and bad press of a human rights complaint by
opting for institutional level mediation. As well, it is possible that managing
these complaints for the purpose of avoiding institutional change may also
hinder the efficient functioning of the EEO in other areas, such as with respect
to an ongoing ESR or the implementation of a unit level employment equity
program. This hindrance will then slow down any attempts at achieving
educational equity via the employment equity agenda. However, in the long
run, co-optation cannot change the reality of whether or not goals concerning
designated group employment have been met within an agreed upon period;
these numbers do not lie and they are monitored regularly by the ESR.
Furthermore, without the structure that employment equity legislation spawns
within the institution, such as an EEO, it would be very difficult to bring about

the kind of systemic change necessary for achieving either employment or educational equity. The employment equity structure also allows people in powerful positions within the institution who are sympathetic to employment and educational equity goals to effect positive change in a constructive and fairly rapid manner; these successes have an important demonstration effect on the rest of the institution.

At the very least, this structure holds up the possibility for change and therefore encourages people to think and speak up about all inequitable practices they have experienced. No doubt, the strategy (or lack thereof) of seeking redress for those experiences will affect the manner in which the complaint is resolved. Here, it is important to learn from those who have attempted to have their complaints redressed via equity processes (see McEwen; Brodribb, *et al.*). The employment equity structure creates the debate necessary for bringing these issues to the attention of the wider university community and indeed the public as a whole. Debates mobilize groups to act and, ultimately, successful employment and educational equity strategies require significant support from faculty, unions, sympathetic administrators, student unions, and even the public to bring about long lasting change. Perhaps the most important aspect of this structure is that it promotes institutional learning about how to achieve employment equity and, therefore, how to overcome institutional inertia. Certainly the point might be made that institutional learning is not confined only to those who want to implement employment equity, but includes those who want to expand on it (as in the case of connecting it to educational equity) as well as those who want to resist it. However it is difficult to completely stall a practice which draws forward momentum from federally mandated reviews and from the ongoing evidence, at both the individual and systemic levels, that inequitable employment policies and practices exist.

Conclusion

Educational equity is about justice. It is about changing political consciousness, social constructs, and institutional systems in order to ensure that all students may learn and grow in an environment which is free from discrimination and which makes creativity, diversity, and open-mindedness the base-line for all educational experiences.

Unlike employment equity, the main focus of educational equity is not on the range of employees in an institution, but on the nature of the programs and the climate in which they are delivered. However, employment and educational equity are inextricably intertwined because the success of employment equity depends on an equitable educational environment. Without such an environment, there will never be a large enough pool of people created from the designated groups from which employment equity programs can draw prospective employees. At the same time, without employees from the designated groups in place, educational equity will be difficult to promote (particularly in the university classroom) since there will be few role models available to promote designated group advancement. Ultimately, this situation constitutes a vicious cycle which is very difficult to break by any one person or sector of the university community.

It is the responsibility of all members of the university community (and indeed of wider society) to make employment and educational equity a reality. This reality can only be achieved if there is pressure from all sectors of the university community (administration, employee groups, students, and designated groups) to move forward on employment and educational equity in a simultaneous, assertive, and collective manner. It is naive and even irresponsible to expect that assigning the task of educational equity to one sector of the university community, such as the Senate or the Deans, will be an adequate way to address a problem which permeates the entire university system and which is linked so closely to the issue of employment equity.

As our society becomes more diverse and complex, the university community will continue to experience increased pressure to provide an equitable educational environment for all students who are part of that community. It is therefore incumbent upon employment equity programming at universities to take part in furthering the goals of educational equity. The most efficient way for a campus-wide grassroots program of educational equity to proceed is for all units to make the issue of educational equity a priority as they implement their employment equity plans and progress through Employment Systems Reviews.

¹The term "university classroom" refers, here, not only to lecture halls but also to seminars, labs, clinicals, and so on.

References

Action Travail des Femmes vs. *C.N.R.* Co. Case (1987) 40 D.L.R. (4th) 193. 210.

Brodribb, S., S. Bardon, T. Newhouse, J. Spencer, and N. Kyba. "The Equity Franchise." *Women's Education des Femmes* 12.1 (1996): 12–20.

Canada. *Bill C-64, An Act Respecting Employment Equity.* 42–43 Elizabeth II, 1994.

Canada. *Canadian Charter of Rights and Freedoms.* 1981.

Canada. Canadian Human Rights Commission. 42–43–44 Elizabeth II, 1994-95, Chapter 44, An Act Respecting Employment Equity. Assented to December 15, 1995. www.chrc.ca.

Canada. Human Resources Development Canada. Assistance for Students With Permanent Disabilities. July 1995.

Canada. Human Resources Development Canada. Special Opportunity Grants for Female Doctoral Students. July 1995.

Dalhousie University. Educational Equity at Dalhousie University: A Discussion Paper. Employment Equity Office, Dalhousie University, March 1995.

Dalhousie University. Employment Equity Through Affirmative Action at Dalhousie: A Policy Statement. October, 1989.

Dalhousie. Employment Systems Review Questionnaire. January 1997.

Dalhousie University. Faculty of Graduate Studies Manual on Policies, Governance and Procedures. Faculty of Graduate Studies, June 1995.

Dalhousie University. Mission Statement. March 1993.

Dalhousie University. The Report of the Senate Advisory Committee on Affirmative Action in Education, Dalhousie University, June 17, 1991.

Employment Equity Council, Dalhousie University. Meeting Minutes. February 11, 1997.

Foucault, Michel. *Power/Knowledge.* New York: Pantheon Books, 1980.

McEwen, Joan. Report in Respect of the Political Science Department of the University of British Columbia. University of British Columbia, June 15, 1995.

MacKinnon, Catharine. *Toward a Feminist Theory of the State.* Cambridge: Harvard University Press, 1989.

Mohanty, C. T. "On Race and Voice: Challenges for the Liberal Education of the 1990s." *Cultural Critique* 14 (1991): 179–208.

Mukherjee, A., and B. Thomas. "A Glossary of Anti-Racist Terms." *Multiculturalism at Work.* Ed. B. Thomas. Toronto: YWCA, 1987.

Ng, Roxana. "'A Woman Out of Control': Deconstructing Sexism and Racism in the University." *Canadian Journal of Higher Education* 18.3 (1993): 189–205.

Ontario Confederation of University Faculty Associations. "Educational Equity." Canadian Woman Studies 12.3 (1992): 99–102.

Pothier, Diane. *Miles to Go: Some Personal Reflections on the Social Construction of Disability.* Halifax: Dalhousie University, 1991.

Spivak, Gayatri Chakravorty. *The Postcolonial Critic.* New York and London: Routledge, 1990.

Taylor, Charles. *Multiculturalism and the Politics of Recognition.* New Jersey: Princeton University Press, 1992.

Tutton, Michael. "In Search of a Breakthrough: Why so Few Women Become Career Scientists." *Dalhousie Alumni Magazine* (1996): 10–15.

Williams, Hannah. "Educational Equity: Background for Discussion." Montreal: McGill University Equity Office, June 1994.

Willis, P. *Learning to Labour: How Working Class Kids Get Working Class Jobs.* New York: Columbia University Press, 1977.

Young, Allison. Educational Equity. Dalhousie University, March 1996.

Race and Equity in the Academy

George J. Sefa Dei

I am not coming to the discussion of race and equity in the academy from a disinterested or a politically neutral position. (Who does by the way?) The politics that drive my position are anchored in a concern about the denial and erasure of race and difference in the academy to present knowledge as a legitimate search for one prevailing truth. Furthermore, equity is far from being a "special interest" concern. Equity issues problematize the core of privilege and power and how we[1] resolve injustice in institutional settings. Indeed for those working in the academy, the political stakes are high.

In *Race and the Education of Desire*, Ann Stoler cites Foucault's response to a question posed by a journalist as to whether Foucault saw his writings as a set of "teachings" or as a "discourse that prescribes." Foucault's reply:

> In my case it's another matter entirely; my books don't have this kind of value. They function as invitations, as public gestures, for those who may want eventually to do the same thing, or something like it, or in any case, who intend to slip into this kind of experience. (Foucault qtd. in Stoler 16–17)

In writing this paper, I humbly identify with Foucault's comments and sentiments. I invite readers, and particularly those working in the academy, to see this paper as an "opening, as a provocation, as an invitation of my own" (Stoler 17).

I am using academy in this text to refer to the social sites of official knowledge production and reproduction, that is, schools, colleges, and universities in Euro-Canadian/American contexts. By "education," I refer to the myriad ways, options, and strategies through which we collectively come to know and understand the world and act within it. Equity is also taken broadly to mean dealing with social difference. Equity encompasses concerns about race, ethnicity, class, gender, sexuality, and how these implicate other dimensions of the human experience and condition. The differential ordering of power relations in society means we not only have to be aware of our "multiple selves" (Kondo 220), but also understand the nature of the "… multiple intersections of structures of power" (Mohanty 1991, 14).

Although I am mindful of the trajectories of difference and the interlocking nature of oppressions, my expressed political direction is to maintain the focus on race as one of the fundamental questions of equity. The intent is to guard against that easy slippage into a bland talk of social justice for "all" that fails to name race and difference in stark terms. As has been repeatedly argued, we cannot ignore or deny race. Neither can we simply believe that race can be theorized "out of existence" (Allahar 27; Omi and Winant). Race is the medium or "modality" through which economic opportunity and social power are lived and experienced in North American society (see also Hall *et al.* 394).

As someone teaching and researching on race and anti-racism, I believe that a genuinely transformative social politics must recognize the situational and contextual variations in intensities of oppressions. I have argued elsewhere (Dei 1999a) that anti-racism politics advocates for social change in which race is acknowledged as a central axis of power, and racist inequities are ameliorated. This politics demands that race comes first, that the salience of race is primary even when coexisting with other dimensions of oppression. There is a growing critique of the seductive language of social and educational justice for all that fails to adequately grasp the severity of the issues faced by identified disadvantaged and minoritized groups in our communities (see Dei 1998). There *are* alternative formulations of balance, equality, and fairness that must enter the dialogue on social justice and equity. We need to change the structures within which the space and voice for equity work are accomplished in the academy.

I find Charles Taylor's work very instructive in formulating my academic/political project for educational equity. Taylor notes that there are a number of reasons why alternative "cultures" should be integral to academic curriculum and public discourse. He argues that previously silenced groups are currently fighting for recognition. The need for recognition emerges not only because of the omission of other voices, but largely because the view of the existing structures of dominance is negative and demeaning. However, what is most profound about Taylor's discussion is that he links this need to the Fanonian conceptualization of the process of liberation. Taylor suggests that, like liberation from colonial occupation, there must be a transformation of the *status quo* to find a basis for incorporating alternative viewpoints. This call for transformation is moral and profoundly political. Alternative voices are part of the catalyst necessary to free the disadvantaged and minoritized from their current situation and position.

In this paper, my discursive approach acknowledges the multiple readings of equity. A race-centric analysis of equity is not without theoretical and political pitfalls, particularly as equity has to be defined broadly to include the axes of multiple identifications, relations of difference, and trajectories of oppression. Nonetheless, we must be troubled by the fact that in conventional discourses articulating multiple oppressions, race is a category that is lost or subsumed. For many of us, it may be said that race is an unsettling issue. Therefore, at this political and academic moment I have decided on a strategic discursive approach to equity that highlights (not necessarily privileges) race. In fact, in the academy, to "enter" into discussions concerning equity and access is to begin to question our own subjective positions and working assumptions about power, privilege, and domination. "Moral distancing" from and "moral condemnation" of injustice may not be enough. Unless, as educators and students, we individually and collectively confront our own oppressions and privileges, we may not be completely justified in merely distancing ourselves morally from another's racisms and oppressions. Those of us privileged to be working in the academy must recognize our specific social locations and relatively privileged positions of cultural, political, and economic power vis-à-vis those of the truly downtrodden. Acknowledging our subjective limitations should provide the needed critical self reflection to pursue a politics of genuine coalition building.

Personally, part of the challenge facing contemporary critical educators and students is to map out our varied complicities in oppressions while at the same time pointing to the interconnections between the social resistance to classism, racism, homophobia, heterosexism, ableism, and sexism. Knowledge explaining how power and privilege can be structured according to race, class, gender, age, and disability cannot be treated as "add-ons" by classroom teachers and educators. As Fine argues, schools continually distribute "... skills and opportunities in ways textured by class, race, and gender asymmetries" (199).

Therefore, our academic disciplines may concretely respond to the existential experiences of a diverse student body. Specifically, this means working with the social categories of race, gender, sexuality, and other forms of difference and what these differences mean for engaging learning and society.

The challenge that "equity" poses for academies of learning is not unsurmountable. The kinds of questions educators ask and address in school settings can assist in transforming schools into sites which serve the multiple interests, desires, and aspirations of a diverse body politic.

The key questions

1) How may academic disciplines and administrations seriously address equity issues when a theoretical understanding of the role of race and difference in the context for power and domination in society is fiercely resisted in public discourses and social practices?

2) What does it mean to self-reflect in the context of increasingly complex understandings of power, authority, and morality in dealing with race, gender, class, and disability in the academy?

3) How do we ensure that what is "theoretical" is not constructed in direct opposition to what is "pragmatic"? How may scholars take "action," thereby avoiding the "political paralysis" that results from the mere intellectualization of transformative political projects? (see also Estrada and McLaren).

4) How do we move beyond the bland talk of "inclusion" to engage in a concrete politics of accountability and transparency and commitment?

5) What are our responsibilities in terms of a critical engagement of the broader community in the struggle for equity and access in education?

Let me focus on three areas in responding to these questions. The questions call for rethinking equity issues in the academy in terms of: (a) dealing with the question of "representation"; (b) developing the idea of multiple, collective, and collaborative dimensions of knowledge that will inform learners about the complete history of ideas and events that continue to shape human growth and social development; and (c), sustaining equity issues in the academy (e.g., curriculum, pedagogy, the spaces that minoritized and dominant bodies occupy).

Representation

Schools are sites and spaces of contestations and resistance. One area for contestation and resistance is the physical representation of multiple bodies in the academy. Physical representation in academic institutions is also a question of educational access and maintaining equity. This means schools must consider how, during these times of reduced state funding, they may attract, support, and retain students from economically disadvantaged backgrounds. Effective recruitment implies that academic assessment measures and evaluation criteria must also be scrutinized to address structural and cultural biases against students who come in from non-conventional spaces and whose credentials may easily be ignored, under-evaluated, and/or misrepresented. We must find a way to deal with the structural and other acts of gate-keeping in our academic recruitment and evaluation policies—for example, the present employment of measurement and evaluation methods that privilege Eurocentric forms of knowledge or human experience over others.

Equally important, racial minority professors are disturbingly absent from the teaching faculties. This problem exists at the same time that students yearn for genuine inclusion of all knowledges. Challenging established definitions of "merit," "success," and "qualification" that are embedded in the cult of individualism and normative knowledge constitutes part of the process of "structural hegemonic rupturing" (see James and Mannette). We must use problematic attempts to decouple the issues of equity from excellence. Furthermore by working with the categories of race and difference as relevant in knowledge production and dissemination, schools can begin to address the challenge of having a diverse student and staff representation. We must deal with the problem of tokenism and seriously enact measures that reflect a sincere commitment to diversity and power sharing in the academy. At the bare minimum, particularly the minoritized students from diverse backgrounds must see the possibility of a space for them in the academy. It is imperative that such students continue their education for hegemonic rupturing to occur.

Knowledge

The search for an alternative, non-hegemonic knowledge base that is able to capture the complexities of social, historical and educational experiences is still on-going in the academy. One form that the search takes is the repeated reexamination of Eurocentricity in its myriad representations. There is a dialectical relation between social identity and knowledge production; who we are has an important bearing on how we come to make sense of our world. The cultivation of non-hegemonic forms of knowledge in the academy requires a critical interrogation of what has come to constitute "valid knowledge" and how such knowledge is being produced and disseminated internally and globally. Hegemonic knowledges and their colonial and imperial representations of the "other," racist, and anti-different popular discourses, as well as "immigrant" formulations of all minorities need to be deconstructed by educators and students in the academy. Progressive educators and learners must continually ask: where is the space and place for alternative, indigenous, and oppositional knowledge forms in the academy?

Furthermore, as argued elsewhere (Dei 1999b) a redefinition of personal politics is tied to our conceptions of the link between the self/personhood and how we come to know and interpret the world and act within it. This is the idea of the inextricability of spirituality, knowledge, politics, and educational change (see also Leah). In critiques of conventional education, the question is often posed as to why certain experiences and histories "count" more than others, in terms of the production and validation of "valid" academic knowledge (see Dei, Hall, and Goldin-Rosenberg).

In my educational practice, I hear particularly (but not exclusively) racially minoritized students agonize about what it will take for *all* educators to recognize the powerful linkage between identity, schooling, and knowledge production. At the heart of this concern is the marginality of indigenous knowledges in the academy, and the implications of knowledge hierarchies for educational transformation and social change. By "indigenous" I gesture to knowledge whose authority resides in origin, place, history, and ancestry. New knowledge is crucial to decolonizing and reforming conventional educational practice. Knowledge about human spirituality offers insights into individual and collective responsibilities in changing the course and direction of educational praxis.

Sustaining equity issues

To bring equity issues to the fore of the academy, instructional courses have to reflect the reality of a diverse student body, and the complexities of global politics. Courses on anti-racism, sexuality, gender equity, and disability studies are important to provide the theoretical and epistemological grounding for learners to understand equity and social difference. Of course, such specific course offerings may not be enough to propel change, but they are an important start. These courses could ensure that learners develop the theoretical and philosophical understanding that race, gender, and difference provide the context for power and domination in society. However, there must be parallel action to integrate equity issues into the curriculum of academic subjects taught in schools, colleges, and universities. We should be concerned that it is usually the "converted" students who are already committed to social action who choose to take courses with prominent race, gender, sexuality, and difference analyses.

To sustain equity issues in the academy, we must deal with what happens to the different physical bodies when they come to occupy spaces in schools. School spaces are contested by different interests and agendas. Spaces can also be imagined and resisted for meaningful political action for educational and social change. Academic spaces continually shift with their constituent physical bodies as learners and educators engage knowledge and knowledge production through multiple strategies. Minority students need to gain access to academic spaces and sites; their collective agency would ensure that the fundamental questions of power and empowerment can be addressed.

Access, power, and empowerment are important, and the mere presence of a diverse student body is not enough—especially if students are not sustained and supported in the academy through continued funding and the removal of oppressively biased environments for learning and social growth. When students ask to research and study on race and equity, responses offered to their enquiries should be welcoming rather than being limited by the absence of bodies. In the academy, we cannot afford to depend upon the same few scholars for the students who ask to work on race and equity. For those faculty working on race, disability, and gender the struggle against "burning out" is a real and present difficulty.

Rethinking the struggle for equity and the future

It is important that educators and administrators move beyond what Michele Fine calls the ideological fetish of "good intentions." This means a shift away from the pre-occupation with "intentions" to the examination of the consequences of human actions and/or social practice. Academic and social transformation demand resistance to the status quo. Social change may be read both in terms of "widespread social and political economic transformation, [and] the micro-politics of tactical manoeuvers" (Moore 4) that minority and minoritized groups employ to seek race justice and equity.

Resistance to the status quo is central to addressing equity issues in the academy. Abu-Lughod has cautioned against the "... tendency to romanticize resistance, to read all forms of resistance as signs of the ineffectiveness of systems of power and the resilience and creativity of the human spirit in its refusal to be dominated" (42). Nevertheless, we can view the "potential for resistance within the structures of power" and social domination (Prakesh 180; see also Foucault 1980, 1983). In fact, resistance should be tied to those in positions of power and influence using their power and privileged positions to challenge social dominance in its myriad forms. Transformative resistance acknowledges our individual and collective responsibilities to challenge and act on privilege, power, and dominance in social and institutional settings. In academic institutions, asking critical questions is crucial to repair the absence, negations, and erasures of experiences, knowledges, and bodies and what they mean for political participation and involvement and for purposeful education. A critical examination of the historical, cultural, and spatial specificities of minority groups' resistance to social domination demonstrates the nature of social politics and everyday local performances in affecting change in the academy. To sustain these performances, minority groups' resistance must be rewarded.

Among socially constructed groups in society there does exist clearly objective and subjective differences. These differences have significant implications, particularly, in terms of power differentials. However, as Mohanty cautioned, as educators the "… central issue … is not one of merely acknowledging difference; rather the more fundamental question concerns the kind of difference that is acknowledged and engaged" (1990, 181). We must point out the dangers of honouring diversity within the context of creating or maintaining unity while ignoring issues of structural inequities. While we celebrate social differences and human diversity we must correspondingly analyze and engage in a critique of the dynamics of power among social groups positioned by race, physical ability, class, gender, and sexuality. Individuals within particular social groupings defined by the social constructions of race, gender, class, physical ability, sexuality, region, and nation are not subjects of a single experience of oppressions. Historical struggles for social justice are different and yet shared. The experience of social oppression is a deeply differential one, experienced in fundamentally different ways by different people. The challenge is to broaden existing ideas and insights into social oppression to account for the instances of oppression and inequality which are structured in the complex social reality experienced by most people.

Similarly, members of the academy do not constitute a monolithic group in the discourse about power and social relations. If the source of bourgeois power is large concentrations of intellectual and economic capital then the academy as a monolithic space becomes problematic. Intellectual capital and the corresponding power to coerce and to unify populations into various hegemonic projects are part of a complex social relation. In institutions, this social relation not only involves macro-relations (e.g., policies, structures, and division of labour), but also micro-power relations embedded in daily school and classroom life, and the face-to-face encounters with teachers, students, and staff representing a range of human and social "differences" (e.g., gender, race, culture, ethnicity, nationality, religion, and philosophical ideologies). Therefore, changing school social relations involves more than class struggle, as other forms of oppression are inscribed in it—racism, sexism, heterosexism, and homophobia. The conflict between competing approaches to equity is one of many dialectics that cannot be ignored in a discussion of race, gender, sexuality, culture, and power relations in the academy.

Ideology is not a false consciousness. It is part of a lived reality particularly when it provides a basis for political action. Ideology is tied to changing systems of values and what we accept as legitimate and/or illegitimate social and political actions. There are divergent and competing claims, ideas, and forces that shape how schools respond to questions of equity and fairness. Insecurities associated with differences may be marshalled and "rationalized" in commonsensical thought and social practice to further colonialist projects of subjugating "others" and remaining silent. Furthermore, certain ideas could be hegemonized as normative knowledge to service the cause of imperialist projects that deny power and agency to human subjects.

As I have already suggested, there are macro- and micro-politics of transformation. If social reality is constituted in praxis and if education is a dialogue then there is a partial basis for a theory of social action. To work toward a theory of social action it is important to focus on macro- and micro-levels of oppression and how they relate and influence each other in school and other institutional settings. It is also important that we recognize the limitations of our own subjectivities as the rationale for coalition politics. This can help us transcend the atomization of our subjectivities and individualities which tend to reinforce alienation from our own communities.

The mobilization of our individual strengths for political action can only succeed with the development of a "community of scholars" starting with our respective work places and schools and engaging local communities (wider public) in the pursuit of concrete actions to challenge racism, sexism, heterosexism, ableism, ageism, and elite economic power at the level of the culture(s) of our institutions (see Sheth and Dei). While a theoretically informed action needs a foundation of common human experience, it does not entail the denial or subjugation of "difference." The need to locate ourselves in our political projects and to define a common ground must be rooted in an understanding of how our differences can enrich a shared concern to address and eradicate social injustices and all forms of oppression. It should be recognized that the emphasis on individual subjectivity for its own sake is itself closely connected to bourgeois philosophy. The individual as a social construct serves the purpose of alienation and social control. An ideology of individualism that therefore heralds "possibilities" without recognizing its limitations for political mobilization can and does reinforce alienation and "political paralysis" (Roman). After all, we define our subjectivities in terms of how whole institutional structures and the dynamics of social difference inter-relate in society.

I am grateful to Irma Marcia James, Eve Haque and Gabriel Bedard of the Department of Sociology and Equity Studies, Ontario Institute for Studies in Education of the University of Toronto (OISE/UT) for commenting on drafts of the paper. I also acknowledge conversations with Nigel Moses, formerly Ontario Institute for Studies in Education (OISE), in developing my thoughts regarding the theory of social action.

[1]Unless where specified, I use "we" in the context of this paper to refer to all who read the paper and share the academic and political project of equity and educational change.

References

Abu-Lughod, L. "The Romance of Resistance: Tracing Transformations of Power Through Bedouin Women." *American Ethnologist* 17.1 (1990): 41–55.

Allahar, A. "'Race,' Ethnic Identity and the Search for 'Home.'" Pres. at workshop on "Cultural Negotiation," Spenser Hall, University of Western Ontario, London, Ontario, April 26–28, 1996.

Dei, George J. S. "Towards an Anti-Racism Discursive Framework." *Anti-Racism and Critical Race, Gender and Class Studies.* Eds. A. Calliste and G. J. S. Dei. Halifax: Fernwood Publishing, 1999a.

Dei, George J. S. "Why Write Back?: The Rule of Afrocentric Discourse in Social Change." *Canadian Journal of Education* 23 (2) (1999): 200-208.

Dei, George J. S. "The Politics of Denial and Difference: Reframing Anti-Racist Praxis." *Race, Ethnicity and Education* (1999b forthcoming).

Dei, George J. S., B. Hall, and D. Goldin-Rosenberg, eds. *Indigenous Knowledge in Global Contexts: Multiple Readings of Our World.* Toronto: University of Toronto Press, 1999 forthcoming.

Estrada, K., and P. McLaren. "A Dialogue on Multiculturalism and Democratic Culture." *Educational Researcher* 22.3 (1993): 27–33.

Fine, M. *Framing Dropouts: Notes on the Politics of Urban Public High School.* New York: State University of New York Press, 1991.

Foucault, M. *Power/Knowledge: Selected Interview, 1972–77.* Ed. C. Gordon. Brighton: Harvester Press, 1980.

Foucault, M. "The Subject and Power." *Michel Foucault: Beyond Structuralism and Hermeneutics.* Eds. H. Dreyfus and P. Rabinow. Chicago: University of Chicago Press, 1983. 208–226.

Hall, S., *et al. Policing the Crisis: Mugging, the State and Law and Order.* London: MacMillan, 1978.

Haynes, D., and G. Prakash. "Introduction: The Entanglement of Power and Resistance." *Contesting Power: Resistance and Everyday Social Relations in South Asia.* Eds. D. Haynes and G. Prakash. Dehli: Oxford University Press, 1991. 1–22.

James, C., and J. Mannette. "Consequences, Contradictions, and Diversity: Reflections on Collegiality in Black and White." Pres. at Learned Societies' Meeting of the Canadian Sociology and Anthropology Association (CSAA), Brock University, St. Catharines, Ontario, 2–5 June 1996.

Kondo, D. *Crafting Selves: Power, Gender, and Discourses of Identity in a Japanese Workplace.* Chicago: University of Chicago Press, 1990.

Leah, R. "Anti-Racism Studies: An Integrative Perspective." *Race, Gender, and Class* 2.3 (1995): 105–22.

Mohanty, C. "On Race and Voice: Challenges for Liberal Education in the 90's." *Cultural Critique* 18.4 (1990): 179–208.

Mohanty, C. "Cartographies of Struggle: Third World Women and the Politics of Feminism." *Third World Women and the Politics of Feminism.* Eds. C. Mohanty, A. Russo, and L. Torres. Bloomington: Indiana University Press, 1991. 1–47.

Moore, D. S. "Remapping Resistance: 'Ground for Struggle' and the Politics of Place." *Geographies of Resistance.* Eds. S. Pile and M. Keith. London:

Routledge, 1997.

Omi, M., and H. Winant. "On the Theoretical Concept of Race." *Race, Identity and Representation in Education.* Eds. C. McCarthy and W. Crichlow. New York: Routledge, 1993. 3–10.

Prakash, G. "Can the Subaltern Ride?: A Reply to O'Hanlon and Washbrook." *Comparative Studies in Society and History* 34.1 (1992): 168–184.

Roman, L. "White is a Color! White Defensiveness, Postmodernism, and Anti-Racist Pedagogy." *Race, Identity and Representation in Education.* Eds. C. McCarthy and W. Crichlow. New York: Routledge, 1993. 71–88.

Sheth, A., and G. J. S. Dexi. "Limiting the Academics of Possibilities: A Self-Reflective Exercise in Freirian Politics." *Engaging the Mentor: A Critical Dialogue with Paulo Freire.* Eds. P. Freire, J. Fraser, D. Macedo, T. McKinnon, and W. T. Stokes. New York: Peter Lang, 1997. 143–174.

Stoler, A. L. *Race and the Education of Desire.* Durham: Duke University Press, 1995.

Taylor, C. "The Politics of Recognition." *Multiculturalism.* Ed. A. Guttman. Princeton, NJ: Princeton University Press, 1994. 25–73.

Symbolic Equity
Disability in Higher Education

Kathleen Rockhill

The university operates as a contradictory regulatory institution with regard to equity. It is a gatekeeper of privilege, interpolating as subjects those bodies that get to be in charge of other bodies. As the major pathway to the professions, the university has become, perhaps, the crucial site for disabling bodies that cannot pass through its doors. It is upon this contradictory terrain, of being regulated out and in at the same time, that bodies get positioned when questions of equity play out through them. As the arbiter of what counts as expertise in our society, the university determines which bodies get to perform expertise upon other bodies—that is the distinction between who gets interpolated as one who knows and/or has the capacity to learn to perform that knowledge—and who gets interpolated as not having that capacity of knowledge.

The university also has the power to define what counts as knowledge, whose knowledge counts, and what counts as excellence in the performance of that knowledge. In this process of "accounting" the specificities of bodily performance are left unarticulated; truly accomplished bodies are seen to perform naturally, as though "gifted" from birth, others are described as "hard workers" or "over achievers." It is into this ideological mine field that the disabled body treads. It is the bearer of "special needs," not of "gifts," but of a whole set of problems. Under negotiation are the limits of the body and the slur upon "capacity" that the "need for support" suggests.

In thinking about equity in graduate education, I wonder how we work the ways in which we are regulated to reinstantiate privilege, and how it is that a whole array of "privileging practices" play out in determining the composition of student and faculty populations. This is also to ask how we participate in the reproduction of social practices that privilege some bodies over others, however ambivalently we may be located with respect to those practices. And it is to ask how apparently neutral practices, like the organization of bodies through time and space, regulate *out* bodies that cannot conform to normalized expectations. How do these normalizing practices systematically marginalize bodies—that is, act as marginalizing practices? How are normalizing criteria deployed through our assumed everyday operating practices, and with what effect, and what is the university's part in that process? These questions come in and out of focus as I scan some of the marginalizing practices which form "the everyday" for faculty and students with disabilities, specifically those with mobility impairments.

In working toward greater equity for marginalized populations in higher education, we have generally politicized around changes in recruitment, admissions, and hiring practices, curricula and program provision. When we work with disability, we have to contemplate yet another dimension, that of structural change in the spatio-temporal arrangements that organize the ways in which bodies are articulated through spaces of academic production. This requires very specific concrete changes, expensive changes, to our buildings, to the way spaces are laid out to regulate the flow of bodies through them, to how time is used to structure movement and productivity, and to how we disseminate teaching and learning resources to make them "truly" accessible.

Without systematic changes, participation is impossible for all but the most privileged amongst the disabled. Money is crucial to acquiring the resources necessary to offset the limits of physical disablement; only with access to financial resources can one know any degree of independence or autonomy so necessary to dominant narratives of "success." This may help explain why disability "success stories" are almost always about white men, and occasionally women, who have the advantage of "family" to help provide support. Think of the resources behind Christopher Reeves, or, on a much smaller scale, Canada's Bonnie Sherr Klein.[1]

The fight for equity with regard to disability has scarcely begun. It has stalled at the level of the symbolic recognition of rights for disabled persons. At stake is a shift in public ideology from a needs-based to a rights-based approach. In Ontario, the inclusion of disabled persons in the Human Rights Code speaks to a very gradual ideological shift towards a rights-based approach, spilling over from the equity struggles of other marginalized populations. Still, in the absence of a concerted political initiative with regard to providing the resources required for disabled persons to realize their rights, the institutional response has been one of compliance, of meeting basic obligations.

For example, the University of Toronto recently approved a policy stating that it "is committed to the principle of equitable treatment pursuant to the 'Human Rights Code' and will accommodate employees and applicants for employment with disabilities in accordance with its obligations under that legislation" (University of Toronto 1995). Note the word "obligations." Perhaps working through the discursive practices of obligatory enforcement is necessary, but its effects are to reinstantiate the status quo. Note, too, that "reasonable accommodation" falls back upon a needs-based rather than a rights-based approach, although equity is theoretically about equal rights. For whom? The unarticulated caveat is that equal rights are for those of equal capacities. How do you differentiate between a "handicap" that limits the realization of one's capacity and limited capacity? With the burden of proof placed upon the individual when "judgement of capacity" is on the line, the institutional gaze is shifted away from questioning how bodily limits and capacities are constituted, and their "disabling" effects.

The effect upon individual bodies is that you must already be in the system to argue for individual "needs" based upon your rights not to be discriminated against because of "handicap." How do you define where the body ends and society begins—that is, what counts as a "handicap," under what conditions? If, by definition, I cannot function as everyone else does, where will you draw the line around what counts as "reasonable" accommodation?

In its work to integrate and accommodate students with disabilities, the university Office of Special Services reports that it served more than 1,000 students with disabilities in 1995–96. Approximately half were categorized as "learning disabled," and about 15 percent were dealing with sight, hearing, or mobility restrictions (University of Toronto 1996). If these data are indicative of a larger pattern, they suggest that dealing with the limiting consequences of physical and sensory anomalies is a very small part of the university's support allocation for accommodating persons with disabilities.

Within a few years, the ubiquitous blue and white wheelchair sign has come to symbolize access. Ramps, retrofitted washrooms, automatic doors, elevators with audio signals are becoming part of everyday life in large, modern public institutional spaces. While I do not want to minimize the importance of these developments, I also want to argue that much of the work of equity for disabled persons is at the symbolic, compliance-driven level. The blue wheel-chair sign is everywhere, but I see little evidence of active outreach to the full range of persons with disabilities, of thinking through and working creatively around the socially imposed limits that constitute the lives of a dazzling array of disenfranchised people.

It is a mistake to think that the work of access is accomplished once a ramp is in place. To state the obvious, a ramp is useful only to mobility-restricted persons who use wheelchairs or scooters; these are very expensive forms of equipment that are affordable only for the financially well-off or the "severely" disabled who manage to qualify for financial assistance. (Standards for approval have escalated dramatically in the last few years, with another five million dollars slated to be slashed from the assistive devices program.) Most mobility-restricted people are somewhere along the continuum of "completely immo-bile" to "able-bodied," and yet this is the discursive and symbolic dichotomy that has been institutionalized. When the use of a scooter or wheelchair is an option, its value is mixed: it expands and, at the same time, dramatically limits your life-space—once in the chair, you can only go where there are ramps that you can access, which requires some way to get to those ramps. Where chronic pain is involved, in constant question are the trade-offs between bodily pain and the autonomy of mobility.

To illustrate my point, I have been trying for over three years to get approval for a wheelchair or a scooter to offset the effects of lower limb paralysis. I am not disabled enough to qualify for the scooter or motorized chair, and since I also have a serious shoulder injury, the rehab consultants will not recommend me for the high quality manual wheelchair that I would need to be able to navigate. Now that I have a wheelchair on loan, I face many situations where I cannot use it. A joy for me would be to be able to access the university libraries and bookstores; I drive round and round the university library, and have yet to see a place to park, even with my disabled parking permit. In fact, I have yet to see a designated disabled parking spot near any ramp anywhere on campus. The exception is the bookstore, where the university usually parks its "disability" van in the one designated disabled parking spot. Even more ludicrous from my point of view, four million dollars were just spent to redesign St. George St.; in the process the possibility of disabled permit parking was eliminated by expensive curb cuts that prevent parking in non-metered spaces.

This is "access," and I'm only talking about getting into buildings on clear days. What happens once you are inside? And what does meaningful access look like for other forms of disability? To work in more meaningful ways with the complexities of access, equity, and rights, people with disabilities have to be centrally involved in policy formation, planning, and implementation, in all aspects of institutional life. As it is now, in meeting university "obligations," we are confined to a little corner designated as "special needs," which is unavoidably to contain a major social and structural situation, translating it into discrete manageable problems and an individualized, client-based approach.

The university is culpable for a situation in which virtually all the research, writing, policy-making, and program implementation that constitutes the lives of people *as* disabled, is performed by able-bodied people. To reverse this situation, people with a full range of disabilities would have to be actively recruited into the university, and their disabilities radically reconceptualized, not as hindrances but as necessary assets, to work in all areas of knowledge production.

Since my accident, I have begun to see how society is organized to consistently disappear, lock out and/or disable those who cannot conform to the dictates of physical normalcy. While normalizing practices define us racially and sexually as well as through disabilities, because disability works through individual bodies to constitute them as economically and physically dependent, it is governed by an infrastructure that is as vast as it is largely invisible to the able-bodied. Four years ago I was hurled, ass-backwards, into what I have come to think of as the medical/legal/insurance/government/rehabilitation maze. This tarantula-like maze is constructed by able-bodied people who have the power of definition, defining our bodies and lives through eligibility criteria and the determination of what they deem to be reasonable resources or accommodation; the able-bodied own the resources that they dole out to the "worthy" disabled. Not only are the "disabled" isolated from society by the disabling practices of everyday life, but so too this tarantula-like maze is seen only by the people caught in its maddening contradiction: the need to prove incapacity in order to be eligible for the benefits that make it possible to participate as a person who can conform to the social demands which shame "incapacity."

Radical differences in physical, sensate, and cognitive abilities bring home how subjects are differently positioned in relation to how we experience knowing. Knowledge is constituted by how we are embodied, by the material conditions that shape our lives, by how we can make sense of our worlds, as well as by our emotional relationships to what and whom we can know. The lives of disabled persons house entire domains of experience, ways of knowing and knowledges that are alien because they are systematically structured out, by the mainstream, by the university, as it reproduces what counts as knowledge and determines whose knowledge counts.

In researching disability and higher education, I am stunned at how little theoretical work has been published. Because of the difficulties I've had in being paid for full-time work, I've been particularly interested in identifying research that relates to accommodations for faculty. I have not located anything to date.

What happens to faculty who become disabled once they are employed? Because the treatment of disability is so privatized and individualized, I cannot find out. Informally, I know of people, all women, who have taken pay cuts, and gradually left the institution. Technically, I am now on 50 percent time, but working all the time. The faculty who become "disabled" are "expected" to be thankful if the institution accommodates us by "allowing" the flexibility of working 50 percent or 80 percent time. We are determined to carry our "full load"; not in any way to be seen as shirking our responsibilities.

I am beginning to think that this is totally wrong-headed. As I read the "Human Rights Code," as long as I can fulfill the essential duties of my job, it is the employer's responsibility to demonstrate that accommodating the "special needs" caused by my disability would create undo institutional hardship. I am currently negotiating to return to full-time work. I am seeking "support" for the work I can no longer do because of the added "drag" of my body, so that I can fulfill my "load" requirements or get them adjusted to maximize my areas of strength. My conversations with administrators, who are supportive in principal, invariably end in the "key of fairness," that is, that they cannot be seen to be granting me special privileges; I must carry my load. Compared to what? compared to whom?

How can we think about "load" when the job is bottomless in terms of time demands, and time is precisely the "special need" that defines the lives of most disabled? What of productivity—how can we think about this in light of the university's ideology of excellence and the traditional way that marginalized peoples have survived under these hostile conditions—survival by being "superworkers"? What's at stake when physical impediments and vulnerabilities are added into that formula for survival? And what happens to the slur upon "excellence" when "disability" requires accommodation at the level of what is taken-for-granted regarding the "physical" and "cognitive," not to mention the "emotional" requirements of academic performance? There is no meaningful codification of faculty load. The ideology of "excellence," of "brilliance," conceals the work involved and the assumptions of "normalcy," or rewarded production, upon which they depend. And then, insurance and legal systems are all premised on 40-hour work weeks. After spending over two hours trying to explain my job to a rehab worker, I was labelled "uncooperative," and they never found a way of recommending more than a back support to accommodate me in my work.

The painful irony of symbolic legitimation is that we now add "disability" as a recruitment category. Given the attitudes I have encountered, I find it difficult to believe that this is anything more than a compliance gesture. I cannot imagine a hiring committee where the question, "but will she be able to carry her load?" will not be the underlying frame of the discussion and decision.

I am concerned about what happens to students in this system. While the numbers are increasing, especially of "learning disabled," and accommodations are making a difference in encouraging more to attend who have to cope with mobility, vision, and hearing limits, I have found little that addresses how students fare once in the system. As a relatively able-bodied faculty member with some resources at my disposal, I cannot help but wonder how people manage libraries, the vast amounts of reading required, the time crunch in fulfilling multiple simultaneous requirements, etc. The research studies that I have seen point out that students also struggle with assumptions of normality, with unreasonable time expectations, with social isolation, with the difficulty of accessing libraries, and with the extra costs that they must absorb to counter these limits. In addition, they must cope with the indifferent or prejudicial attitudes of faculty, students, and field placements. Most disturbing, research-ers report that students distance themselves from other students with disabili-ties, do not want to be identified as disabled, to be seen as a "problem" or a "troublemaker." Students are represented as hesitant to seek out the help that they need, let alone fight for their rights.

Because disability is deeply sedimented in the ideology of individual incapacity or inability to perform basic human functions, rather than in the hostile social conditions that produce disablement, human rights for disabled people are always conditional on their not coming at too great an expense or inconvenience for the able-bodied. Because disabled people, especially the severely disabled, are not seen to be fully human—that is, "normal"—full participation in education or the work force is seen to be a privilege for us, not a right. Recently I was told by a disabled student who must drop out of study that she is no longer eligible for disability benefits if she attends university, because it is argued that if she can do the "work" of going to school, she is not disabled, and should be among the ranks of the "employable." If this logic is operative, it means that one cannot even use the time freed up from being employed to pursue further study. I faced a similar logic; when I returned to part-time work, I was cut off accident benefits because I was deemed to be, self-evidently, "employable" and therefore, by definition, not disabled.

In these mean-spirited times, when unemployment is high and the public purse is closed tight, the right to education and work is fundamental. I have my doubts about how far we can move the university in the direction of greater equity when retrenchment suggests the shoring up of privileged strongholds. Still we need to work with equity in ways that interrupt the flow of privilege. In the domain of disability, this means actively offsetting how disablement works structurally, temporally, and physically as well as socially, so that the most able-bodied, and the most economically privileged, are not the only ones amongst the disabled for whom "access" is workable.

[1]Bonnie Sherr Klein is a filmmaker at the National Film Board of Canada and the author of *Slow Dance: A Story of Stroke, Love, and Disability.*

References

Baron, Steve, Rena Phillips, and Kirsten Stalker. "Barriers to Training for Disabled Social Work Students." *Disability and Society* 11.3 (1996): 361–377.

Klein, Bonnie Sherr. *Slow Dance: A Story of Stroke, Love, and Disability.* Toronto: Knopf, 1997.

Low, Jacqueline. "Negotiating Identities, Negotiating Environments: An Interpretation of the Experiences of Students with Disabilities." *Disability and Society* 11.2 (1996): 235–248.

Meekosha, Helen, Andrew Jakubowicz, and Andrew Rice. "'As Long As You Are Willing To Wait': Access and Equity in Universities for Students with Disabilities." *Higher Education Research and Development* 10.1 (1991).

Stewart, Donald, Peter Cornish, and Kent Somers. "Empowering Students with Learning Disabilities in the Canadian Postsecondary Educational System." *Canadian Journal of Counselling* 29.1 (1995).

University of Toronto, Equity Issues Advisory Group. "Annual Report (July 1995–June 1996)." Pub. in *University of Toronto Bulletin* 25 Nov. 1996.

University of Toronto. "Accommodation in Employment for Personal with Disabilities: Statement and Guidelines." Attached to memo from Michael Finlayson, Office of the Vice-President. 29 March 1995.

Selected University Experiences
A Preliminary Discussion of Equity Initiatives for Aboriginal Peoples

Patricia Monture-Angus

The job advertisement for the position of Dean of the Saskatoon Campus of the Saskatchewan Indian Federated College[1] is sitting on my desk beside my computer. Every now and again I "eyeball" it, thinking. Three years after coming to Native Studies[2] at the University of Saskatchewan, I am debating another move. I am tired of the energy leaving takes. I am also tired from the energy staying takes. Over the last nine years that I have been an academic, one of the survival skills I have elected to exercise is leaving (Halifax in 1991, Ottawa in 1994). When I came to the University of Saskatchewan, it was with the plan never to be leaving again. Now, I am left wondering if I am stuck in a three- or four-year "leaving" cycle. The job advertisement still sits beside my computer.

It seemed very ironic that the decision (law school versus Native Studies) I faced was about whether or not to agree to be marginalized. I was individually marginalized in the law school and knew that Native Studies as a discipline was marginalized. I had the choice of different varieties of the same condition. In the end, and I am not sure this was a conscious decision at the time, I chose the "collective" marginalization of the Department of Native Studies. All of this does not really matter because what my decision came down to was not really about power. It was about self-respect. It was about quality of life.

I am reminded of another time when I was thinking of surviving by leaving. In Ottawa—I think I had been there for a year—I applied for a job at the Royal Commission on Aboriginal Peoples as director of research for women. That is not the exact title, but that does not really matter to this story. I was granted an interview. During that interview, one of the Commission's senior officials (I choose to protect his identity but will note that he is a white man because it is important to the story I am telling) looked at my curriculum vitae, wrinkled his nose, and asked me "why have you had so many academic jobs?" (I had only had two.) I left a contract position in Halifax for a tenure-track job in Ottawa. I did not understand in this picture what did not make sense for my interviewer. "Don't you think leaving again would hurt your career?" Remember this was a job interview (for a job that at that moment I still thought I wanted). I pushed down my initial reaction to deconstruct the various offensive stereotypes immersed in that white man's questions.

The basic offense was in his assumption that my career path could and should look a particular way. There was no realization that this standardized career path (self-evident to the interviewer only) had been developed almost exclusively on white (and male) experience of the university. I do not remember how I answered that question, but I know I did not tell the whole truth. This is but one example of the strain that is caused when you do not fit into the established patterns or expectations. These patterns, expectations, and rules are not always obvious or expressed in the operation of the institution. For those who are not crossing cultural boundaries these patterns, rules or expectations are so self-evident that they are held to be obvious, unquestioned truths. This is not how I experience them.

One of the survival skills I rely on is the power and privilege of possessing a legal education. In the face of oppression (that is, the not so self-evident patterns, rules, and expectations), people sit up a little faster and listen a little harder when they hear you are a lawyer. Sometimes, because I look "Indian,"[3] mentioning I am a lawyer really puts people out of balance as though they cannot quite understand my words. This strategy always leaves me frustrated. It is an exercise of privilege that the majority of "Indian" people cannot even dream of exercising. I am aware of this each time I use it on my own behalf or for the benefit of someone else. Beyond this my experience of Canadian law has been about experiencing a principle source of "Indian" oppression and colonization. Having a legal education is about experiencing power concurrently with experiencing historic and recurring oppression.

This recognition of the dualism of Canadian law (that is the concurrent experience of both power and oppression) forced my decision to "retire" from teaching law in law schools. My leaving law teaching was calculated. Most of my life is calculated. Not calculating is not a privilege that I own. Just because it was calculated does not mean it was easy. I am pleased to report that I do not really miss anything about the law school.[4] It has only been quite recently that I have resolved my relationship with Canadian law. I think sharing this story might be important to the larger story I wish to tell about equity and graduate studies.

One morning last spring, I got up really early to hear the keynote speaker at a conference here in Saskatoon. My friend insisted that I go. I am glad I listened to her urgings.[5] The speaker was Terry Tafoya, a Skokomish-Pueblo storyteller (see Bruchac 75). One topic in his presentation was "clowns." This image must be fully understood as an Indigenous image (and not the western image of circus clown). I understand the "clown" that Dr. Tafoya spoke of to be one of the many trickster figures that are common in many Aboriginal cultures. The clown is like Weesagechack of the Cree, or coyote. As I am beginning to understand, the trickster role is not just so much to teach but equally to make us think and reflect. Dr. Tafoya said (and this sentence has stayed with me): "the clown will say things like, my older brother who is younger than I am." Clowns live and love dichotomy. They are contrary and I have long known I possess some contrary qualities. In this culture, when participating in ceremony they often wear black and white to symbolize the natural contradictions in the world.

I am a little wary of borrowing the imagery of another Indigenous nation that I am unfamiliar with. I do not know the people or their territory.[6] I am not telling their stories. To do so without the consent of the people would be a fundamental breach of "Indian copyright laws" as well as being a cultural appropriation of great magnitude. I do not even know the right way to ask permission in their way to hear a story (a lesser standard than having an earned right to tell the story). My understanding is simplistic. In fact, I understand that what I heard in Dr. Tafoya's presentation was something of myself reflected in his words, as though he held up a thought mirror. This story I am now telling is not a teaching about his people's way. It is not a traditional story as I tell it. It is only a story about what I learned about myself and my own experience of legal relations while listening to him.

In talking about the role of the clown in the social structure of his people, Dr. Tafoya made one small reference to law. Nothing more than a few sentences. In his tradition, it is the clown who presents any new laws to council. The clown[7] does this in a manner that ridicules the new law. I did not hear the next little bit of the presentation because I was consumed by my own thoughts.

Since graduating from Queen's Law School in 1988, I have been constantly drawn back to the question of whether to practice law or not. Over the years I have never been successful at putting to rest the question (often experienced as a taunt, "to practice or not").[8] After listening to Dr. Tafoya, I understood that in a very small way I am in the same relationship to the law as the sacred clown. My relationship with law is to ridicule, to challenge.

Hearing this man's words and knowing there is a cultural place for what I do (and feel) in at least one Aboriginal culture neutralized the "ought" feeling I had been carrying about my own engagement with legal practice. It allowed me to shift my resistance to Canadian law (an experience that had reinforced feelings of difference and isolation) to feeling the comfort of realizing that what I had been feeling was always a "cultural" response. My relationship with law moved from the experience of "outsider" to one of belonging; to one of being in the flow of tradition. It transformed my experiences of law as someone who is relegated to "outsider" status (which often feels like no status) to a relationship where I have both a role (which could become a relationship) and a place with regard to Canadian law.

Especially because I had yet to develop a clear cultural image to understand my relationship with the law, I first experienced my arrival at Native Studies as an incredible relief. I had found a place where I could work, and think, and be. I first experienced Native Studies as an insider. I felt appreciated as an Aboriginal academic especially in the classroom. I was thrilled to have the institutional space where I could devote myself to teaching Aboriginal justice, including law, and nothing else. At the law school I taught courses like property, constitutional law, and legislation. These are all courses in which I had little commitment or true interest. And although I do not like to admit it, this fact must challenge even a committed teacher's ability to teach well. This difference in teaching assignments (and, therefore, my experiences of law schools and Native Studies) is largely a result of both the focus and structure of the law curriculum.

In order to reach this paper's objective, graduate studies, I need first to talk about two things. My own university education fundamentally shapes how I think about "equity" in graduate studies. Secondly, my experiences as professor in both law schools and one Native Studies department are also essential to understanding my position with regard to equity and graduate studies. Although I was once a graduate student, that was almost a decade ago and I do not presume that I can now speak for graduate students, Aboriginal or not. Perhaps my experience of the university and how I organize my experiences of exclusion, as Mohawk, as woman, and as professor, helps to inform others (including graduate students) who are also striving to understand their own experiences of the university.

As I just indicated, I need to speak to who I am. This is a methodological, practical, and theoretical starting position. How and where I have been educated influences how I think and who I am. It gives you, the reader, access to the personal information that informs and shapes my writing so that you can read and do your own figuring as you move along with my thoughts. This is a fundamental process of teaching within my tradition. My aunties told me you cannot understand where you are going unless you know where you have been. More importantly, you cannot understand where you are going unless you are also responsible to the future, to the next seven generations.

I earned an Honours B.A. in Sociology from the University of Western Ontario in 1983. I earned a law degree from Queen's University in Kingston, Ontario. I am a proud survivor of gender wars at Queen's University (see McIntyre 1987; 1988). I started an LL.M. at Osgoode Hall Law School in the fall of 1988. I did not finish this degree and I did not have a lot of will to finish it.[9] At the time I made that decision, I knew I was jeopardizing my continued life at the university. My experience then of the university was, at times, a contest between surviving the moment and surviving the months and years to come.

The reasons I did not finish my LL.M. thesis are important to share. What I learned through the process of my education in law is that I did not want to be known as a lawyer. In many ways, this is a theoretical response (and not one grounded in the practicalities of exercising legal skills). I have a total repulsion for Canadian law. It is oppressive. It is colonial. For my people (and I believe for other Aboriginal peoples), it is not a solution. It is, in fact, the problem. It is not justice. It is merely what we have to survive. As an individual, legal education just asked too much of me. My leaving was a matter of survival.[10]

I would likely go back to graduate school in a minute on two conditions. The first is if I could find a program where I could be all I dream to be. This would be a place where I could learn from a position of cultural respect. It would be a place where I could look at knowledge including how I understand knowledge from my Mohawk woman's place; a place where people would not look at me as if I was crazy when I based my scholarly work on what grandmother told me (that is one example of Aboriginal epistemology). Very clearly, that place does not yet exist within educational institutions that grant graduate degrees.

The second condition is even more onerous. I have responsibility to six children. In 1994, we located our family back on the reserve. This was a conscious choice. My children are settled, happy, and have access to culture, language, and ceremony. They reside in their territory and have a relationship with the land that is nurturing. It is a difficult task as an "Indian" parent to consider disrupting this relationship with family, community, language, and land. I would only consider accessing further post-secondary education if it did not significantly disrupt the children's well-being. Residency is not a matter of comfort, it is a matter of safety—that is ensuring that my children are raised in an environment as free of racial hatred as I can find—where they have access to culture, language, and ceremony. This means I have the choice of attending two different universities. The University of Saskatchewan is three hours from home. The University of Alberta is four-and-a-half hours away. If there were, now or years earlier, a graduate school where I could go, where I would truly benefit and my children would not have to suffer, I would go. By suffering, I do not mean that as a family we would not have to make sacrifices in pursuit of the goal of higher education. That is not the standard I refer to.

If universities are ever going to practice equity beyond the level of literacy (that is, writing down good things about equity), then my expectation is that they will be able to make space for my life as an "Indian" woman. This means that the university must come to terms with the conditions of my life as an "Indian" woman. It (still) means I more than likely got a late start at university (and this is the result of the history of educational exclusions of "Indian" people). It means I more than likely have greater family obligations including the fact that I am more likely responsible for more children and belong to an extended family in an active way. There is also a greater likelihood that I am a single parent. Further, the disposable income within my immediate family and my extended family is more than likely insufficient to support the family let alone provide additional resources to support me while I go to school. Attending university also has the unfortunate consequence of isolating me from my family if they live on a reserve as most reserves are generally a fair distance from universities (and this increases the further north one goes).

This is the foundation for my definition of equity. Equity means finding a place I can be while maintaining my connection with who and what I am. This definition of finding a place to be, in my mind, is a minimalist position. When I am talking about equity, access is not the only criterion. Although access is essential to anything else happening, it should not be considered unless the institution is willing to consider both retention and quality of experience. Equally important is the consideration of whether or not the educational experience equips an Aboriginal person in any meaningful way for their life after the post-secondary institution. My experience of legal education was that almost everything taught was irrelevant to a practice of law in an Aboriginal community.

It is impossible for me to consider graduate education and equity in the abstract. One way to ground this discussion is in my own experiences of the university and of Native Studies. With no intention of limiting Aboriginal students' choices, it does seem reasonable to conclude that opportunities are more likely to be available in Native Studies for Aboriginal students (and I suspect these options are often more attractive to Aboriginal students). These conclusions indicate that it is important to consider the discipline of Native Studies as a home for Native graduate students who wish to further their arts and science education. If relevant and respectful opportunities are not available in this department of the university, then it is unlikely (but not impossible) that such opportunities will be found in other graduate programs.

Native Studies programs began developing in the United States prior to their development in Canada. The first program in Canada was at Trent University in Peterborough, Ontario, in 1969 (see Asikinak 1997). This means that Native Studies is a very young "discipline" (if indeed it is a discipline) (see Thornton qtd. in American Indian Studies Center 1980). My experience with Native Studies points clearly to the significant need for Native Studies scholars, both Aboriginal and Euroamerican, to engage in both dialogue and reflection on the first three decades of the discipline's development. This dialogue has been undertaken to a greater degree in the United States than it has been in Canada (for example, see Stein, Reyhner, and Asikinack). My comments in this paper about Native Studies are preliminary observations which recognize that a detailed and critical analysis of the emergence and development of Native Studies as a discipline in Canada is urgently required. Without this analysis, any dialogue about change in the discipline cannot fully occur.

In January of 1998, I began teaching a fourth year Native Studies theory class for the first time. I have always enjoyed theoretical pursuits. After volunteering to teach the class, I began to panic. How could I teach a class in Native Studies theory when I remained unconvinced about what the "discipline" of Native Studies was. I resolved this crisis by devoting the first two classes to the examination of this very question. In the first class, I asked students to locate articles which examined this question. Part of the design of the exercise was to demonstrate to students the lack of literature, particularly "Canadian" authored,[11] in this area. In the second class we sat in a circle and each

of the students presented the article they located. After each of the presentations, I offered a synthesis of both the themes as well as what I thought were
the important points.[12]

One of the possible differences between the development of Native
Studies in Canada and the United States may be that, in the United States, it
was groups of Aboriginal professors coming together in the university to form
a concentration of their scholarship that resulted in the development of
American Indian Studies as a separate department.[13] In Canada, I believe the
opposite is true. I believe the call went up from Aboriginal students—the
Indian Teacher Education Students in the case of the University of Saskatchewan—for the creation of Native Studies (Department of Native Studies,
University of Saskatchewan, 1–3). The rationale for establishing a department
of Native Studies at the University of Saskatchewan is described in a document
generated for the review of the department by the College of Arts and Science,
as follows:

> It recognized that, of all the provinces, Saskatchewan had the highest
> proportion of Native people. It was mindful of the fact that the
> University of Saskatchewan, as early as 1961, had pioneered the first
> Indian Teacher Education program (ITEP) in Canada, and the profes-
> sional colleges at the University, including Law, Agriculture and
> Commerce, either already had or were contemplating special pro-
> grams for Native students. The establishment of liberal arts classes in
> Native Studies in the College of Arts and Science was seen by the
> committee as an important means of affirming the value and dignity
> of Native cultural traditions: their histories, life-styles, philosophies
> and languages. (Department of Native Studies, University of Sas-
> katchewan 2)

The call for Native Studies was taken up by Euroamerican academics as
there were so few Aboriginal academics in any Canadian university (including
the University of Saskatchewan). Two decades after the "birth" of Native
Studies in Canada, it seems essential to create institutional spaces to discuss the
future of this new initiative called "Native Studies." This dialogue in my
opinion must include a discussion of both the role of Euroamerican scholars of
Native Studies as well as Aboriginal ones. We must face this challenge head on.
Facing this challenge includes recognizing that Canadian universities where
critical masses[14] of Aboriginal scholars do not exist in some departments must

face the problem of creating new positions for Aboriginal scholars in times of fiscal restraint. The other alternative is to accept that the majority of scholars in some Native Studies departments will continue to be Euroamericans for the foreseeable future. This alternative carries serious limitations for creating a "discipline" of Native Studies.

I am reassured that the struggle I face to dream a good place (with a reasonable measure of control and independence) for Aboriginal people in Native Studies fits into this historic pattern. The struggle and tension I have experienced and retain is not personal. The struggle is the result of an inability to attract Aboriginal scholars (and a significant part of this exclusion is the way the universities, at least in the recent past, create hiring criteria: those without degrees need not apply).[15] As a result, departments of Native studies were (and are) all too often largely staffed by Euroamericans. The consequence is that without the good will of Euroamerican professors, Aboriginal people did not and do not have a significant and certain voice in either the control or development of the departments. My concern is not so much about who is doing the teaching, but what and how the substance of Native Studies is being taught and how the discipline can in fact develop if Aboriginal voice and experience is significantly excluded, isolated, objectified, and marginalized. After all, how can Aboriginal epistemology be included in the university without the inclusion of Aboriginal scholars who are connected to their communities.[16]

Reflecting on the first meetings of American Indian scholars in the 1970s, Elizabeth Cook-Lynn (Crow Creek Sioux) shares this vision of what Native American Studies was meant to be:

Tribally specific, nation-to-nation, and Pan-Indian theories were the bases for the development of disciplinary principles such as sovereignty and indigenousness. General knowledge, specialized knowledge, and applied knowledge were organized into specific course designs. The discipline was defined in general terms as the *endogenous* consideration of American Indians or, more specifically, the *endogenous* study of First Nation cultures and history. This meant that this discipline would differentiate itself from other disciplines in two important ways: it would emerge from *within* Native people's enclaves and geographies, languages and experiences, and it would refute the exogenous seeking of truth through isolation (i.e., the "ivory tower") that has been the general principle of the disciplines most recently in charge of indigenous study, that is, history, anthropology and related disciplines all captivated by the scientific method of objectivity. (11)[17]

Compare this to one description of the discipline of Native Studies in Canadian materials:

> … the primary goals and functions of the Native Studies Department [at the University of Saskatchewan] are as follows:
> 1) to promote academic and teaching excellence;
> 2) to understand and appreciate the nature of Aboriginal societies and to acknowledge the contribution of those societies to both the national and international communities;
> 3) to foster cultural awareness and reinforce Native pride, while simultaneously bridging cultural gaps and challenging racial intolerance and stereotypes;
> 4) to encourage the development of specific Native Studies paradigms and theoretical frameworks;
> 5) to foster and conduct original scholarly research on Aboriginal history and life;
> 6) to promote and encourage Native scholars and Native scholarship; and
> 7) to develop research skills relevant to the needs of Aboriginal communities. (Native Studies Department, University of Saskatchewan 10–11)

Consider how different this vision is from the position that Professor Cook-Lynn enunciated.

It is patronizing to suggest that Native students need Native Studies to reinforce pride and foster cultural awareness. I am not convinced that these are legitimate goals of Native Studies. I am also suspicious of any suggestion that a goal of any university department is to promote "certain" scholars. This suggestion is steeped in a notion of Euroamerican superiority and the colonial construction of Indigenous peoples. It is flatly unacceptable. The notion that research should be developed to meet the "needs" of Aboriginal communities must be seen as a half-answer. Although it may remove the force of objectifying Aboriginal people it is worse as it asks Aboriginal people to consent and accept research paradigms that were developed outside of our experiences and knowledge base. I do not accept that Native Studies is about any form of objectification of Native people. Instead, the recognition and respect for Indigenous systems of knowledge must become the key goal of Native Studies. This characterization of Native Studies in the Canadian school in which I teach falls dramatically short of the vision of American Indian Studies that is being articulated in some places in the United States.

I have been at Native Studies for a little more than three years now, long enough to get the sense of the place and some sense of the discipline. As I have indicated, I have not been here long enough to know, with conviction, what Native Studies is. This is not a personal shortcoming. I do not get the sense that my colleagues (inside and outside the department, Aboriginal and Euroamerican) know any better, or with more clarity than I know what Native Studies is. Written in 1986, the introduction to the *Abstracts of Native Studies* noted:

> The overwhelming majority of studies done of Native peoples in Canada continue to reflect the techniques and concerns of the traditional disciplines and most scholars continue to operate within the parameters of their traditional disciplines. This is not surprising given the recent birth of the discipline of Native Studies, and *the lack of graduate study opportunities.* [emphasis added]

This lack of a coherent and recognized methodology unique to Native Studies results in the lack of coherent theories in the area as well as grounding my concern that the field is not yet a discipline. My experience of the "discipline" at least from my vantage point at the University of Saskatchewan is that little has changed since 1986. If Native Studies remains without a coherent methodological framework (other than those borrowed from the cognate disciplines of history, anthropology, geography, and so on) and lacks recognized theory then this recognition must be translated into a concern about the existing structure of the curriculum.

In the course calendar for the University of Saskatchewan, Native Studies is described as

> a thorough academic examination of all aspects of Indian, Métis and Inuit life and *histories.* Examining both the Canadian and international context, Native Studies *seeks to link the processes of the past with contemporary issues.* Students will be exposed to a variety of *perspectives, world views, sources and intellectual traditions.* (University of Saskatchewan Calendar, 1997–98) [emphasis added]

I am troubled by a number of aspects of this description (and have indicated this by the use of italics in the quotation). In fact, only four other departments in the college (art history, classics, paleobiology and women and gender studies) offer definitions of their field of study in the university calendar. In my experience, words such as "perspective" or "world views" are often used instead of words that recognize Indigenous ways of knowing as systems of knowledge. Despite the reference to intellectual traditions, it appears that what is being examined in Native Studies in my department is a historical analysis with a few contemporary problem solving skills. This is very offensive in the way it reinforces the stereotype of the vanishing Indian.[18] It also does not meet the standard that Professor Cook-Lynn (1997) articulated in her discussion of the programs in the United States. My Native Studies department is clearly exogenous. This is backwards to my Aboriginal way of thinking and being.

A review of the courses we offer substantiates this concern. It reveals that 69.2 percent (18/26) of the courses have history as their sole or a significant focus.[19] A comparison with the courses offered by the Saskatchewan Indian Federated College, an Indian controlled institution, reveals that 37.7 percent (17/45) of their courses have as a sole or significant focus, history. By the second year of study history courses offered by the Saskatchewan Indian Federated College are organized along nation lines with courses in Cree, Saulteaux, Assiniboine, Dene, Dakota, Inuit and Métis. Each of these courses is described as "culture and history." At the University of Saskatchewan we offer only two second year history courses under the generic heading of "Indian." I believe that both these factors inflate the amount of "history" apparently being taught at the Federated College. More disturbing, the courses taught at the University of Saskatchewan demonstrate that our curriculum is clearly based in both exogenous and historical thought. At the Federated College, only four of their third year courses and none of their fourth year courses have history as the focus. In the Native Studies department at the University of Saskatchewan, five of our third year and three of our fourth year courses have history as a principle focus. The "history" that we present to our students is most often a western perspective on Indian and Métis history including a focus on archival research. We do not consistently present a course that provides a parallel opportunity for students to undertake oral history projects. Although we offer two classes in methodology, neither appears to examine in a rigorous way Indian or Métis methodologies. I am not suggesting that this western based perspective on history should be excluded from Native Studies (even though it is available at other sites on campus). For example, the history department at the University of Saskatchewan offers one course on "Indian-White Relations in Canada" as well as four courses which appear to have a significant section on Indigenous peoples. History also lists six courses in Native Studies that will be given credit to a history degree with prior permission of the department. The Native Studies department does not engage in such cross-listing. My central point regarding historical perspectives is that the course offerings in Native Studies need to be balanced between western, Indian and Métis "perspectives" and practices. A balanced curriculum in Native Studies is not necessarily one that equally (numerically) offers courses across these paradigms or knowledge bases. In my view, Native Studies should be weighted in favour of Indigenous knowledge.

Professor Cook-Lynn (1997) in one of the most recent articles on Native Studies notes that

> … just offering a group of courses did not make a discipline, that the interdisciplinary examination of "cultural conflict" was not what this work was about, and that finding ways to understand the history of education among indigenous peoples in the United States could not be done efficiently through the exogenous social-science disciplines of anthropology, sociology, and psychology. (10)

Given this standard and the analysis of course offerings completed, I see clearly that what has been accomplished curriculum-wise within the Native Studies department in which I work has been a failure if the standard is meeting an Aboriginally-defined discipline of study.

Most troubling, the discipline (equally, my department) has not addressed in a principled way the relationship between Native Studies as either a place or as an intellectual space and Aboriginal people (students and professors) or Aboriginal communities. No one seems to want to commit to having this conversation, especially if this commitment involves crossing cultures.

As I have noted, there are five tenure-track faculty at the Native Studies department at the University of Saskatchewan. We are educated in different disciplines. There are two historians,[21] an anthropologist, a sociologist, and a legal scholar. The three who hold tenure are all Euroamerican men.[20] (I know that at least one of them will take offense at this discussion. I am breaking rank and unspoken rules. I know I am risk-taking.) Then there is me. I have been a member of the department for a little more than three years now. I have had my probation renewed once. The most recent member to join the tenure-track ranks is a Métis man. He has held this position for nearly two years. However, this Métis man has been involved in our department for longer than I have in various contract capacities. If you have been following this conversation carefully, you will have noted that I am the only woman in the tenure track "gang."[22] I am the only Indian. I am the only Mohawk.

Graduate students in the department therefore only have a 40 percent chance of having an Aboriginal professor teach their classes or sit on their committee. This figure is optimistic. It presumes that graduate teaching will not be assigned according to the "status" of the professors. As the most recently hired, it is less likely that the two Aboriginal professors will have the opportunity to teach the core graduate courses. Although I have several times now made an offer to do this teaching, that offer has never been accepted. It is usually met with blank stares as it is obvious to me that my colleagues still see me as far too "junior" to do this teaching.

In a sense I agree. Oddly, I think, I have never been a student of Native Studies. I have never even taken a single course in Native Studies. (Do you see trickster dancing across the page?) In fact, none of our tenure stream faculty have a degree in Native Studies. This must influence the way that we teach Native Studies: I am not convinced that we have had the opportunity to rigorously discover Native Studies if in fact we have never been students of the discipline.

I was educated as a lawyer. I was hired to teach in Native Studies without a Ph.D.[23] It seems obvious to me the fact that I am an Aboriginal person (Mohawk woman) must have something to do with the fact I am here. Can you imagine a history department hiring a professor who had never taken a single history course? This leads me to conclude that Native Studies must in part (and at least) be about providing space for Aboriginal scholarship and Aboriginal people in the university. Understand that making space is different from "promoting" or "advancing."

Although often a marginalized space within the university, I was attracted to Native Studies as a place where my principle individualized experience would not be of marginalization. What I have learned in the last three years in Native Studies is that marginalization is a complex experience. As a department in the university Native Studies is marginalized. It is under-resourced and that is a form of institutional marginalization. Institutional marginalization also operates in a number of other forms including the physical space we occupy. There was no room for us in the arts tower so along with the math department and modern languages, we occupy a renovated residence just on the edge of campus. Although I understand this was the choice of the department in order to create "separate" space, it does not feel this way to me. It feels like marginal space which contradicts the desire of the department to be interdisciplinary. It seems to me that it would be easier to be an interdisciplinary department if we had close connections to other disciplines that were enhanced by the physical space we occupy.

The Native Studies department at the University of Saskatchewan is the only Native Studies department that I have ever experienced.[24] I am, therefore, uncertain if my department is representative of other Canadian departments of Native Studies. In a document describing the department drafted by Dr. Jim Waldram[25] at the end of 1997, it is stated:

> The Department was formed as a "program" in 1982 with three professors, including the founding head of the department, A.S. (Tony) Lussier, a Manitoba Métis scholar. In 1983, it became a "department" within the College of Arts and Science, offering three and four year general and honours degrees. In 1989, we graduated our first Master of Arts in Native Studies student under the "special case" formula (and we believe that this was the first ever graduate degree from a Native Studies department in Canada).[26] In 1997, we were given approval for a permanent Master's program and admitted our first special case PhD (sic) student.[27]

There is no doubt that Native Studies has been developing over the three decades since its "birth." It is the shape and content of the "development" that I believe needs to be examined. The problem is that Native Studies was created in response to the structure of the university and the existing disciplinary boundaries. I wonder if (Euroamerican) scholars studying Natives felt marginalized within their own disciplines of history, anthropology and geography and sought camaraderie together. If this is the case, then this is one of the subtle texts that causes change within the field to be so difficult; returning to their disciplines of origin is not attractive to them because they felt marginalized by their interests in Native people.

It seems almost by default that Eurocanadian scholars have a legitimate claim to be in Native Studies (that is because they were there first—coyote sure has some fancy moves eh!). The reality is that the question is not what space should Native Studies provide for Aboriginal students, professors, communities but what space (or relationship) does Euroamerican scholarship have within the Native Studies academy. To suggest otherwise is to ask the appropriate question in reverse and is to entrench patterns of colonialism.

It is absolutely my view that Euroamericans belong in Native Studies. One of the things that I am quite sure belongs in the definition of the field is the concept "relationship." Not only is kinship an important cultural component in every Aboriginal nation I have experienced but my conclusion is also a reflection of the reality that Native Studies does exist within mainstream institutions. Non-Native students (including Euroamericans) are also attracted to and participate in Native Studies. These two facts alone demonstrate to me that the field of Native Studies is equally about the "relationship" between Euroamericans and Aboriginal nations. However, I do not yet accept that this is the central concept around which Native Studies should be built. Nor do I accept that "equality" of Euroamerican inclusion is necessarily the next logical step in developing Native Studies as a discipline. What is required for the discipline to develop is a critical mass of Aboriginal scholars.[28] What confounds me about the hesitation of my Euroamerican colleagues to consider (publicly) their role in the discipline as Euroamericans (any attempt to open this dialogue is usually seen as a personal attack) is the realization that if we cannot have the conversation in a microcosm then how can we ever resolve the relationship issues nationally?

There are several problems in constructing this dichotomy in Native Studies. I recognize that my raising the question of the role of the Euroamerican scholar in Native Studies causes tension in the discipline (and more specifically in my department). I would note emphatically that my raising the question is not instigating or even initiating but responding to the silence of Euroamerican academics—I recognize that not all Euroamericans academics are the same— who *ought* in my opinion to raise the question themselves. I do not view their silences as inaction (or nothingness). The usual consequence of my raising the issue is becoming labeled as non-collegial, instigating, difficult, and so on. Trying to name this problem forces the majority of Euroamerican scholars further away from committing to the need for Aboriginal knowledge and asserting their privilege in ways that have negative consequences for both the individual Aboriginal scholar and advances in the discipline. It creates two distant camps. For me personally, the problem is quite a conundrum. If I do not raise the issue with my Euroamerican colleagues then I feel dishonest. Worse, I feel like I have failed the community I "represent." If I do raise the issue, the consequence is disastrous in my work relations. These are the reasons I take such great offence at the unreflected exercise of privilege by Euroamerican academics, their silence and failure to rigorously examine first their own privilege and then the larger question of the privilege of Euroamerican academics in general.

The idea of being a single academic but at the same time as being representative of a community is also problematic. In the structure of the university my community had little input in situating me in this place of power and prestige. I was not elected as the Chiefs are. It's an inside-out kind of representativeness. I speak from a "representativeness" pedestal within the university but face calls at home not to speak for too many. It is equally important to understand that I belong to a community—both mine (Mohawk) and my partner's (Cree). And this creates a set of responsibilities to the community that I do not think universities even see let alone understand. For example, sitting on my porch and talking to someone with a drinking problem or raising my sister's child is not what they mean by community involvement. Yet these are the daily realities that I face as an "Indian" person. Ironically the university recognizes my "Indian-ness" and my representative-ness when it is to their advantage, yet when it is a question of benefit to me (such as when issues of "status" are raised in the department)[29] it is conveniently forgotten.

My experience of the university generally is that the structural barriers are illuminated to me as I slam into them head on. Equity, and the expertise I have developed, have come at personal consequence and have been very painful for me. Equity in the university is largely about access. My own experience of equity in the university is about delivering equity to others. I have never been asked what equity concerns I have about my own position within the university. There is no consideration given to those few of us who have been attracted to and hired by the university. The consequences are often evidenced in the retention rates of Aboriginal faculty and of Aboriginal students.

In fairness to the University of Saskatchewan, I must note that I do believe there are individuals who are really trying to change things. The problem as I see it, despite eloquent mission statements[30] and equity documents, is that achieving equity is not a condition or rule within the regular structure of the university. It is an additional responsibility on the list of tasks for administrators and, therefore, is often ignored or worse, resented. This is the fundamental shift in university structure and philosophy that I see as essential.

Thus far my writing has focused on my own experience of the university campus. However, this narrative is not really about me. I use the narrative to teach softly about equity as well as with the hope that the reader will do some of their own figuring (see *Thunder in My Soul* 11–12, 44–45). I have here adopted an academic style that parallels one of the principle teaching methods in Aboriginal society. I have really been writing about what I understand to be missing from the university's practice of equity. I am also suggesting that my experience of the University of Saskatchewan parallels other "outsider" experience at other Canadian universities.

It may appear to some readers that the discussion of Native Studies I have presented does not have a direct relationship to these collected papers on graduate studies. However, if as a professor (that is as privileged) I feel the tension, carry the impact of institutional marginalization, and have these questions about my relationship with equity, then how does an incoming graduate student experience the department and the institution? If I feel overwhelming pressure to silence, and I am not being graded or given course credit, then how does a student experience the environment? As the only female, tenured (almost) faculty member, what message does this send to graduate students? What institutional space and environment does it create for them? As students learn of my tenure experience including the fact that the two "regular" members of the department (that is, two Euroamerican men) did not support my tenure application, how does this operate to silence, foster fears instead of confidence, and exclude? If I experience the university as alienating and I have a position on the hierarchy well above students (even graduate students), then I fear the quality of their experience is negated as a possibility. This must be a serious concern as it is about the quality of their educational experience.

To speak more directly about graduate studies and equity, I want to share my experience in this area. I became a member of the College of Graduate Studies and Research in 1995; this appointment carries through to the year 2000. This is my first involvement in graduate studies, never having had this opportunity in a law school. I have never supervised a graduate student thesis. I am on the committee for three students, all Aboriginal women. All of these students are still in the preliminary stages of thesis completion, their course work being done. The College of Graduate Studies and Research also has an equity committee. I have been a member of this committee for a year. The committee has met only once. My experience as a professor of graduate studies has very much been an experience from the periphery.[31]

Early in 1997, the department of Native Studies secured the approval of the College of Graduate Studies and Research to offer a regular Master's program.[32] The department believes they graduated the first person in Canada with an M.A. in Native Studies in 1989. Securing the regular Masters program in Native Studies (one of only a handful in the country) is exciting. It now allows us the opportunity to offer a Ph.D. in Native Studies by special case. I do not believe that there is a "regular" Ph.D. program in Native Studies anywhere in Canada. Unfortunately, my celebration of our "regular" program and the special case Ph.D. opportunity is somewhat hollow. I am pleased by the accomplishment. I am more profoundly saddened though by the missed opportunity. The paperwork for the regular program was already well underway by the time I joined the department. Obviously, the major influence in the structuring of this program was based almost solely on mainstream academic understandings of knowledge and the systems that create that knowledge. The opportunity lost was to create a graduate program that fully reflects the understanding of Native Studies that Aboriginal peoples themselves may imagine based on Indigenous knowledge systems.

The "regular" Master's program at the University of Saskatchewan developed by Native Studies is described as "Applied Native Studies." An early draft of this proposal provides a definition of Native Studies. I will provide segments of this proposal followed by a discussion:

> In general, the history of the relationship between Native peoples and academia has been one of exploitation. Native people were the subjects of inquiry, passive voices shaped in the literature by scholars who felt little need to return research to the community or to help the people with pressing, more current issues. (Waldram)

This idea that Native Studies must return research to the community is a very noble one. However, this notion does little to change the shape of the relationship between Aboriginal communities and the researchers. In this picture, the power of the researcher over the community is still maintained as it is the researcher initiating the program of research and not the community. Until control of every aspect of the research is vested in the community, the objectification of our people and communities has not been changed.

The proposal continues:

> The Department of Native Studies eschews such intellectual colonialism. Applied Native Studies is taken here to mean the production of data, and the generation of knowledge of relevance to the Native community (defined as communities, organizations or individuals). It involves the establishment of relationships with Native peoples for the purposes of research. (Waldram)

This is a real problem. The relationship must precede the research. If the relationship with Aboriginal people or communities is not paramount and primary in the process, then the research will never be in the control of the community. Nor will the relationship ever be based on equality and respect. This demonstrates that the colonial thinking (or the objectification of the group studied) has not yet really ended. The colonial nature of the relationship is not removed but embedded. The fact that the colonial relationship remains objectifying and is disguised creates a further potential to harm Aboriginal people as the relationship of objectification is removed from our gaze.

The document continues to state:

> It insists on accountability to those involved in the research. Applied Native Studies represents the effort to train students to be sensitive to the needs of the Native community. The emphasis in the program will be on training in research skills that are in demand by the Native community, in combination with the sharpening of minds and the intellectual development that accompanies solid, theoretical education. Graduates of the Applied Native Studies program will be equally prepared to undertake PhD (sic) work or to work with Native groups in research and policy development. (Waldram)

I have several concerns with the closing sentences of this paragraph I have presented in segments. First, the graduate studies program in Native Studies at the University of Saskatchewan gives preference in admission to Native students. I think this is a good initial policy. However, how is it that the department (which consists of a majority of white men) can presume to train students to be sensitive to the communities that they belong to (and the trainers do not). Second, being sensitive to community needs also does not end the relationship of colonialism (or "power over"). Returning research results is just one small step, perhaps necessary, but not the final outcome that is required to create intellectual relationships that are truly not grounded in one culture's superiority. What I find most disturbing about this statement which defines our graduate program is the fact that it fails to recognize Indigenous systems of knowledge as well as the corresponding methodologies. Finally, the last sentence exposes an interesting omission. Why is it presumed our graduates (remember we are now admitting only Aboriginal students to our graduate program) will only work for "Native groups?"

The program was not developed in response to the demands of an identifiable Native community nor was it developed in consultation with Aboriginal people or communities. In this way it parallels the development of the department. The Aboriginal people who got to speak to the proposal were those of us privileged by education and already belonging to the department. This evidences the fact that the Native Studies department (note the reference is not to individual faculty members) has no clear institutional ties with any Aboriginal community in Saskatchewan of a long-term or sustaining nature.

I want to conclude where I began. Recently, I was invited to a conference hosted by the American Association of Law Teachers (which I sadly note I was unable to attend). The task, as it was given to me, was to participate in a conversation about what society, law, and the law school would look like if (a rather large if, I admit), women, persons of colour and Aboriginal peoples had been the ones with the power to define those places. I thought that was an awesome idea. I do recognize that the list of the disempowered and disenfranchised who suddenly got power is not a complete list. However the brilliance of the way this conference was being organized was that I was being asked to dream. Usually, my life is consumed with acts of resistance (see Monture-Angus). Even equity is about "tell me why you do not fit." "Tell me what is wrong with the university?" It was so wonderful to be asked the question, "what can you dream?"

It was really important for me being asked to dream. The last two years I have been really struggling to accept the amount of resistance in my life. In fact, I have been struggling to resist resistance, if that makes any sense. I have been struck by how much of my life is about resistance as opposed to just being, or just being an academic. Think about that for a moment. When I walk into the university it takes so much of my energy just to be there. Everything around me reinforces that I do not belong there (even in a department of Native Studies). This space and what we do in this university space was not envisioned around how I (as representative of a different culture, world view, system of knowing) look at the universe.

This is an open invitation to everyone to spend their time not resisting but dreaming. Dreaming of the kind of space that we could provide if we did not have to resist. The most important equity question for me is what do I need in my world to learn? What environment do I learn best in? How do I learn? What do I think knowledge is? How did I get to that knowledge? What kind of environment is going to encourage me to be the best thinker, the best person that I can be? I believe every human being deserves the gift of excellence. I want all of us to understand that we all deserve this.

*An alternate title to this paper presented itself. I considered "Flint Woman Encoun-
ters Weesagechack on the Prairies" as most appropriate. However, I was concerned
that many academics would not understand the imagery. I wish to thank Debra
Laliberte for the work she did transcribing the audio tape to text. I would also like to
thank the research program at the University of Saskatchewan for their financial
support.*

[1] I have been writing this article for a little more than a year. In that time, there
have been at least three or four job advertisements on the desk beside my
computer. Sometimes I apply and sometimes the deadline for applications
passes without notice or regret. I have had interviews for new positions in the
last year but I have yet to attend another interview. I remain unconvinced that
leaving this university for another (or Native Studies for another discipline)
changes anything but geography.

[2] I am not comfortable with this description of what I do or as the name of the
department. "Native" is a word which for me exemplifies colonial reality, that
we were here to be "discovered" in a "primitive state." In the United States the
general phrase is "American Indian Studies." This is marginally better in my
opinion. Neither label reflects my experiences as a Mohawk woman (more
accurately as Kanien'kehá:ka).

[3] There is no fully comfortable word to express in English, my race, culture, and/
or nationality. I use quotation marks around "Indian" as a way of reminding that
this is a word ascribed by colonial activity (and misunderstanding). I also defer
to Canada's constitution and adopt more borrowed words, Aboriginal Peoples.
These peoples are the "Indian, Inuit, and Métis."

[4] As 1997 unfolded, I have come to understand this is not as true as I once
thought. In law school, I had collegial, supportive, and sustaining relationships
with other faculty members. It is likely that this is partially the result of sharing
a discipline and educational background. In Native Studies, however, my legal
education distances me from other colleagues who have been trained in the
social sciences and humanities (in my department we have a historian, geogra-
pher, anthropologist, and a sociologist). Increasingly, I have felt marginalized
and isolated in the Native Studies field (ironically to a degree that I could not
have imagined in a law school). This experience is juxtaposed with my
classroom experience which is more clearly rewarding in Native Studies where
I teach solely in my areas of interest (Aboriginal justice, Aboriginal law, theory,
and First Nations women). I do not discount the fact that gender plays a large

role in the marginalization I experience (all four of my tenure track colleagues are men).

[5]Thank you Patricia Sasakamoose Tait.

[6]You cannot understand the people without maintaining kinship relationships with those people. Such relationships cannot be sustained away from the land.

[7]I have purposefully stayed clear of making any gender references to this clown as I do not know if both women and men carry this responsibility.

[8]I was a called to the bar in Ontario on January 28, 1994. I maintained that call only until June of 1994 as my family had permanently left the province in May. In all honesty, this call was really more a celebration (and closure) of the oath case. For a discussion, please see Grey.

[9]As a result of a set of extraordinary circumstances and the initiative of Dr. Mary Ellen Turpel-Lafond at the time of writing this paper, I was again an LL.M. candidate at Osgoode Hall Law School. I am pleased to report that in June of 1998, I received my LL.M.

[10]I was only able to begin my graduate legal education because I won a national scholarship. The Department of Indian Affairs refused to fund me. I did not have the opportunity to turn down a job offered in June of that year and stay another year in the graduate program writing my thesis. I offer this comment primarily because it is not well understood that being a "status Indian" does not guarantee educational funding.

[11]This is a profound contradiction for a person who considers themselves neither Canadian nor American, but a citizen of the Mohawk nation. However, I recognize that the development of Native Studies (and post-secondary education in general) has been different in Canada and the United States.

[12]I have been influenced in my teaching pedagogy by Paulo Freire. His book, *Pedagogy of the Oppressed*, is one of the texts for this class.

[13]This fact was raised in class by one of my students, Cathy Wheaton.

[14]If term and sessional appointments in my department are included then a critical mass of Aboriginal scholars might be said to exist in the department. Further, if I cross the campus, I also see a critical mass of Aboriginal scholars (at least five other Aboriginal professors in some form of "permanent" relationship with the university). However, from my vantage point in Native Studies, this is insufficient to positively change my daily experience of the university.

[15]Recounting the hiring history of the department, the 1990 departmental report states:

> Between 1983 and 1985, the Department lost the two Native faculty

who had been members since the inception of the Program: whereas Professor Currie chose not to assume a tenure-track position and retired in 1983, Professor Lussier decided to leave the Department in favour of a position at Keewatin Community College in 1985. *Ultimately, both were replaced by non-Native faculty largely because suitable Native candidates were not available but also because non-Native candidates were well suited to the positions.* [emphasis added] At the same time, however, it was clearly recognized that, because all three existing members were non-Native, future tenure-track appointments would have to be filled by Natives, or held in abeyance until suitable Native candidates could be found. In 1986, the Department passed a formal motion to that effect and continues to honour the principle that, at very least there must be an equitable representation of Native people among the regular faculty. (*supra.*, 54)

[16]Again, I would note that these are my own preliminary observations and further research on these issues is urgently needed. I believe it is important to note that more recently created departments (such as the Indigenous Studies Program at McMaster University created in 1990) may well have a different history. Also, other departments may have been more successful at securing positions and attracting and retaining Aboriginal professors.

[17]I think it is important to clarify the terms (as I was not familiar with them). Endogenous simply means growing from within. Exogenous, obviously then, is originating outside.

[18]Recent Statistics Canada figures indicate that this is no longer the concern. The Aboriginal population in Canada is not vanishing but "baby booming" (*Globe and Mail*).

[19]Based on the University of Saskatchewan Academic Calendar, 1996–1997. This does not include the two courses which I have developed as they are not yet listed in the calendar. The courses are "Justice in Aboriginal Communities" and "First Nations Women and the Law."

[20]As of January 9, 1998, I received the unanimous recommendation for tenure from the University Review Committee. This decision overturned the negative decision of the College Review Committee. Once the Board of Governors of the University of Saskatchewan affirms the University Review Committee's decision, my tenure will take effect on July 1, 1998. I believe I will then be the only "Indian" person tenured in the College of Arts and Science at the University of Saskatchewan.

[21]Professor Winnona Stevenson (Cree), one of the two historians, was a member of this group but left the department in June of 1996 to accept the headship of Indian Studies at the Saskatchewan Indian Federated College. I miss being in her Cree woman's energy.

[22]The 1990 department evaluation states:

> The Departmental Standards, which were approved by the College in 1986, were designed to facilitate the hiring of Native faculty who, at entrance level, seldom have completed doctoral degrees. While candidates may be admitted to a probationary contract with a Master's degree, the final appointment and professional development of the candidate are conditional upon further graduate studies. To be eligible for tenure, a candidate must demonstrate a commitment to doctoral studies, and to be promoted beyond the rank of Associate Professor he/she must have completed a Ph.D. It is understood that, as soon after the initial appoint (sic) as departmental priorities will allow, the new faculty member would be granted an education leave of one or two years in order to complete at least the necessary field work for the doctoral program. The overall intent is that while there may be disparities in academic background at the entrance level, all members of the Department eventually will have the same academic credentials. (54)

[23]As far as I am aware, there is only one Ph.D. program in North America that allows for the opportunity to earn a degree in Indian Studies. That program is the University of Arizona in Tuscon, and started in 1997.

[24]My visit to St. Thomas University as a guest lecturer in 1997 was too short to qualify as an experience of that program. My involvement as a participant at numerous Elder's Conferences at Trent University also does not qualify.

[25]I do not know if this drafting by Dr. Waldram was an assigned duty by the department. I have been excluded from department meetings since September of 1997. The department moved the meetings from Thursday afternoon to Monday afternoons. I have a teaching commitment (in addition to my University of Saskatchewan duties) in Prince Albert on Monday afternoons. Prince Albert is one and a half hours north of Saskatoon.

[26]In the *Abstracts of Native Studies* (1984), supra, vi, it is also noted in the introduction: "Trent University has again led the way by developing the first Master of Arts program in Native Studies."

[27]Email of Dr. Jim Waldram dated December 16, 1997, 1 (copy of message on file with the author).

[28]I include in my definition of Aboriginal scholar both Aboriginal students and Aboriginal professors. I have no desire to to draw lines across our Aboriginal nations. Further, it must be recognized that the historic exclusion of Aboriginal people results in the fact that some Native scholars come to seek mainstream academic credentials later in their lives.

[29]An example would be the assigning of graduate teaching which has already been discussed in the text of this paper.

[30]The University of Saskatchewan Mission Statement approved by the Board of Governors on May 20, 1993 refers by name to Aboriginal people in a standard equity clause. The clause reads as follows: "To advance employment and education equity through our policies and practices, and, in particular, to address the needs of aboriginal (sic) people, persons with disabilities, visible minorities and women." For the provincial university in a province with such a high percentage of Aboriginal persons, and a population that is clearly growing, this is at best a missed opportunity to express an eloquent statement of vision which truly reaches out to Aboriginal aspirations. The message this statement sends to me is simple. In order to achieve the standards the university community aspires to, they must "help" me and "advance" me. The focus is on me, and on changing me. There is no inkling that the problem is not me but the structure which I am being forced into.

[31]The comments on graduate studies reflect my experiences as of February of 1997.

[32]The difference between the granting of Master's degrees by special case is largely an administrative one as I understand it. With a regular Masters program, the department now only completes paperwork on each application whereas in the special case situation additional paperwork to approve the program is also required. The special case M.A. program impacts graduate students in two ways. Often their acceptances are delayed and a higher undergraduate average is required for admission to a special case program. Second, it means that without a regular program courses are more likely to be completed as independent studies.

References

Abstracts of Native Studies. Introduction. (1996).

American Indian Studies Center. "American Indian Studies as an Academic

Discipline: A Revisit." *American Indian Issues in Higher Education.* Los Angeles: American Indian Studies Center, 1980.

Asikinack, William. "Why Native American Studies: A Canadian First Nations Perspective." *American Indian Studies: An Interdisciplinary Approach to Contemporary Issues.* Ed. Dane Morrison. New York: Peter Lang Publishing, 1997. 111–116.

Department of Native Studies. "Preliminary Departmental Report to the College of Arts and Science Review." Saskatoon: University of Saskatchewan, May 1990.

Freire, Paulo. *Pedagogy of the Oppressed.* New York: Continuum Publishing Company, 1996.

Grey, Catherine. "Patricia Monture v The Queen." *Canadian Woman Studies* 10.2–3 (1989): 146–147.

Lynn, Elizabeth Cook. "Who Stole Native American Studies." *wicazo sa review* 12.1 (Spring 1997): 9–28.

McIntyre, Sheila. "Gender Bias Within the Law School: 'The Memo' and Its Impact." *Canadian Journal of Women and the Law* 2.1 (1987–88): 437–467.

Monture-Angus, Patricia. "Considering Colonialism and Oppression: Aboriginal Women, Justice and the "Theory" of Resistance." *Native Studies Review* (forthcoming).

Monture-Angus, Patricia. *Thunder in My Soul: A First Nations Woman Speaks.* Halifax: Fernwood Publishing, 1995.

Stein, Wayne, Jon Reyhner, and William Asikinack. in *supra.*, Morrison , 71-116.

Tafoya, Terry. *Roots of Survival: Native American Storytelling and the Sacred.* Ed. Joseph Bruchac. Colden: Fulcrom Publishing, 1996.

Waldram, Jim. E-mail circulation. 16 December 1997.

Waldram, Jim. "Draft Proposal for a Master's Program in Applied Native Studies." 1 September 1994.

Webster's English Dictionary. Ottawa: Pamco Publishing, 1994.

2.

Re-Loading the Canon

Making Que(e)ried Bodies?
The Politics and Practices of Special Topics

Jodi Jensen and Erica Meiners

The purpose of this discussion is to highlight examples of how strategies to address equity and diversity "work and are worked" within the natural sciences and in a particular medical structure. Our intent is that these slightly out of place critiques will inform the policies and practices within post-secondary education.

As a starting point we take seriously Spivak's discussions about essentialism: that bodies working towards social justice need to "assert the performance of positionality and refuse to essentialize it" (157). In evaluating the cost of taking the "risk of essence" we also take frameworks and questions from Cindy Patton. Patton articulates the necessity of theorizing how structures, discursive and material, shift and frame strategies that attempt to work towards equity in institutions:

> … My reading of the new right rhetoric suggests that while we are deconstructing identity, the new right is deconstructing the social space that our identity predicates. Defending social space (*if this is indeed so desirable*) while avoiding the problems of identitarian politics requires a broader critique than so far has been offered by critics of essentialized identity: if, as many argue, identity is always performative or a performance, then identity is necessarily always in context or in practice. In order to be useful and not merely nihilistic (*not that I object in principle to regular doses of nihilism*) the deconstruction of this

identity must be accompanied by an analysis of the spaces posited by or through identity. (227) [emphasis ours]

This discussion is an attempt to think through Spivak and Patton's points in our situated contexts: as a researcher within a medical sphere and as a feminist in/out of the natural sciences. We ask: *what does it mean to take Spivak's "risk of essence" and simultaneously begin an analysis of the spaces posited by or through identity?* We do not intend to point to the/a mythical solution to achieve this state called "equity," nor are we interested in privileging one strategy or tactic for social change over another. We want to emphasize two points: the necessity of rethinking inter-intra disciplinary coalition work; and the necessity of theory as inseparable from practice.

Placing bodies in disease

For the past year one of the authors has been conducting fieldwork for a dissertation, studying medically affiliated support programs for women with addictions to see how these structures discursively negotiate relationships between trauma, identity, memory, and the body. In this fieldwork, the programs and the governing/organizing structures and their relationship to the pharma/medical nexus have been researched. The clients have not been studied.

The theme for a series of publicity campaigns in 1996 and 1997 for raising awareness about depression, eating disorders, and schizophrenia was "diversity." In British Columbia, posters and radio commercials were the primary means of advertising and providing information for each of these campaigns. The intended message is that "depression" or "schizophrenia," or an "eating disorder" can afflict anyone and that the disease is equitable in its distribution throughout the community. Gender, ethnicity, and socio-economic status (more visible markers of difference) are highlighted in these ads as irrelevant factors to the acquisition of these diseases.

These campaigns attempt to deconstruct a stereotype that only white, middle-aged, middle-class housewives are depressed or that eating disorders are confined to white, heterosexual women. However, it is important to look at the spaces in which these definitions and performances of diversity are circulated. Discussions of difference can negate philosophical and socio-cultural factors that contribute to or even make disorders. These "glosses" of diversity can negate complex histories of how the medical structure has produced and continues to produce pathologizing discourses to manage identities for other social institutions: education, state, church.

We are not arguing that the proponents of these campaigns want to erase the relationships between gender, poverty, and racism and these disorders, nor is the intent to invite debate on the organic or cultural "nature" of mental illnesses. These posters, while attempting to highlight diversity, reify a medical category and collapse the ways cultural contexts (racisms, heteronormativity, misogyny) *affect, infect, and effect* bodies. As Miche and Warhol state in their work on alcoholism and models of recovery:

> The repeated term alcoholic then is orthographically displayed as a primary identity ... the disease makes no distinctions.... Categories are supposed to collapse under the weight of common humanity, a common body and soul under attack. (338–339)

There are also more explicit contradictions that exist between identity, capital, and the psycho-medical nexus. For example, why has there been a poster advertising to the mainstream public that depression affects everyone when the advertisements in medical trade journals target specific bodies (women/other) as the marked recipient of anti-depressants and tranquilizers? Why are the diversity posters for depression sponsored by a major pharmaceutical manufacturer? Pharmaceutical companies have a significant and increasing impact in the definition and organization of identity categories within medical spaces (Lowe).

Within this medical sphere, not unlike academic spaces, even if they are conceived and executed under the best of intentions, these performances of diversity function as "add ons" and often do not challenge the foundations of the larger structures. In addition, a valid argument can be made that the recent drive to promote diversity and equity is about profit for the pharmaceutical companies, not social justice.

But, what if these campaigns make medical services "more accessible" to a few? If this is the only strategy offered or available, is it naive to refuse it—and the corresponding access to resources—on theoretical principles? As articulated earlier, strategies for social change are always multi-dimensional, contextual, tactical, etc. However, in repeated situations this researcher's push to deconstruct identity categories has been positioned against, instead of with, the practice of the health care organizations and activists within those organizations, thus rendering her, as Habermas and Nancy Fraser charge of Foucault, a "young conservative."

In pushing for persistent, situated analysis of how identifications work, and an ongoing assessment of the cost of strategic essentialism, theory should not be placed in opposition to practice. It is precisely these binarized scripts, with their tendency to premature closure that we are refusing in this paper. It is not a question of having "special topics" or not, or having a diversity poster or not. Rather, different questions need to be asked, to move the discussion to different spaces:

> ... Recovering a progressive project requires an understanding of the limitations of performative personae as well as evaluating the role of the field which they posit and struggle on behalf of themselves. One of the crucial analytic issues, then, is considering how to think about the space in which performative identities are in play, how to interrogate identity as it is situated in fields of power. Power must not be treated monolithically or viewed as isomorphic or continuous across the various forms of space ... new ways of understanding the "successes" ... must be imagined ... not by reintroducing once (and properly) discarded ideas about the subject or the state, but by queering social theory. (Patton 227–228)

Patton stresses the necessity of ongoing work (the theory/practice divide is refused) looking at where in social spaces identities and identifications occur. In addition, it matters who executes this work. How should these discussions transpire, and by whom, and who pays for this labour?

Two points Patton has raised require brief highlighting. (1) How to assess whether defending social spaces is indeed desirable? While this query might be a little rhetorical, here we apply de Certeau's discussion about tactics. We wonder if more productive possibilities to "refigure" access to resources and more equitable social relations are occurring outside the academy. (2) What might queering social theory resemble? Although we hesitate to invoke queer theory, displacement or "re-figuring" the terms equity and diversity are required. Does this involve re-figuring or queering the body?

Placing bodies in science

Popular conceptions of equity for women in the natural sciences can be used to address similar questions. Namely, what does it mean to take Spivak's risk of essence seriously, and what impact does this have on oppositional practices? How do strategies to achieve equity work within, and how are they worked by, institutions?

How the concept of equity is deployed in the literature on women and science provides an opening to this discussion. One of the authors is an ex-scientist whose research explores how scientists make strategic use of feminist critiques in standpoint epistemologies. The intent here is not to consider why there are few women in science, but to consider the directed and controlled circulation of specific bodies, identities and epistemologies within educational institutions.

In the natural sciences, equity for North American women is often conceptualized as a pipeline, intaking the bodies and outputting scientists for tenure-track jobs. For example in 1992, *Science* magazine issued its first annual "special section" titled "Women in Science." One article examines why American women hold only 18 percent of tenure-track positions in neuroscience when over the previous decade women comprised just under half of graduate students entering the field. The article notes "that although the pipeline supplying the field of neuroscience starts out with lots of women in it, it is leaking—like a sieve" (Barinaga 1366).

Pipeline and other equity statistics are constructed on assumptions regarding appropriate entry and exit points, career paths, and by the practices of collecting and constructing disappearing bodies. This study of women's participation in neuroscience measures intake to the pipeline at graduate school, not counting those who dropped out or were filtered out before reaching this point.

Non-white women are visibly absent from the 1992 "special section" on women in science, with the exception of their inclusion in an advertisement by a major laboratory designed for recruitment—something which did not go unnoticed judging by the letters in response. In Canada, women who identify as belonging to a visible minority are almost twice as likely as white women to receive a university degree in the natural and applied sciences (Statistics Canada 1995, 60). And yet the literature on women in science rarely considers how race/ ethnicity (together with more invisible identity categories of class and sexual orientation) might affect women's participation at all levels in science and technology.

Many feminist science critics focus attention on integrating attributes historically associated with the feminine, such as subjectivity and empathy, into scientific methodologies. This approach has implications for bodies with multiple identities and contributes to the strong skepticism that some women scientists hold towards feminist revisions. For example, gender essentialism is easily problematized by one Asian woman scientist, who points to similarities between the cooperative management styles attributed to white women and to Asian men, and to the contradictions between notions that women cannot do math and that all Asians are math brains (Knecht 409). In addition, when popularly translated in scientific contexts, these strategies become located/ fixed in essentialized bodies, with the result that women scientists' identities and practices become the grounds for debate and contestation, rather than putting the institutional practices at stake.

By invoking pipeline statistics, women scientists have secured support for limited institutional changes. However, the political motivations behind these changes have less to do with equity than with competition, profit and nationalism. The projected decline in the number of white males of college age by the late 1990s has created concerns about possible declines in the scientific workforce. Increasingly, scientific workers are recruited from so-called alternative communities to preserve the health of the industries of science and technology and as human resources for national economic strategies. Industry seeks to create the perception of diversity among its workers, recognizing that replacing the image of science as a community of elites with that of a community accessible to all is necessary to maintain support for public financing of scientific research (see Crosby; Etzkowitz *et al.*; Statistics Canada 1988; Widnall).

Pipeline and other equity statistics raise questions about which bodies/ identities get counted and why; about which identities are real, visible, significant; about who among the bodies disappearing from the pipeline has value or represents loss. While the metaphor of the pipeline is invoked to draw attention to inequities, in practice it functions to cleave off or eliminate diversity. As noted earlier, within certain medical structures disease functions as a primary identity, making no distinctions between the bodies infected or the conditions of infection. Similarly, the pipeline cannot distinguish between the individual elements or the resources it carries. Each potential scientific worker drawn into the pipeline, from increasingly diverse pools of reserves, is pumped out with "scientist" as a primary identity.

The special sections on women (and more recently on minorities) in popular science magazines and recruitment literature contribute to the construction and commodification of specific identities. As Patton argues, if identity is performative then it is necessarily always in context or practice. "Interrogating identity as it is situated in fields of power" is crucial (11). Any consideration of equity needs to focus not just on numbers of particular kinds of bodies, but on the forces at play on, and within, institutional fields.

Special topics courses and programs, for example Women's Studies, Native Studies, and Gay/Lesbian Studies, have been created as a form of, or route to, institutional changes within education. Equity and diversity function in much the same way in special topics as in the special sections on women in science; however, special sections in science literature contribute towards the construction of alternate reserves for the pipeline to draw from, whereas special topics in the academy siphon essentialized bodies off the pipeline into marginalized sites within educational institutions.

That increased recognition for special topics departments, programs, and courses has been achieved in the U.S. during the era of Reagan and Bush, and in Britain under Thatcherism, indicates a shift in the nature of discriminatory and oppressive politics (Evans; Perez). Special topics create additional academic and intellectual space; however as educational theorists Evans and McGee have noted, special topics may also serve to contain political challenges within disciplines and allow institutions to respond to the consumer demands of students without introducing fundamental changes (Evans; McGee). In addition, Laura Perez argues that special topics assist in creating the illusion of equal access and proportionate representation of minorities.

We want to nuance the discussion to show how essentialized identities, when linked to conceptions of disciplinarity, might impact oppositional practices within education. Special topics construct an institutional home for essentialized identities. While conceived as interdisciplinary, in practice, special topics merely juxtapose a number of disciplines from the social sciences and humanities, so that the boundaries between disciplines remain intact and practitioners continue to speak from positions of authority and expertise (Trinh T., Minh-Ha). For example in Canada, there are currently more men teaching women's studies than there are natural scientists (MacDonald).

In her discussion of oppositional identity and education, Laura Perez concludes the following:

> Conceiving both politics *and* identity as mobile and tactical can be liberating and empowering, as well as a defense, for the minority within the educational system.... This kind of politics depends precisely on the exploitation of loopholes and blindspots within the structures and practices of institutions, and the broad building of alliances based on intersection of interests rather than on orthodox allegiances that cannot respond to the difference and array of Chicana/o interests. (276)

Perez suggests undertaking coalition work within institutions across the boundaries of discipline and identity. In a similar vein, Chandra Mohanty, in an article identifying the necessity of looking critically at the strategies western feminists have used to work towards social justice, posits coalition work as an active "politics of engagement." Because coalition work is always contextually and temporally situated it avoids the reification of identity categories. Mohanty states that it is the coalition among struggles that leads to this theoretically informative and active "politics of engagement."

While coalition-based politics is a useful place to begin, a politics of engagement should not translate into an evacuation of discussions on the genealogies of strategies. Cindy Patton stresses the necessity of continued "rigorous" detailed work which looks critically at the circulation and execution of identity politics.

In lieu of a conclusion, we want to reiterate that our intention has not been to provide pat solutions. Our use of slightly out-of-place critiques is not intended to raise questions of whether or not there should be diversity posters or special topics, but to illustrate how policies and practices work and are worked within institutional fields, including education. As we have stated, strategies for social change with and in institutions are multi-dimensional. Our situated critiques are intended to encourage collaborative inter/intra disciplinary theorizing about the effectiveness of strategies for social change.

The two points we have emphasized are first, interdisciplinary coalition work is necessary, and needs to be supported at the institution—financially, textually, and politically. Second, we believe that theory is necessarily inseparable from practice. We view these as partial, temporal possibilities that will continue the process of ensuring that strategies for social change are, in the words of Linda Alcoff, "transgressive not recuperative."

References

Alcoff and Gray. "Survivor Discourse: Transgression or Recuperation?" *Getting a Life.* Eds. Smith and Watson. Minneapolis: University of Minnesota Press, 1996.

Barinaga, M. "Profile of a Field: Neuroscience." *Science* 255 (1992): 1366–7.

Crosby, T. "Minorities: Underrepresentation, Education and Careers in Science." *Journal of College Science Teaching* 17.5 (1988): 342–3.

de Certeau. *The Practice of Everday Life.* Berkeley: University of California Press, 1984.

Etzkowitz, H, *et al.* "The Paradox of Critical Mass For Women in Science." *Science* 266 (1994): 51–4.

Evans, M. "Whose Direction? Whose Mainstream? Controlling the Narrative and Identity of Women's Studies." *Graduate Women's Studies: Visions and Realities.* Ed. A. Shteir. Toronto: Inanna Publications, 1996. 109–120.

Kelly, M. *Critique and Power: Recasting the Foucault Habermas Debate.* Cambridge, MA: MIT Press, 1994.

Knecht, K. "Letters." *Science* 261 (1993): 409.

Laundry, D., and D. Maclean. *The Spivak Reader.* Routledge: New York, 1996.

Lowe, D. *The Body in Late Capitalist U.S.A.* Durham: Duke University, 1995.

McGee, P. "Decolonization and the Curriculum of English." *Race Identity and Representation in Education.* Eds. C. McCarthy and W. Crichlow. New York: Routledge, 1993.

MacDonald, Marilyn. Personal communication, 1996.

Mohanty, C., "Feminist Encounter: Locating the Politics of Experience." *Social Postmodernisms: Beyond Identity Politics.* Eds. Seidman and Nicholson. New York: Cambridge University Press, 1996.

Morton, Donald, ed. *The Material Queer.* New York: Westview Press, 1996.

Patton, C. "Refiguring Social Space." *Social Postmodernisms: Beyond Identity Politics.* Eds. Seidman and Nicholson. New York: Cambridge University Press, 1996.

Perez, Laura. "Opposition and the Education of Chicana/os." *Race Identity and Representation in Education.* Eds. Cameron McCarthy and Warren Crichlow. New York: Routledge, 1993.

Spivak, G. "in a word." *The Essential Difference.* Eds. E. Schor, and E. Weed. Indianapolis: Indiana University Press, 1994.

Statistics Canada. "Women in Canada, A Statistical Report." Ottawa: Industry Canada, Catalogue number 89-503E, 1995.

Statistics Canada. "Human Resources for Science and Technology." Ottawa: Supply and Services Canada, Catalogue number 88-508E, 1988.

Trinh T., Minh-Ha. *Framer Framed.* New York: Routledge, 1992.

Warhol, R., and H. Michie. "Twelve Step Teleology: Marratives of Recovery/ Recovery as Narrative." *Getting a Life.* Eds. Smith and Watson. Minneapolis: University of Minnesota Press, 1996.

Warner, R. *Recovering From Schizophrenia: Psychiatry and Political Economy.* London: Routlege, 1985.

Widnall, S. "AAAS presidential lecture: Voices from the Pipeline." *Science* 241 (1988): 1740–1745.

Institutionalizing Postcolonial Studies

Kofi Asare

At the outset, let me begin by saying that I am speaking to the challenge posed by Postcolonial Studies in the academy as a student. In fact, as a graduate student, first and foremost. Obviously I share other identities (some useful, others not so) in my daily transactions within culture and society. I have been for example, depending on the occasion, a man, a father, a Black African, Ghanaian, Canadian resident (which incidentally also makes me an "immigrant"—a loaded word in our culture today), and the list can be extended.

I have decided to begin this way because as one African writer, Chinua Achebe, said in a recent interview, issues of identity have a logic all their own, and are rarely neutral. As Achebe sees it, "each one of these tags has a meaning, and a penalty and a responsibility."[1] Hence I would suggest that extreme care should be exercised each time we assume an identity or have one thrust upon us. Because in large part, how and what we wish to be known is at the heart of a lot of our concerns as a community of humans—our identities, we know, will continue to inform the very character of the relations we form in life. Indeed, I am sure some of you may have already made a connection between me and Fanon's classic quandary from *Black Skin, White Masks* by asking yourselves, "What does [this] Black Man want?"

Clearly, issues and questions of identity are at the basis of a lot of the quarrels in both Academy and society in general. Indeed, I will wager that at the heart of the postcolonial project itself is its doubtful status as something one can truly hang anything on. What then, we may ask, is Postcolonial Studies?

What is the condition of postcoloniality? What does it mean as a theory and as practice? How is it constituted and what consequences, if any, attach to a postcolonial identity? These are questions which should engage us as we attempt to formulate a theory—any theory of the margin, from such a privileged centre as the western Academy.

Stuart Hall has said in a fine formulation that "cultural identities come from somewhere, have histories." He goes on to add that our "identities are the names we give to the different ways we are positioned by, and position ourselves in, narratives of the past" (qtd. in Gates 210). How is a postcolonial self positioned or posed in the narratives which interest us? And how does it become a part of these narratives? As I see it the problem of postcoloniality as a state of being, a mode of consciousness, a discipline, is one of status. Does having a name confirm and confer untroubled and incontestable identity? Like all new and emergent fields, Postcolonial Studies is also struggling to constitute its boundaries even while it pursues its passions. And as it faces these large and troubling questions, it does so with the knowledge that the success or failure of its insertion in the academy will, to borrow from Hall again, hinge on how it is "positioned by and in" the academy. So my question—what does it mean to have Postcolonial Studies in the academy?— must first answer the urgent one of its identity as a discursive practice. What in short is the postcolonial self after?

Why should it matter, in the final analysis, to have Postcolonial Studies instituted as a discipline relevant to our needs today as students and/or educators? What is the nature of this inclusion? What does it mean in the context of earlier occlusion? What is the nature of this inheritance? How is it positioned in the "hierarchy of cultures" (Fanon's phrase) and discourses? What is the specificity of its status in the academy? What does the classroom as a site represent? What is postcoloniality vis-à-vis canon formation and curriculum development? Is it in fact a discipline? And finally, is the postcolonial about process or arrival? Does the post in postcolonialism inaugurate a new beginning or merely anticipate one?

In Kwame Appiah's rewarding survey of the period in *In My Father's House: Africa In The Philosophy Of Culture*, he characterizes postcoloniality as

the condition of what we might ungenerously call a comprador intelligentsia: of a relatively small, Western-style, Western-trained, group of writers and thinkers who mediate the trade in cultural commodities of world capitalism at the periphery. (149)

Referring specifically to African postcolonialism, he goes on to add that most of these writers are "known through the west they present to Africa and through an Africa they have invented for the world, for each other, and for Africa." Even more significantly, Appiah is of the view that all aspects of contemporary African cultural life "have been influenced, often powerfully, by the transition of African societies through colonialism, but that they are not all in the relevant sense postcolonial. For the post in postcolonial, is "the post of a space clearing gesture" (Appiah 149)—the staking of a narrative ground in the sense suggested by Stuart Hall. As Sarah Suleri contends in "Feminism and the Postcolonial Condition,"

> the concept of the postcolonial itself is too frequently robbed of specificity in order to function as a preapproved allegory for any mode of discursive contestation. (qtd. in Ashcroft *et al.* 273)

Denis Ekpo has entered the fray by suggesting that, whatever its meaning, Postcolonial Studies today faces a crisis of "performative impasse" (121).

Increasingly, the debate around postcolonialism as an oppositional practice is being staged as a contest of theories. It has been suggested that the absence of a theoretical certitude in Edward Said's works emerges from the fact that he borrows from the brilliant strategies of Michel Foucault in his own inquiry into the epistemological violations of Empire, without moving beyond it. And that Said is caught as it were, "in Empire," unable to theorize a way out of an oppositional practice caught perpetually between a yearning for national belonging and the sanctuary and freedom of exile:

> What is there worth saving and holding onto between the extremes of exile on the one hand, and the often bloody-minded affirmations of nationalism on the other? ... Are they simply two conflicting varieties of paranoia? (Said 1984, 161)

A lot has been made about Gayatri Spivak's impossible attempts to frame a postcolonial identity away from the strategies staked out by Jacques Derrida and the deconstructionists—a strategy incapable of looking beyond the text (what Asha Varadharajan has termed "phonetic rain" (xxv)).. And Homi Bhabha? Bhabha suggests that through Lacan, the "poetics of narcissism" replaces the "politics of nationalism"—interiority, we are told is everything. In Bhabha's work we confront the self-absorbed and continually self-referential subject of postmodernity:

> The split subject of colonial identification is characterized by ambivalence: the subject both desires and desire to deny the other. *There is no origin of Self or other, no place or time at which identity is definitively established, where Self and Other begins.* (Goldberg xix) [emphasis mine]

This statement by David Goldberg is most bewildering and baffling. While I am fully aware that subject formation is a complexly variable phenomenon, to posit a self in a perpetual state of paranoia and self-negation is a forbidden luxury to a lot of us. Recently a new voice announced itself by attempting to rescue the postcolonial subject from her disabling quietism through the power and mysticism of Theodor Adorno's "negative dialectics." I am speaking of Asha Varadharajan's study of Spivak, Said, and Adorno in *Exotic Parodies: Subjectivity In Adorno, Said, and Spivak.* Varadharajan asserts that her epiphany emerges from a true and extraordinary irony:

> The Post-colonial intellectual (like Spivak) is in danger of reducing her language to "phonetic pain" and her experience to "the suffering of the victim," but compelled both to resist that pain and to envisage the task of decolonization and the condition of postcoloniality. (xxv)

What has emerged clearly from the crises and contradictions of Postcolonial Studies should give us more than mere pause. Surely, we need more than this if we are to recover the initial promise implicit in the postcolonial purchase, the promise implied in Fanon's bold declarative that the challenge remains the "veritable creation of the new man" (1991, 36)—and of course, the new woman. Secondly, the intense socio-cultural construction and deconstruction of subjectivity has had the strange effect of blurring lines, although clear lines are needed in these most harrowing of times. Through all the clamor and din, we must not lose sight of the fact that the specificity of location ought to form one of our major concerns. What after all is this borderlessness? Are we equal in our capacities to negotiate this new boundarylessness? Crucially these questions begin to insist themselves. For my purposes, I nominate postcoloniality oppositionally, re-situating its agenda within the broad project of an ideology of liberation. More to the point, postcolonial studies ought to remain an "epistemological stance" also committed to the project of moving beyond the margin, in transcending otherness (not difference)—becoming.

If I have implied otherwise, I want to suggest that Postcolonial Studies is important, not least because as a practice of epistemological recovery, it seeks to add fullness to the picture. Today we know that knowledge about ourselves has been enriched by the writings of many erstwhile others. Still, our bid for inclusion must be framed within the caution put so forcefully by Spivak:

> As this material begins to be absorbed into the discipline, the long established but supple heterogeneous and hierarchical power-lines of the institutional "dissemination of Knowledge" continue to determine and overdetermine its condition of representability. *It is at the moment of infiltration or insertion, sufficiently under threat by the custodians of a fantasmatic high Western culture, that the greatest caution has to be taken.* (1993, 56) [emphasis mine]

Simply put, postcoloniality can be read as an act of recuperation—*sans* apology. For some years now, and recently in his book, *Culture and Imperialism*, Edward Said has correctly maintained (and with some irony) that we are all in a sense made possible by imperialism and empire. I believe that by the same token we are also un-made by imperialism and empire. Therefore, it seems to me, the task of postcolonial practice in the academy is to contribute to the reconstitution of the de/formed subject of colonialism. As Fanon reminded us in *Wretched of the Earth*, by its very nature colonialism is always an act of violence. It not only denies the self a place of its own, it also destroys whatever the self had to begin with.

Postcolonial Studies must of necessity be posited as an ongoing and active negotiation with its own protocols of engagement. This is how its work should be done. After all, every query of the self can only enrich it as a practice, continually reminding it of its limits as well as its status as provisional. In a sense, Postcolonial Studies is uniquely positioned as a discourse, beset as it is with the highly problematic question of how emergent discourses can safely appropriate the models—the conditions of whose constitution are imbricated in the very oppressive and hegemonic processes of epistemological de/formation—of its colonizers. Our call for equal representation must also be distinguished from the positions staked out by the extremes on both sides of the cultural battle currently raging—battles not only over the canon or the curricula, but lately over the very terms we use in our relations in society itself.

Not long before her unfortunate death, Audrey Lorde, commenting on the state of human relations, noted in words whose power bears full citation, how to harness difference:

> Difference must be not merely tolerated, but seen as a fund of necessary polarities between which our creativity can spark like a dialectic. Only then does the necessity for interdependency become unthreatening.... Within the interdependence of mutual (nondominant) differences lies that security which enables us to descend into the chaos of knowledge and return with true visions of our future, along with the concomitant power to effect those changes which can bring that future into being.... We have been taught either to ignore our differences, or to view them as causes for separation and suspicion rather than as forces for change. Without community there is no liberation, only the most vulnerable armistice between an individual and her oppression. But community must not mean a shedding of our differences, nor a pathetic pretense that these differences do not exist. (111–12)

Surely, Postcolonial Studies' engagement with society and the academy must be shored by similar sentiments. So we seek representation, because more than the fact that our right to be represented is enshrined by the mysticism and practical necessity of a democratic culture we valorize, but also because we know we can bring another perspective to our sense of the world we collectively inhere.

Today we no longer have to insist on the fact that some knowledge about Africa, Asia, and the others have always been present at the constitution of the West itself, and that acculturation is not specific to Africa, but the very character of all histories. The task of Postcolonial Studies is given added urgency when we realize that increasingly globalization has come to mean Americanization and corporatism—the vertical integration of structures for control, order, and sovereignty. We cannot afford to think in the current terms which equate the triumph of multinational capital with the arrival of a new era of human development based in equity.

As students, educators, and administrators, we must constantly remind ourselves that the partial institutionalization (some will pejoratively call it "normalization") of the emergent and broad field of Postcolonial Studies in the academy opens up fresh challenges and issues forth new concerns. Importantly, it inaugurates a whole range of problematics, even while it generates new and surprising alignments in relations. Secondly, contrary to some recent claims, a lot has been accomplished in society at large; still, a lot still remains to be done in the academy itself.

It seems to me that our ongoing need to secure the initial promise of Postcolonial Studies by a reworking and retheorizing of some its key concepts, however, should not be an end in itself. We must take seriously Spivak's reminder that "knowledge and thinking are halfway houses," and "that they are judged when they are set to work" (1996: 246). The race for theory has often ended up as an end in itself, missing the "curious guardian" at the margins of our own discourse, to say nothing of the "Master" text. We have to maintain one very obvious position: that there is a reference outside the text. In the end our dealings with knowledge must be informed by what we may call the possibility of circulating knowledge without domination—knowledge as the power to conceive new possibilities, the power to breach and extend boundaries, the power to found the self. Our gaze must remain focused on the hidden subject of the address, the subject of inequality, wherever we find her, because our work remains unfinished until decolonization can truly make of us new men and women. The writings of peoples previously denied even a history—a record of their presence here on earth—is important in the academy precisely because they desire to know how they got here in the first place. And yet we must not in haste ignore the lessons we have learned on our journey here. As an act of cultural retrieval, a postcolonial practice will mean very little if it is incapable of submitting its own concepts and assumptions for critical scrutiny.

Our departments and the policies attaching to them have to be re-tooled to serve pressing needs. We must challenge the very notion of an interdisciplinarity constructed historically on the false parceling up of territory into manageable colonies for order and control. Like the history of imperialism/colonialism which gave birth to it, the order of knowledge we inhere in the academy is itself the product of colonial violence. So, as we seek representation and inclusion, we cannot do so at any cost. Our call for a broadening of the field of inquiry should not mean the abandonment of previously canonized texts. Rather, our goals must consist in making the academy relevant to the diverse needs of a new community determined, firstly, to see a reflection of themselves in the academic mainstream, and secondly, to restoring balance and scrutiny to the whole field of knowledge production and dissemination.

This process is by necessity premised on the real and eventual dissolution of borders. We need to find new ways to articulate subjectivity, new methods that would enable us to actively engage with canon formation. We should welcome non-canonical readings of canonical texts, readings from various contestatory, marginal, or subaltern perspectives. And in this endeavor, postcolonial and feminist theory have been in the forefront of these epistemological shifts. Indeed, I will go further to recommend that a second language is crucial to this undertaking for forging connections across borders, race, gender, and essences which will continue to be the real challenge of Postcolonial Studies.

Importantly therefore, as students, educators, and academics, we have to seek out fellow travelers in the formerly colonized areas of the world, in order to form bonds of partnership which transcend institutional structures of validation and legitimation. Michel Foucault once asserted that his "archeological project" was committed to depriving "the sovereignty of the subject"— the Western subject—this exclusive and instant right to discourse. To this must be added V. Y. Mudimbe's observation that "the geography and history of Africa," to take one example, "also point out the passion of a subject-object who refuses to vanish." As Mudimbe continues, "He or she has gone from the situation in which he or she was perceived as a simple functioning object, to the freedom of thinking of himself or herself as the starting point of an absolute discourse" (200). And rightly so.

In conclusion, I want to propose that there is a false choice contained in Frank Lentricchia's re-formulation of John Dewey's famous challenge, "Education as a function of society or society as a function of education." Clearly, we can say that it is not an either/or position. More often than not, what is at work in such processes of exchange is something in the manner of a dialectical antinomy: we determine as we are determined.

This is what is embodied in the initial promise of postcolonial studies. We are now slowly waking up to a truth the ancients have always known: everything, in the final analysis, is a part of "The Whole." And in the end if language remains our one unique gift as humans, it also confers a special burden on us. So, in the face of this ongoing reconfiguration (at all levels of society and culture) let us bear in mind the full implication of Fanon's idea that each individual existence is a motion toward the other, the affirmation of our humanity in the other, and that "to speak" as I do here today, "is to exist *absolutely* for the other" (1968, 17) [emphasis added].

[1]I am thankful to Kwame Appiah for this observation from Achebe. See Kwame Anthony Appiah, *In My Father's House: Africa in the Philosophy of Culture* (New York: Oxford University Press, 1992), p. 173.

References

Appiah, Kwame Anthony. *In My Father's House: Africa In The Philosophy Of Culture*. New York: Oxford University Press, 1992.

Ekpo, Denis. "Towards Post-Africanism: Contemporary African Thought snd Postmodernism." *Textual Practice* 9.1 (1995): 121–135.

Fanon, Frantz. *The Wretched of the Earth*. NewYork: Grove Press, 1991.

Fanon, Frantz. *Black Skin, White Masks*. New York: Grove Press, 1968.

Foucault, Michel. *Power/Knowledge: Selected Interviews and Other Writings 1972–1977*. New York: Pantheon Books, 1980.

Gates Jr., Henry Louis. "Looking For Modernism." *Black American Cinema*. Ed. Manthia Diawara. New York: Routledge, 1993.

Goldberg, David Theo, ed. *Anatomy of Racism*. Minneapolis: University of Minnesota Press, 1992.

Lentricchia, Frank. *Criticism and Social Change*. Chicago: University of Chicago Press, 1983.

Lorde, Audrey. *Sister Outsider*. Freedom, CA: The Crossing Press, 1984.

Mudimbe, V. Y. *The Invention of Africa: Gnosis, Philosophy and the Order of Knowledge*. Bloomington: Indiana University Press, 1988.

Said, Edward. *Culture and Imperialism*. New York: Alfred Knopf, Inc., 1993.

Said, Edward. "Reflections on Exile." *Granta* 13 (Winter 1984): 161.

Spivak, Gayatri "Diasporas Old And New: Women In The Transnational World." *Textual Practice* 10.2 (1996): 245–269.

Spivak, Gayatri. *Outside in the Teaching Machine*. London: Routledge, 1993.

Suleri, Sarah. "Woman Skin Deep: Feminism and the Postcolonial Condition." *The Post-Colonial Studies Reader*. Eds. Bill Ashcroft, Gareth Griffiths, and Helen Tiffin. London: Routledge. 1995. 273–280.

Varadharajan, Asha. *Exotic Parodies: Subjectivity in Adorno, Said and Spivak*. Minneapolis University of Minnesota Press, 1995.

Women's Studies in Post-Soviet Totalitarianism
Between Institutionalization and Realpolitics

Irina Zherebkina

The topic of equity is very symbolic for the former totalitarian countries. The notions of "equality/equity" were crucial to communist discourse. The totalitarian space is considered an utopian social space in which everyone must *a priori* be not only equal but happy. In reality, however, from the point of view of the external, democratic discourse where everyone may be equal, because of the lack of individual opportunities as well as the current brutal economic crisis, everyone is unhappy.

Post-socialist development suggests a variation of utopian social space in which a new ideology of *social inequality* appears to guarantee social happiness. As a result, today (as it was during totalitarianism), in the East European social sciences there still exists a deeply-rooted binary division into two types of discourse: Western/"democratic" and East-European/"non-democratic." The former, with its roots in social inequality, is profoundly concerned with equality issues at the ideological level. The latter, which continues to be based on totalitarian structures of family, state, and equal impoverishment of people at the highest level of political discourse as well as mass media, is "celebrating" the ideology of inequality as a sign of deliverance from totalitarianism and an indication of "democratic" achievements.

On the whole, the political situation in Eastern Europe is characterized by several types of global contradictions. Taking the Ukraine as an example, there are three major contradictions that are of the greatest importance.

First, on the one hand, there are contradictions between the "democratic," "politically correct" types of discourse in the former Soviet Union, and the reality of violence, racism, anti-semitism, and anti-feminism on the other. What does a "politically correct" discourse mean? It has precisely the same meaning as it does in western practice and it is likewise applied to language and performative behavior. Thus, to be perceived as "politically correct," it is enough to be careful about how one speaks and how one behaves in public, although privately one does not have to endorse the beliefs underlying such politically correct rituals.

As long as individuals submit themselves to such political discourse, they are not threatened. Thus, in totalitarian society there is no fixed identity as its place is occupied by a "double consciousness" and a "double standard." The secret of power lies in the fact that unless it is called into question in public, it continues to exist unquestioned.

Second, there are contradictions between the official state policy of "national independence" and the new alliance of nationalists and communists actively controlling the privatization process in the country. This alliance of nationalists and national communists in the Ukraine has served to strengthen the patriarchal structure of the Ukrainian society. The current outbursts of nationalism in East European post-socialist countries are a reaction to the fact that long years of Communist Party rule, by destroying the traditional fabric of society, have dismantled most of the traditional points of social identification. When East Europeans attempt to assume a distance from the official ideological universe, the only positive reference point at their disposal is their national identity. In the current struggles for ideological hegemony, national identification is used by the ex-opposition as well as by the old Party forces. With the collapse of the Soviet Empire, its material resources, coercive capabilities, and legitimacy system, the communists quickly realized that the manipulation of popular nationalism is their best hope of retaining power. Nationalism is, therefore, grasped by the national communists both as the best means of legitimating their challenge to the centre (Soviet Russia), and as a reintegrative strategy for the territories they hope to control.

Third, there are the contradictions between the proclaimed official state ideology of the "new role of woman" in society and new types of discrimination against those women who do not conform to the stereotype of the "ideal model." In the Ukraine, the "new role of woman" is closely connected to the revival of the old, national images of Ukrainian woman. Post-soviet national communism opposes the role women had under the socialist regime. Its ideology plays on the hard life women had under socialism and touches on the problems and challenges posed by motherhood. Post-soviet national communism regards socialism as a system that downgrades motherhood, and thus, does not allow a "woman to be a woman," that is, a housewife and a mother. This fantasy about women is based on the belief that women and the nation share the same desire: to give birth.

National politics and women's politics: the crisis of identification

In a classic study, "Feminism and Nationalism in the Third World," Kumari Jayardena shows the connection between feminism and nationalism in Asia in the nineteenth and early twentieth centuries. The movement towards women's emancipation in Third World countries developed on the basis of the national liberation struggle, the main goals of which were to gain state political independence, create national identity, and modernize society. At this stage of the movement for national independence, feminism and nationalism were complementary and compatible.

Today, the situation has completely changed. All over the world feminists and nationalists view each other with suspicion if not hostility. Within the last decade, conflicts in Eastern Europe and in the USSR successor states, have contributed a great deal to this situation (Moghadam 3). Ukraine today is one of the countries of the former Soviet Union where nationalism is elevated to the rank of state policy and plays the role of macropolitical discourse, striving to unite all the varieties of social and cultural discourses and politics. The women's movement that became active in Ukraine after the collapse of the Soviet Union sees itself primarily as a continuation of the traditions of the Ukrainian women's movement and women's organizations of the end of the nineteenth and beginning of the twentieth century, movements that identified themselves with the ideology of the Ukrainian nationalist movement.

In the beginning of the 1990s in Ukraine, there was an increase in the number of women's organizations which have as their goal making an impact in different spheres of public life. The number of officially registered women's organizations in Ukraine grew from 11 in the summer of 1995, to 85 at the beginning 1997. The most popular women's organizations in contemporary Ukraine are traditional in nature. For example, among them are a) organizations that are successors of former state structures; b) women's associations that emerged as a result of the need to solve specific social issues (e.g., committee of soldiers' mothers); and c) organizations connected with the activity of political parties and non-government associations. Women's organizations in the Ukraine are rooted in a traditional vision of women's social role and, on the whole, are of neo-conservative orientation. The characteristic feature of women's organizations and the women's movement in the Ukraine is the fact that their activity is based, first of all, on the idea of nation-state building in Ukraine.

As a result of their strong nationalist course, the position of the leaders of the Ukrainian women's movement becomes extremely ambivalent. On the one hand, the leaders of Ukrainian women's organizations see the women's movement in Ukraine as a part of the international democratic women's movement and recognize achievements of women's movements in West-European countries and the U.S. At the same time, they emphasize that feminism in the Ukraine is special because Ukrainian women "live deeply rooted in their nation." That is why Ukrainian women's leaders try to assure the Ukrainian authority that their organizations "do not appeal to militant feminism" (Dratch 177) and that "the western form of feminism will not get accustomed to our place" (Krandakova 14). Ukranian women understand that "the western form" of feminism implies "the recognition of a man to be guilty for all misfortunes of woman" and think, for example, with Elena Krandakova, the Chairwoman of the Committee on Women's Issues, Maternity and Childhood at the President of Ukraine, that

> it's necessary to change public consciousness in such a way that there would be no separate "women's" and "men's" issues in the society, in order for them not to contradict each other and not to fight with each other. (14)

Why is it that the advent of the politics of nationalism signals in Ukraine the subordination, if not the demise, of women's politics? What does it mean to speak about one politics in terms of another, or how is a genuinely representative national consciousness to be spoken for by feminism and vice versa? It is very important to try to answer these questions in order to evaluate the contemporary political situation in Ukraine as well as in the post-Soviet region as a whole.

"The woman's Ukrainian idea"

Today, the Ukrainian woman, in practice removed from the level of real political participation, has acquired a role as the main political symbol in the structure of Ukrainian nationalist ideology. As the national movement at the beginning of '90s in Ukraine gained momentum, *"Berehynia"* a model of the ideal Ukrainian woman also gained popularity and was, in fact, adopted—as a symbol—by a number of women's organizations. Berehynia is a combination of Christian Godmother and an ancient Slavic goddess—mother, protector of health, native language, and national identity. Berehynia, "the one, who is, protects, and takes care," is the incarnation of the ideal wife and mother that is at the centre of the Ukrainian family as well as the custodian of moral, cultural, and national values. Berehynia is the Ukrainian woman-peasant, whose main sphere of activity is taking care of the home and bringing up children. She is striving not to be the leader of the family but to be a reliable support to her husband, children, and older parents.

At the same time, in Ukrainian anthropological and historical literature a national myth about the special status of women in Ukrainian history denies that Ukrainian women are discriminated against in comparison to oppressed and dependent Russian women. Modern Ukrainian anthropology gives a variety of historical examples such as Yaroslavna, Queen of France, the Ukrainian-Turkish Sultana Roksolana, and the opposition of the democratic Ukrainian *Russkaia Pravda* ("The Russian Truth") of Yaroslav Mudryi to the patriarchal Moscow *Domostroj* (the "household law"). Each stresses the historical superiority of the social status of Ukrainian women over Russian women (Bondarovska 82).

As anthropological theory, the Berehynia theory emerged not very long ago—about 10 years ago[1]—and is a classic example of the "invention of tradition" in the politics of nationalism as suggested in the work of Erick Hobsbawm. The idea of Berehynia became very popular both in Ukrainian anthropology and in the Ukrainian women's movement. The name Berehynia is, in fact, included in the names of many Ukrainian women's organizations (for example, the first Kharkov women's organizations, which emerged in the period of post-*perestrojka*, were called "Berehynia" and "Miroslava"). Three moments in the modern politics of Ukrainian nationalism are consonant with the theory of Berehynia. The first stresses the role of village people in Ukrainian national consolidation; the second deals with the overlap of Ukrainian national moral values and religious morality; and the third stresses the national importance of reproductive activity for women.

The promotion of the ideal of Berehynia in Ukraine sought to restore not only village culture, but also peasant consciousness which presupposes the obedience of children to their parents, youth to seniors, wives to husbands, and by extension, citizen to state. Today, supporters of the politics of national consolidation of Ukrainians emphasize the important role of village people who "traditionally are carriers of classical features of national mentality" (Skrypnyk 35). The support of national consolidation of the Ukrainian people by village people and, above all, village women, is increasingly significant because "city Ukrainians more and more lose the Ukrainian initial deep ethno-psychological orientations and acquire another structure of values, another form of thinking" (Skrypnyk 35). The basis of the revival of Ukrainian cities where people speak Ukrainian, and the rise of the prestige of Ukrainian culture must become a "purposeful language-cultural policy of the state" that includes "state protection of national language and culture, introduction of new TV channels in the Ukrainian language, etc" (Skrypnyk 35).

As demonstrated in the work of American-Ukrainian Marjana Rubchak, the modern creation of a number of images of ideal femininity, and above all, icons of maternity, to substitute for Ukrainian women's images of socialist iconography—women tractor-drivers and dairy-women, "women-heroes of Socialist labour," etc.—disguises the true gender inequality that exists in modern Ukrainian everyday life (see Rubchak 1996b). "Those modern women," writes Marjana Rubchak,

> who believe that in such symbols they would find themselves as woman in the dynamics of our present life—do not realize that they just strengthen by that the opposite myth—[the] myth of women's secondary status. (Rubchak 1996b: 148) [author's translation]

Western and, above all, American feminism embarrasses the traditional Ukrainian women's movement by its re-evaluation of traditional morality, its re-evaluation of the role of women in the family, of the role of women in the church, and its recognition of the rights of sexual minorities, etc. It is necessary to pay attention to the fact that representations of women's sexuality are completely excluded from the Ukrainian national women's iconography, and erotic and sexual issues in Ukrainian culture have been studied neither in Ukraine nor in the main international centres for Ukrainian studies. The political symbolism of women's images in Ukrainian culture presupposes the complete "innocence" of Ukrainian young girls or women. Most "unsuitable" for the Ukrainian women's movement and their national leaders is the perceived hostility and aggression of western radical feminists with respect to men and to patriarchal social traditions. On the whole, the notion of "patriarchal politics" is not typical for the lexicon of the Ukrainian women's leaders. Male images in Ukrainian national political symbolism usually correlate with feelings of male vulnerability and suffering: Cossacks suffering in the Turkish-Tartar captivity; a serf and then exiled Shevtchenko; soldiers of the Ukrainian Insurgent Army dying for Ukrainian independence, etc. The role of Ukrainian women is to support the men, to be like Berehynia not only towards men but also to the state. That is why when the Ukrainian women's movement and women's organizations claim to have a place in the international women's movement, they find themselves in a situation of existential choice between the real struggle against gender discrimination and their iconographic mission to support the nation and the national state.

In contemporary western feminist literature devoted to the problem of nationalism and the women's movement, what is emphasized first is the divergence of the women's movement and the nationalist movement, noticed at the beginning of the '90s (in Algeria and the South African Republic), and secondly, the growing destructiveness of nationalist politics and their connection to violence against women (see McClintock; Moghadam). The authors pay special attention to the destabilizing character of ethno-nationalism in the East Europian countries and the former USSR, where the threat of conflicts and violence against women is especially great.

In *Hatreds: Racialized and Sexualized Conflicts in the Twenty-First Century*, Zillah Eisenstein looks at the growth of aggressiveness of national politics with respect to women. She stresses that in Eastern Europe democracies have come with male domination that in turn defeated ethnic nationalists. "Democracy supposedly replaced communism," writes Eisenstein, "then nationalism displaced democracy. These new-old nationalisms define the twenty-first century" (45). These "new-old" nationalisms utilize old kinds of hatreds: racism, anti-Semitism, gender hostility. When Benedict Anderson wrote about nation as an "imagined community," and about nationalism as a new method of thinking about brotherhood, power and time, he thought about the nation with love (qtd. in Eisenstein) But today this "imagined community" is a fantasy world with women present, but silenced. The fraternity is masculine. As mother of the nation, woman is a symbolic fantasy; she is at once present and not seen. "Because nations are symbolized by women," writes Eisenstein,

> ethnic cleansing directs its fears and desires onto the bodies of women. On the one hand, women are idolized and revered; on the other hand, they are brutalized, tortured, raped, and often killed. (58)

154 | *Irina Zherebkina*

The connection of nationalism with violence against women, to which western feminists point in their works, is what the leaders of patriotic Ukrainian women's organizations forget about. The situation of political and civil choice, in which the Ukrainian women's movement finds itself today, is not simple. Ukrainian women truly have grounds to fear that western feminism will remain a hegemonic modern women's discourse in publishing, mass-media, education, and the economy, and that this type of feminism cannot be adopted by women who live under different social conditions (see McClintock 384). The leaders of Ukrainian women's organizations feel it is their right not to trust western feminists and their methods of protecting their rights, preferring to keep their own methods and to appeal to authories with demands to set quotas for women in government structures. Nevertheless, no matter how unusual the ways of the western women's movement may seem to Ukrainian women, and no matter what future relations between western feminists and post-Soviet/ post-colonial women's movements may be, in a situation of choice, making alternative decisions is always possible. In a situation of direct violence against women, which is connected with the politics of nationalism, there is no alternative for women at all. Violence is the last argument of nationalism against women, which the women's movement may oppose only by conducting anti-nationalist politics.

The characteristic features of the contemporary Ukrainian women's movement

During the long years of Soviet power, Ukraine had no experience of social movements, because for totalitarian authorities the existence of social movements would mean the Soviet inner political situation was beyond state control. The situation has not changed today. Contemporary state administration and main government institutions in Ukraine are based on a union of the former Ukrainian opposition—nationalists—and the former party nomenclature, "repainted" into national and "democratic" colors—national communists.[2] On the level of ideology there is nothing common between communists and nationalists. Communists, according to their own words, are internationalists who criticize any types of nationalism; nationalists are usually anti-Communists. At the level of political unconscious, however, a connection between nationalists and communists is easily seen: both discourses are built on the basis of exclusion of anything "different," and both are guided by the latent energy of sexism, homophobia, and authoritarianism.

The chief barrier for the development of a democratic and independent women's movement in Ukraine is its clearly expressed nationalistic and neo-conservative character. On the whole, Ukrainian women do not identify their rights and interests—such as reproductive rights, reproductive health, ecological health—as specifically women's issues, different from the national interest of building a nation-state. State national priorities dominate in the modern women's movement the same way as in the Ukrainian women's movement of the nineteenth century.

The modern Ukrainian women's movement has no classical basis such as the grassroots activity of western social movements. In post-Soviet societies the notion of women's activity is associated purely in mass consciousness with women's activities in communist society. Women who have reached the top of the party governing structure under the communists normally had a specific way of behaving: dressed in gray, featureless suits with bushy "hairdos" and blank eyes—more bureaucratic than their male colleagues—with a command of men's manners, they were symbols of the terrible monsters of the Soviet totalitarian machine. This political symbol of the socially-active woman was refused above all by post-Soviet mass consciousness.

The main reason, however, for the lack of women's grassroots activity in post-Soviet Ukrainian society is a disjunction between official conservative ideology (both the Soviet and nationalistic) regarding women, where women's main function is seen to be maternal (reproductive), and the actual life of Ukrainian women, both in the Soviet and post-Soviet period, where women are, in fact, the chief productive force in society.

Only with the change of official ideology with respect to women is it possible to become aware of gender discrimination in Ukrainian society and for Ukrainian women to realize their rights within the society. This can only happen with the mobilization of a women's mass social and civil activity driven by a desire for a change in society. Women's grassroots activity does not have to be built according to traditional political examples. The western women's movement demonstrates that women's mass activity on local levels today appears to be more effective than the activity on a general, national level. Woman today usually avoid taking part in traditional forms of power or entering official political parties and structures. However, on the local level, western women unite in various NGOs and communities (according to their interests, neighbour's, city, professional communities), through which they can influence social life at the local level.

The women's movement in Ukraine did not develop a feminist tradition in the nineteenth century. The interests of the nation, but not those of women as social subjects, dominated the Ukrainian women's movement in the nineteenth century; the question of women's rights was secondary in comparison with that of the independent Ukrainian state.

The conservative character of the modern Ukrainian women's movement is explained by the influence of a political discourse characterized by the alliance of nationalist and communist ideology. A few women's organizations of feminist orientation have been actually pushed out to the periphery of women's movement.

One of the attributes of the modern women's movement in Ukraine is its susceptibility to political manipulation. After the United Nations Fourth World Conference on Women and the NGO Forum held in China in 1995, "women's issues" have become more popular both in various political parties and in the Ukrainian state. As a result, state policy regarding women can be divided into two main periods: 1) "before Beijing": a politics of "throwing away" women's situation from women's issues in the country; and 2) "after Beijing": ratification by Ukraine of international documents regarding women. This is a stage of simulative, theatrical attitude of state policy to women's issues.

The logic of the simulative solution of women's issues in modern Ukraine is moreover becoming a real threat for the modern women's movement, because the communist regimes of the republics of the former Soviet Union had the same simulative "double standard" with respect to the solution of women's issues. On the level of ideology and official life, equal rights of women and men were affirmed, but at the level of "real life," Soviet society was deeply patriarchal. In the same way, at the level of public life, in Soviet society everyone spoke of the achievements of communism and followed party rituals, but in private life, people were guided by completely opposite models of survival and absolute distrust of communist ideology. This distance of cynicism and theatrical behavior is a double standard that allowed the communist regime to hold power for so long. The secret and effect of power, according to Michel Foucault, lies in the fact that in order to support its regime there is no obligatory need for the conscious belief in this regime; it is enough to pretend to execute its rituals and not to put it under the microscope in public.

The simulative attitude of state policy to women's problems and theatrical strategies inside the women's movement itself is today one of the main barriers to the development of an independent and democratic women's movement in the Ukraine. As a result of nationalist politics, the women's movement in the Ukraine glorifies the traditional female role in society and the problem of patriarchal domination concerning women becomes officially invisible, which also means that its effects become much more difficult to recognize.

The national women's movement is based primarily on identification with the nation and not with woman's subjectivity. It is necessary to emphasize that in strategies of nationalism, identification with the nation ("our nation") is based on a fantasy of the Enemy—the Other that threatens our standards of living by its habits, discourse, and ritual, alien to our way of living. The attitude towards this Other is strongly ambivalent and is built through the system of the following (non-exclusionary) imperative: if it does not master the language of our culture, or does so badly, it displays its latent imperialism; if, on the contrary, it masters and assimilates "our" way of life and "our" habits, then it wants to take "our" nation from us. The logic of nationalism is a binary logic of exclusion of any Other from the system of proper values, and to the category of Other belongs proper women's heterogeneous subjectivity that does not cope with the logic of binarism.

In today's Ukraine, mass rejection of the Other is demonstrated by discriminatory strategies with respect to the Russian-speaking population, which makes up 27 percent of the population in the country. During the election campaign in 1994, Ukrainian President Kuchma deliberately appealed to the Russian-speaking population of Ukraine, promising "soft" language policy, that is, the approval of the two state languages: Ukrainian and Russian. After his having won the elections, however, all the promises were forgotten and discriminatory policies with respect to the Russians became stronger. Russian-speaking women in today's Ukraine are considered to be a reflection of the moral disintegration and fragmentation of the society.

Introducing women's studies in post-Soviet societies

How do we introduce women's studies programs into the system of higher education in Ukraine and Russia?

Previous oppositional feminists have lost their ground since the Eastern European countries have started to function as "normal" capitalist societies. They are feeling abandoned because under the socialist regimes they had a specific utopion sphere of privacy, created to elude Party control, that made possible a very particular kind of agency and enjoyment that does not exist in democratic society. They dream of returning such losses of intellectual enjoyment through new university women's studies programs because, as it is known, "the university in our society remains a relatively utopian place, a place of great privilege" (Said 24).

In the countries of the former Eastern Block, various western foundations have given money which indicates the growing level of democratization in post-Soviet societies. Special merit belongs to the Soros Foundation which supports the idea of introducing women's studies programs into the system of higher education. The role of western initiatives here becomes a stimulating one. For example, in the Ukraine, before the United Nations Fourth World Conference on Women in Beijing, with the support of the Soros Foundation, a series of women's actions in preparation for the NGO Forum were held and a number of new women's organizations were established. At the same time, before the UN Conference and NGO Forum in China, the Ukrainian state also became more active. On June 12, 1995, the first Parliamentary Hearings on Women's Status in the Ukraine took place. Furthermore, a state program on women's status was officially represented at the UN Conference by a Ukrainian delegation ironically with a man at its head—the then vice prime-minister, Ivan Kuras.

In Russia, the establishment of women's studies programs has occurred more rapidly. In 1994 a women's fraction in the Parliament "Women of Russia" was founded, and since 1995 a State Research Educational Program on the social-legal status of women has existed. At the level of higher education in Russia, so-called chairs of "feminology" are actively forming (but they emphasize they are not connected with feminism or with that "type" of women's studies that exists in the West). Why? Consciously, the differences in strategies are not articulated anywhere, but as far as I can understand this difference, the chairs of feminology, on the whole, want to establish "the high role and predestination of women" (maternal function in this hierarchy of values is of top priority) and, that it is assumed that woman "as such," "in her essence" is a very valuable object, but historically, circumstances do not allow this value to show itself. The notions of "value" and "maternity" in this discourse are correlative. As far as western women's studies programs are concerned, in post-Soviet discourse feminism is interpreted as aggressive and amoral. Questions of power, exploitation of women, or women's sexuality are dispensed with as "amoral" or considered almost inadmissible.

Parliamentary Hearings in Ukraine in 1995 also passed a resolution to introduce gender studies in academic institutions and educational systems. The irony, as usual, lies in the fact that no budget has been granted, nor has the question of a budget been raised. This demonstrates once again the symbolic character of such Ukrainian resolutions; they are caused not by the "internal" needs of the system but by the "external" performative strategies, striving to meet western levels of "democratic discourse."

It is remarkable that even when women's issues enter the system of higher education, the usually-neutral word "gender" (because it is not understood) is chosen instead of more explicit words such as "feminism" or "women's." In fact, at a meeting of the Chair of the Theory of Culture in Kharkov University, when approving five lecture courses of a joint women's studies program, the professors of this chair asked that the words "feminism" and "women's" be removed from the names of the courses; the former, from their point of view, carries an aggressive connotation, and the latter a frivolous one.

How do we finance women's studies programs? Without solving this important problem we cannot seriously speak of introducing women's studies into higher education.

Universities in Russia and Ukraine now have two types of financing: 1) either state financing—these are mainly all old, higher educational establishments of a universal kind (students, as it was in the former socialist society, do not pay for their education); 2) or self-employment, at the expense of fees for education; these are new, so-called "commercial" universities with three major subjects: economics, law, foreign languages.

With respect to the first type, state financing, there is only one possibility—the state is able to finance only one privileged women's studies program. There is not one of this kind in the Ukraine yet, but there is one in Russia— "Women of Russia" under the leadership of professor Olga Khasbulatova. With respect to the second type of financing in "commercial" universities, disciplines such as "feminology" must serve the rigid patriarchal views of the students. That is, it is necessary to include such courses as "good manners" for female students, "image making," etc. (for example, such as the program proposed by "Panna" University in Kharkov). In fact, both possibilities of financing contribute to the general tendency of establishing new types of inequality in the society.

The final point of discussion is how women's studies is perceived by the students. In the Soviet and post-Soviet system of education there was no practice of choice, no practice of "credits"; if a discipline is included in the curriculum, then all students must take it. Student consciousness, on the whole, is very patriarchal and stereotypical. The students reacted to feminist theory with a kind of horror, with a fear that their whole identity would collapse if they embraced feminist thought. One student responded, "I will lose my femininity if I keep reading this feminist stuff." Further, the students (it's a Soviet habit) feel hostility towards everything that is forced from the upper level.

This situation poses two questions. The first is connected with the attributes of post-Soviet discourse as such and post-Soviet reality. In the assessment of modern political strategies in Eastern Europe it is necessary to take into account the fact that the fraudulent similarity of democratic political vocabularies of the West and post-communist countries of Eastern Europe confuses more than it clarifies. Post-Soviet reality hides itself behind the conventional democratic terminology that is disjunctive with respect to Western Europe because it is still totalitarian in its basis, preserving full state control over all forms of social life. Women's studies university programs within this system are doomed to have a performative and simulative character.

The second question is connected with the attributes of feminist theory on the whole. To explore the question of feminist identification and possibilities of the institutionalization of women's studies in the Ukraine and other post-communist countries, I want to ask what has become of the notion of women's rights and women's studies since the collapse of socialism. I think that the whole set of questions related to feminist theory as such has become deeply problematic. Feminist notions of women's rights that are so central to western social theory suddenly lost their established meaning when communism collapsed. The first thing East-European countries came across after the collapse of communism was the emergence of new types of racism and social inequality instead of democracy. And, it seems to me, western feminists did not notice this change; rather they think that the collapse of communism only confirms the notions of feminist theory.

All these problems demand a rethinking not only of the problem of institutionalization of women's studies in the ex-USSR, but also the premises of feminist theory which feminists have for too long taken for granted.

[1]The issues of Berehynia were introduced into Ukrainian anthropology by Vadym Sckuratovskij (1988) and Vasyl Ruban (1992).
[2]Leonid Kravchuk, the first President of Ukraine after Perestroika answered the question "How a Communist becomes a nationalist?" posed to him by Professor Michael Ignatieff (University of British Columbia), by stating: "The only people available at independence who knew ... 'the art of governing' were

the 3.5 million members of the Communist Party. We will bring on new people, but they need to be educated and trained. And besides, he says, what is so bad about the Communists? Some are more democratically inclined than the so-called democratic opposition" (qtd. in Ignatieff 114).

References

Bondarovska, Valentyna. "Psychological Status of Woman in Ukraine: The Way to New Psychological Models." *Woman and Democracy. The Materials of the International Scientific-Practical Conference.* [in Ukrainian] 82 Kiev: Zhinocha Gromada, 1995.

Dratch, Marija. "The Speech of the Head of International Organization 'Zhinocha Gromada' Marija Dratch at the First Parliamentary Hearings on Realization in Ukraine of the Convention of UN About Liquidation of all Forms of Women's Discrimination." *Woman and Democracy. The Materials of Scientific-Practical Conference.* [in Ukrainian] Kiev: Zhinocha Gromada, 1995.

Eizenstein, Zillah. *Hatreds: Racialized and Sexualized Conflicts in the 21st Century.* New York Routledge, 1996.

Hobsbawm, Erick J. *The Invention of Tradition.* Cambridge: Cambridge University Press, 1977

Ignatieff, Michael. *Blood and Belonging: Journeys into the New Nationalism.* New York: Farrar, Straus and Ciroux, 1993.

Jayawardena, Kumari. *Feminism and Nationalism in the Third World.* London: Zed Books, 1986.

Krandakova, Olena, (Head of the Committee on Women's Issues, Maternity and Childhood at the President of Ukraine). "Decisions of the IVth World Women's Forum and Propositions to the Ukrainian State Programs," "Planning of the Family," "Children of Ukraine," and "Woman of Ukraine." *Beijing Strategies: The Program of the Actions in Ukraine.* [in Ukrainian] Kiev: Zhinocha Gromada, 1996.

McClintock, Anne. *Imperial Leather: Race, Gender and Sexuality in the Colonial Context.* New York: Routledge, 1995. 383–386.

Moghadam, Valentine M. *Feminism and Nationalism. Gender and National Identity. Women and Politics in Muslim Societies.* Ed. Valentine M. Moghadam. London: Zed Books, 1994.

Rubchak, J. Marian. "Christian Virgin or Pagan Goddess: Feminism Versus the Eternally Feminine in Ukraine." *Women in Russia and Ukraine.* Ed.

Rosalin Marsh. New York: Cambridge University Press, 1996a. 315–330.

Rubchak, Marian. "Woman as Icon in Ukranian Post-Soviet Culture." *The Beijing Strategies: The Program of Actions in Ukraine.* [in Ukrainian] Kiev: Zhinocha Gromada, 1996b. 144-149.

Skrypnyk, Ganna, and Lidija Orel. "The Problems of National Consolidation of the Ukrainian Society in the Context of General Democratization of the Country." *Woman and Democracy. The Materials of the International Scientific-Practical Conference.* [in Ukrainian] 35.

Bitter-sweet Fruits
The Institutionalization and Professionalization of Women's Studies and Gender Research in Germany
Hildegard Maria Nickel

After North Rhine-Westphalia, Berlin has the most chairs in Women's Studies or Gender Research of all university towns and federal states in Germany. In 1994, we had a total of 13 chairs at the Free University, Humboldt University, and the Technical University of Berlin. These chairs bring with them more than the requisite numbers of departmental professors whose research and teaching have given them scope to address women's and gender issues, and all the teachers and postgraduates working in these fields as part of their research.

The other universities in Eastern Germany can boast neither a similar number of research professorships in women's or gender research, nor a similar proportion of women on their teaching staff, nor, indeed, any such institution as the Centre for Interdisciplinary Research (ZIF). Although we have no cause, then, to complain, neither can we rest on our laurels.

I shall be examining, therefore, ambivalences about the opportunities and risks created by institutionalizing women's and gender research. My perspective is that of an East German woman, fully aware that I have leapt up the career ladder after the events of 1989 while other women in the GDR's universities lost their jobs. I am writing as a sociologist, that is, from the angle of a scientific discipline with its own idiosyncrasies which can nevertheless be regarded as a paradigm. And finally, even if there is a lot more that could be said about the history of the GDR's demise and German unification, I shall be keeping my sights on the future.

I postulate six theses in order to express my position.

1) As far as women's studies and the institutionalization and professionalization of these studies are concerned, there is nothing to be gained from looking back with nostalgia to the academic system in the GDR. In my opinion, there was no feminist women's research in the GDR, although there was research about women. This research was methodologically limited in that women were essentially considered in functional terms, and therefore reduced to their economic, biological, and/or political functions. Women were of no interest as subjects, that is, within the complexity of their real lives, but as labour, political officials, executive personnel, child bearers, and/or mothers; "objective," male-centred analyses were about the "optimum" distribution of women among skill levels, occupations, or managerial functions. With male performance as the yardstick, the question was whether women were already scoring "quite well" on some things, but still having to learn about others. In this sense, the research was largely forcused on women's perceived deficits rather than their differences vis-à-vis men.

These "deficits" needed to be addressed and overcome in the interests of "higher"—usually economic—objectives, mostly by means of hard work and effort on the part of women themselves. There was less a focus on the objective inequalities between the sexes in access to economic and cultural resources as well as availability of time, because traditional research about women was considered partisan in the sense that it served the dominant ideology and apparatus. It was not, however, consistently partisan towards women. Rather than a women's movement at its shoulder, it had the "Woman Department" at the SED Central Committee on its back. Research had to supply legitimation, and thus collaborated in the creation of myths about the successful advance of equal rights in the GDR and of establishing taboos about women's true conditions. It collaborated in the atrophy of women's consciousness and public desensitization to the gender question because gender was reduced to a box in the statistical records and not treated as a structural category.

Women were involved in carrying out this kind of academic research, and they profited from it. This did not automatically sharpen their senses for feminist women's studies, nor professionalize their efforts in this direction. That deficit cannot be wiped out by a double salto.

2) The changes after 1989 brought an opportunity to modernize Germany's universities, and East German women, feminist or not, were real or potential protagonists in reforming teaching and research. However, before this opportunity took shape, women on the staff of East German universities

were already fearing for their jobs. On the whole, East German women had little to show for themselves in the restructuring, either in terms of jobs or in terms of the planning process. But West German women were also poorly represented in the central positions. The opportunity to renew the universities genuinely in favour of women, women's studies, and gender research has been lost, and decreasing budgets alone are surely not the only reason. At best, what is currently happening will lead to some cosmetic repair.

3) By the end of 1993, when the restructuring process was more or less complete in terms of personnel, 38 professors of sociology had been appointed in the territory of former East Germany, but only four of them are women, and only one of the eight institutes offering Sociology or Social Sciences as a major degree has a woman in the chair.[1] "A male conspiracy" or "boys' networks" are hardly adequate explanations for what I would call a dramatic structural process. According to Kreckel, this is

> the unfortunate flip side of probably the most important break-through for German sociology as a whole, achieved by the re-establishment of East Germany's universities: the original recommendation of the Scientific Council regarding the four indispensable pillars of sociology (theory, methodology, macro- and micro-sociology) has been universally accepted and by and large implemented in the East German universities. Many West German universities can do no more than dream of this. It would represent a tremendous advance to them if this model were to be acknowledged throughout Germany as the normative standard. (9 [author's translation]).

So are women, and women's and gender research, the victims of a deficit in the status of sociology? Or are they the price to pay if a scientific discipline needs to project a new, more professional profile? Kreckel maintains that the "most promising strategy" for establishing sociological research on women and gender is "simply to 'butt in' on the main themes. Why should it be so impossible to sensitize the sociological core—theory, methodology, macro- and micro-sociology—increasingly to gender issues and thereby to enrich it?" (9–10). Kreckel draws reassurance from the comparatively high number of women on the intermediate academic scale in Eastern Germany.

The women among these academic assistants (who fare rather better in the East, accounting for 42 percent of the academic staff compared with only 20–

25 percent in the West) are expected to "sensitize" and "enrich" the core areas of the discipline. The dissertations which these scientific researchers have to submit to achieve their qualifications are "allocated directly to a particular chair." This means, in Kreckel's view, that it is "not unlikely that many dissertations by (a professor's) female staff will be conducted in the central fields of sociology, and not in peripheral fields, such as gender research" (Kreckel 10). In other words, not only does Kreckel ascribe women's studies and gender research to the periphery of the discipline; he also places it under male leadership (professorship)! Is this the general trend underlying the "professionalization" of women's studies and gender research in Germany? Are the new federal states a training ground for items on tomorrow's university policy agenda?

In *The Social Sex*, Agnes Dietzen beautifully describes the consequences of institutionalizing and professionalizing genus-centred research in Germany and of the problematic relationship between sociology and (sociological) women's and gender research. I shall try to define my own experience of this problematical relationship. At the Sociology Institute at Humboldt University, instead of the usual four chairs, there are eight, including one devoted to the sociology of the family, youth, and gender relations, to which a woman was appointed. In Berlin, the Sociology Institute and the Political Science Institute constitute a single structural entity offering a common course of study. Thus, alongside the eight professors of sociology there are eight professors of political science. Not one of them is a woman. The lack of acknowledgement which is supposed to be overcome via the "orthodox cores" of the discipline, apparently applies even more to political science, where it has led to the total exclusion of women.

I can gloss over the irritating interplay of cooperation and competition which this unequal constellation entails, and over the mechanisms of specific exclusion or inclusion in the framework of informal relationships. I shall concentrate instead on "institutional resistance" to a theme which is regarded as ridden with conflict, which arouses uncomfortable feelings, and which places stones in the path of what Merton calls "sociological euphemism." Sociology's "institutional resistance" to the gender theme is implemented not only by means of isolation and marginalization, but also by means of delegation and cordoned-off enclaves. Women are still free to engage, as Kreckel describes, in "pure" teaching. And, it is from "pure teaching" that we derive definitions of what work, theories, and findings are relevant (including examinations). This has certain consequences for ("peripheral") women's and gender research.

5) Sociology has what Dietzen calls an affective relationship with neutrality or objectivity. It has derived its profile and professionalization from a set of ("objective") methods and (core) theories which do not make it easy in sociological women's and gender research to avoid the resulting disciplinary pressure. In feminist women's and gender research, this creates a dilemma which cannot be solved individually by isolated women on the university teaching staff. If we are talking about institutionalizing and professionalizing women's and gender research at the universities, then the qualifications which students acquire must be recognized within the discipline, marketable, and sustainable in terms of its future relevance. These qualifications must help women to compete equitably with male applicants. Women's and gender research during a degree course which blocks women's access to the academic labour market and confines them to small playgrounds would be irresponsible.

My own personal solution is to bridge the dilemma by doing the "splits": I obtain research projects which are mainstream (or else they would not be funded) and conduct feminist gender research within that context. I choose my students very deliberately, and the majority, though not all, are women. I try to encourage them to pursue an academic career, not by creating space for women's dreams, but by obliging them to make their mark on the existing academic system by means of their own accomplishments. That may not necessarily be what undergraduate women come to me for, but it may well be their gateway to an academic career.

6) To conclude, let me say a few words about the Centre for Interdisciplinary Research or ZIF, and its options for institutionalizing women's studies in Berlin. Although the ZIF has often tottered on the brink, it is now able to celebrate its tenth anniversary. That is a good reason to look backwards and forwards. These are years in which the world has changed radically, when many women at Humboldt University and the ZIF saw their working world collapse and their hopes of finding a new role burst like bubbles. For members of the old Humboldt, they were years of reorientation and rethinking, of finding new sustenance, and thrashing out new phenomena. This has left little time for serious reflection about institutionalizing and professionalizing women's studies, for strategic debates and conceptional blueprints. This makes the questions all the more urgent now, with personnel renewal at Humboldt more or less concluded and, alongside the dismissals—which above all affected academic women (Wissenschaftlerinnen 2000)—new recruitment beginning to bear fruit.

This staff restructuring has created new tasks for the ZIF. Whereas it used to focus its energies largely on the "Ost-Fem"[2] and on East German women, its main task now is to build a bridge between women researchers in East and West. This could help to tackle the prejudices about broody mums in the east and bra-burners in the west (such as described by Rommelspacher). From the outset, this was the idea behind the regular ZIF ring lectures. Many will remember the first cycle in the summer semester of 1990, entitled "Women's Studies Without Borders," then published under the very fitting title (in German) "So Close together and So far apart: Women's Lives in East and West." In spite of all the efforts to achieve co-operation, what then drove a wedge between women's researchers from the East and West, rather than drawing them closer? Rivalry over meagre resources? A tendency to know it all on the one side and to moan and groan on the other? Quite likely. But an even more important factor seems to me that our shared German language has generated (feminist) concepts which are attached to very different contexts of experience. At the conceptual level, we thought we understood each other, but we knew very little about each other's experience.

Now there is a significant opportunity for the ZIF to offer an arena where East and West German women can think together about what institutional-izing and professionalizing women's and gender research means at Humboldt University. A number of university teachers and scientific researchers from various Berlin establishments are meeting at the ZIF to consider an institution-alized form of gender studies in Berlin and to pool their resources. It is still too early to predict whether a new institution will result. What is important is that women involved in women's and gender studies have come together and are talking to each other about the prospects for research.

Unlike the United States, Canada, and other European countries, how-ever, where Women's Studies were established at an institutional level early on, in Germany this differentiation is in no way reflected in the structure of universities and departmental teaching. It is paradoxical that, for all the measures aimed at assisting women in recent years, there are no indications of any structural change in the academic landscape. Quite the contrary. At present any movement towards academic professionalization which might have occured appears to have been forced backwards. The structural weakness of feminist teaching is most obvious in two respects: a high proportion of teaching posts are not firmly established and the subject is hardly anchored in examination and course requirements. Women's Studies are still on the sidelines.

In Germany, although Women's and Gender Studies are offered in various forms, there is to date no academic bachelor or master degree as in Northern

Europe, Canada, and the United States. Humboldt University at Berlin is the first educational institution in Germany to offer a Gender Studies degree.

[1]The reference is to the Humboldt University and the woman in question is me. See Kreckel.

[2]Ost-Fem is the name of a regular meeting where women academics from the East discuss issues pertaining to women's studies. Western women have sometimes been deliberately excluded from active discussion. This was done to permit Eastern women to escape from the hegemonic culture of discussion the Western women bring with them and discuss questions which thus were exclusively or predominantly their own.

References

Dietzen, Agnes—Soziales Geschlecht. *Dimensionen des Gender-Konzepts.* Opladen, 1993.

Kreckel, Reinhard. Soziologie an den ostdeutschen Universitäten: Abbau und Neubeginn, Der Hallesche Graureiher 94-3.

Nickel, Hildegard Maria. "Frauen in der DDR." *Aus Politik und Zeitgeschichte.* Supp. to *Das Parlament* 13 April 1990. B16–17.

Merton, Robert K. "The Unanticipated Consequences of Purposive Social Action." *American Sociological Review* 1.5: 894–904.

Wissenschaftlerinnen 2000. *Berliner Perspektiven für die Gleichstellung von Frauen in der Wissenschaft.* Berlin: Senate Department for Labour and Women, June 1995.

3.

Pedagogy

The (Un)Specified We
(Re)Creating (Di)Visions
Through Words

Terry Provost

The national subject splits in the ethnographic perspective of culture's contemporaneity and provides both a theoretical position and a narrative authority for marginal voices or minority discourse. They no longer need to address their strategies of opposition to a horizon of "hegemony" that is envisaged as horizontal and homogenous.
—Homi K. Bhabha (180)

The only way I can hope to suggest how the center itself is marginal is by not remaining outside in the margin and pointing my accusing finger at the center. I might do it rather by implicating myself in the center and sensing what politics make it marginal.
—Gayatri Chakravorty Spivak (35)

What I am about to share with you, here, is a subjective thought that has been progressively reaching lucidity, a thought instigated by a dis/covered problem in using certain personal and possessive pronouns. They have the power to create psychological dis/ease when verbalized, and can be passively violent in their ambivalent address for some listeners. These pronouns I call collective terms and substantives. But I mostly refer to them in my analysis as "the (un)specified we" or simply "we." Although they are the linguistic norm in popular culture, in classrooms, they become increasingly troubling to listen to—over and over. But here, too, for the purpose of elucidation, I shall also mention certain points over and over. Absorbing and interpreting these terms has chased me into different emotional realms—anger, fatigue, anxiety, resignation, and finally resistance. After much pondering, I have come somewhat closer to finding answers and substitutions. But I am still only at the beginning of articulating awareness and realising activism. To read the emphatic slashes and parentheses in this text is to glimpse the different angles of ambiguity and allegory in my reflections. Here is my thought.[1]

The problem of plural pronouns in classroom discourse

The collective terms *we, us* and *our* seem to be used everywhere and by everyone in Canadian culture.[2] Broadcasters use them *ad nauseam*. Politicians use them gratuitously to create a sense of homogenous nationalism, albeit false. People utter them automatically in ordinary and formal situations. And written material—books, novels, magazines, scholarly journals—display a profusion of these words. I have noticed, though, that they are often used in academic settings without much critical regard. So then, my concern is, in classrooms, is there really an inclusiveness experienced with the utterance of these words? Or do they act as linguistic agents that result in excluding and recolonising the marginalized subject?

Like Others who do not fall into any one or all of the conventional categories of White, male, straight, middle-class, Canadian-born and "first-world," I find it especially disturbing in class when an interlocutor in *a position of power*, particularly one who has made his/her differences verbally apparent, utters "we." Once articulated, I spend more time trying to contextualize, decode, and interpret the "we" than I do listening to the rest of what the speaker has to say. I wonder, do I identify with that "we"? Was it meant inclusively? Or do authoritarian speakers realize that their use of these terms has the potential to exclude—literally as well as symbolically, and in many cases, succeeds in doing just that?

Moreover, seeing that these terms are deictical elements—in other words, that their interpretability is contingent to the context being constructed, created, described or explained during speech acts, the interlocutors themselves become signs of their own personal beliefs as well as living, breathing, animated referents and signifiers of macrocosmic social ideology. An additional problem with *we's, us's* and *our's* is that they have been so well-appropriated and absorbed in elitist discourse that, in many cases, when uttered, they blur the distinction between the we-Hypothetical(s) and the we-Real(s) of the ruling class/ dominant culture and marginalized subjects. Says Shi-xu:

[O]n the one hand, if ideology were a system of ideas—or interests, norms and principles—in the (un)conscious, the analytical data of these "ideas" are discourse-bound: they are always situated in the social context and used to perform social tasks. These ideas are part and parcel of discourse. On the other, *if ideology were social and institutional structures and relations of domination and power, such structures and relations, too, are materialized in discourse. Therefore, discourse constitutes ideology.* (648; emphasis mine)

With the discourse articulated in academic settings being contextualized by the ideological "us," unattributable power becomes structured through the utterance, which then proliferates subliminally in the communicative relationship being temporally (re)presented and established between listener and speaker. Thus, the hazard with certain discourses containing such substantives is that authority (usually western) finishes by (un)intentionally and presumptuously speaking for and (mis)representing marginalized subjects.

Problematizing explicitness and implicitness in text production and reception, Desmond Allison states that the Hypothetical-Real relation in meaning is based on discourse comprehended "as either factual or non-factual" (374). Although this relation has already been tackled by numerous linguists (see Allison 379; Mey 145–148), Allison, like Shi-xu, realizes the significance of discourse relations. "The important question about explicit signalling in a text surely concerns not merely numbers of cohesive signals or discourse markers, but precisely what relations are explicitly signalled and what relations are left to be inferred in a (valid) representation of the text's meaning(s)" (378).

The (im)palpability of discourse relations, namely that of their (in)visible implicit/explicit occasioning of power and subjugation, which creates ranks by sieving out subject from non-subject, is an ongoing obstacle in basic communication and in academic interlocution.

Particularly in classroom settings, at the university level (undergraduate and graduate alike), where academic discourse ideology is kinetic, intense, and peaking, these terms are bounced around amongst interlocutors excessively and automatically. Here, impartial thought becomes articulated in *we's* and *us's*, uttered and enlivened by speech acts that are absorbed sensorially, reproduced psychically, and then thrown back out orally, only to be absorbed again, rethought, re-internalized, and reproduced in consequent utterances. In fact, in verbal situations of learning, dialogue and intellectual exchange, arbitrarily uttering "us" in speech acts indicates the speaker's initiation of a projection—whether done mechanically or mindfully, and thus the immediate creation of a proposed yet non-consensual unnegotiated agreement, arrangement, or relationship with a listener or audience.

To be on the safe side, I shall explain my sense of academic discourse ideology, which I use interchangeably with ideological academic discourse. It is an ideology/discourse that advocates elitist as well as competitive ways of being and expressing—both verbally and behaviourally—in a classroom setting, competitive ways that are made mandatory in order to survive or excel in the academic system. For example, student oral presentations, a compulsory component of curricula, enable speakers generally to ameliorate their communication skills, and particularly to refine the skill of quickly but coherently translating thought into verbal language. Additionally, with this exercise, speakers are able to overcome the sense of intimidation usually associated with talking in front of several people or a large audience.

Yet at the same time, oral presentations demand that interlocutors speak clearly and intellectually, with theoretical vocabulary and "key words." The "proper" use of the jargon signifies "mastery over topic." Scholastic authorities who also present and lecture are likewise expected to use key words. In this respect, the application of the jargon (ideology) and the jargon itself (discourse) become psychically and sensorially inculcated, and thus inescapable, given their idealization and normalization in academia. But it is frequently the *we's* and *us's* (re)appearing between the key words that further obfuscate meaning, identity, and positionality. This is the root of the problem with the ideology/discourse I am here defining and examining.

Moreover, the use of a specific nomenclature is a telling sign of an intelligence transforming ambiguously, an intelligence perhaps fighting to resist and subvert the system, but nevertheless lingually complying with and cognitively conforming to it in degrees. Coercive compliance and conformity denote maximal exposure to the colonialist use of the *we* in academia, as well as a strain, an exigence in resisting its articulation. As conventions, collective terms are constantly re-atomized in language, unwittingly drummed into oracy. This is another way in which they inhere in academic discourse and become elitist—by regular transmission in speech acts and by oral, mental, and (con)textual bombardment. Circulated as such, these terms become subliminally naturalized, artificially homogeneous, and thus empty when uttered to a diversified audience.

In this regard, disciplining and saturating the mind and tongue with *we's* and *us's* eventually lead to a problematic linguistic construction. In other words, it is through frequent practice, or rather by severe militant conditioning and reiteration, that the uttering of collective terms becomes mutationally grooved into a person's speech and cognitive patterns; thereafter, its constructedness becomes *habitual*, transformed as and deemed "second nature." Even I my/Self,[3] here, am presently falling into the trap of academic discourse ideology by using a certain jargon with *we's, us's* and *our's* to articulate better my ideas. Yet paradoxically, it is with this same discourse that I can try, or am trying, to subvert norms by explaining my observation, an observation that simultaneously places me inside and outside of the elitism and oppressive structures of academic language.

From my perspective, the militant conditioning of this discourse in learning commences, and is internalized, at an early age. Preschool, kindergarten, elementary, and junior high school are some educational institutions where the *we* starts to come into regular usage. Senior high schools, colleges, and universities that continue to cater to colonially oppressive curricula compound the problem of the *we* and solidify its use in oral discourse and written text. This is another reason why the *we's, us's* and *our's* of academic discourse ideology frequently go unnoticed and unquestioned in the classroom—given their being passed around (un)consciously and constantly from person to person, textbook to person and professor to student, from second to second, year to year. Thus, in addition to early-life socialization, the aspect of *lingual and cognitive sublimation* built into this ideological discourse is key to grasping how these terms have become so pandemic and so difficult to eradicate from scholarly and everyday speech in western cultures. Seeing that eradication might be an impossibility at this point in time, it is important to examine how this sublimation takes effect.

Educators' use of the exclusionary we

As scholastic guides and presumable role models who are exponents of the Establishment, many professors and lecturers (un)knowingly practice ideological academic discourse on a daily and hourly basis. They (un)consciously reinforce its problematic nationalism and western biases by regularly uttering "we" and "us" to listening subjects. The aspect of (un)knowingness in the practice is achieved by (dis)integrating and coercing will through lingual conditioning. The (dis)integrating of will concomitantly signals the subliminal (dis)integrating of subjecthood in the Establishment's pre-existing framework of *choosing* or *self-determining* individual/national identity. Ostensibly, the collective terms produced from this (un)consciously militant speech-act conditioning also reproduce intellectual, textual, and verbal thought, which promotes conformity in thinking, expressing and—through its rigid, reiterative and limited scope—(neo)colonial ways of knowing. These ways become patterns, which then become emulated as western "epistemology," which is then churned into "authoritative" canons, ready to be (re)produced and (re)disseminated for the next set of students, the next generation, the next listeners who themselves will turn into, (un)knowingly and thus to varying degrees, exponents of the Establishment.

Ellen Messer-Davidow also recognizes this catch-22 in academia. As professor-scholar-theorist, Messer-Davidow speculates that education concomitantly emancipates and oppresses intellect. It hinders as well as liberates consciousness. Using the collective terms to describe the dilemmic advancement of feminist change, she writes:

> Universities and colleges … constitute our behaviours and desires, and we academics, through our daily practices, constitute their structures and processes…. Universities and colleges, because they educate, perform structuring mediations between those who constitute them and the system of multiple oppressions that order our culture…. We have been existing both in the discipline and in opposition to them…. We have built an academic apparatus that has enabled *and* constrained feminist inquiry. (282–283)

Thus, to varying degrees, academics are pro-exponents of the Establishment, continuing its power as epistemological authoritarians; however, they are also its anti-agents, breaking down that same power through different strategies and methods.

But occasionally, the *we's, us's* and *our's* uttered by authority figures *are* noticed; and when this happens, they create a greater degree of dissonance and divide for Other(ed)s in the context of identifying and learning. Consequently, the more identificational distance visibly existing, perceived, or contingently created in speech acts between the speaking interlocutor and the marginalized listener, the greater the dissonance experienced by the Other(ed) when these collective terms are spoken. At this moment, when thought is actively splintering, questions abound intrasubjectively. The listener might therefore ask, Who is the "we" representing? For whom is it intended? Is it prescriptive or descriptive? Inclusive or exclusive?

At the risk of redundancy, I shall define what I mean by "we-Hypothetical" and "we-Real," my appropriated remodified terms.[4] From a pragmatic perspective, these are oscillatory modes of interpreting and locating Self, individually as well as collectively, within situation. These modes fragment, refragment, interface, and solder, only to split apart again to repeat the whole process of agentially finding and orienting Self in context. These modes are thus linked to ontological and experiential identity in the context of different degrees or worlds of reality. More precisely, they are connected to the subjective perception of, and interrelationship with, whichever actual phenomenon a person *qua* "experiencer" determines as real and valid. Moreover, the repetition of the process of filtering subjective identity through the already experienced and the now experiencing resultingly pluralizes Self. For example, I can say "we in this room" now, and be understood on a basic level as referring to us in this classroom, physically occupying and experiencing the same place and space, although differently. But were I to say "we socialists," for instance, or "we non-smokers" or "our ackee tree," certain listeners' identification—both collective and individual, temporal and historical—would start to diverge and fragment from that of mine. If no Self-re/cognition is experientially made in the historical space that links the subjective past with the always-becoming subjective present, this plurally (un)fixed fragmenting identity may travel into the realm of the hypothetical, where it would then transform into non-identity, non-experience, and non-real.

The political ambiguity of the we

Conversely, certain concepts and realities in speech acts, when interpreted or intended as ambiguous, could create problems with self-positionality—for speaker and listener alike. For the message-receiver/listener, identity in such a situation could end up caught somewhere between the we-Real and the we-Hypothetical. Given the aspect of conceptualizing the experiential, an identity with its many Other Selves can be in numerous places at once; it can identify, not identify, and be unresolved all at the same time. This indicates that the we-Real(s) and we-Hypothetical(s) within subjective identity are not necessarily "dichotomies" in the traditionally western sense; though when codified in speech acts and referring to a specific collective or a specific nationalism in academic discourse, they are often (meant to be) represented or understood this way. Within the process of cognizing, I additionally see these modes as b/orderless fluid categories embedded in an interlocutor's broad interpretation of time and space, of psychical belonging, of historical and experiential memory, of the real and the imaginary, and of the individual and the collective.

From the scope of linguistics, particularly that of grammar and syntax, part of the problem with these terms is that they operate as nominative, possessive, and objective pronouns. Therefore, they are inherently linguistic disguisers, efficient in creating indirectness and ambiguity. They represent "*persons or things without actually naming them. The functions of pronouns can be explained by its relationship to that of nouns: pronouns stand for persons or things indirectly*, by taking the place of nouns which name them directly" (Vivian and Jackson 257; emphases mine).

The active (re)construction of indirectness, contingent to the utterance of these terms, denotes that an interpretive rupture is continually at play for speaker and listener. There is a severing, an ongoing (syn)tactical crisis in interpretation in trying to perceive when and where the subjective Self becomes (in)directly (re)coded as the problematically objective *us* of dominant culture.

This said, it becomes obvious that, at the interstices of the degrees delimiting reality and phantasy, and at those intersections where the marginal and mainstream we-Real(s)/we-Hypothetical(s) hybridize and compete, lives the omnipresent determining *I/i* of situation and experience.[5] At these numerous centres and peripheries constantly p/resides the *I/i* of re/cognition and deduction, for the facility in uttering "we" is based on a subjective assurance, preconception, or problematical generalization of there being not only multiple *I/i*'s experiencing or having experienced a given context, but possessing an identical understanding of it.

Nonetheless, in the numerous classroom situations I have experienced in Canada, the we-Real(s) of the professor/lecturer/speaker, who is usually still of, or representing, the White mainstream (although this is slowly changing), become(s) universalized and made into we/self they/Other dichotomies. This results in the masking of the we-Real(s) of the marginalized. The universalizing of the hegemonic we-Real through speech acts renders invisible the various we, us- and our-Reals of marginalized subjects, while simultaneously deriding heterogeneity. But this rendering of marginalized (in)visibility, this hegemonically becoming invisible of the Other is a recolonization, a (sub)liminal type of passive/active violence that allegorically subjugates and silences. It is this process—the subtle act of (re)othering the already Othered and dominating listening subjects into categorial marginalization through an implied/imposed experiential homogeneity—that I consider a form of (neo)colonial exclusion. This is not to say that collective *we's* do not exist in terms of perceived consensual "realities." Rather, the point being stressed here is that an aleatory ulterior oppression becomes constructed and activated in discourse when one person, in a western context, *decides* to translate the subjective *I/i* into the "objective" *we*, and then globally (super)imposes it onto everyone and every experience. This demonstrates the verbal/psychical (re)colonization of Others made possible through terms as simple as pronouns.

Besides being specious and discriminatory, these pronouns which indirectly provoke (neo)colonial exclusion and (re)colonization are intangible sophisticated agents innate to ideological academic discourse. They partake in the hegemonic knowing and manipulating of metalanguage. This is to say that speaking interlocutors, through the use of *we*, are able to mystify their national/political/personal stance on serious sociocultural issues, and gain power, rank, and primacy from this mystification. Applicable to this matter is Pêcheux's description of subject making and concealing. He claims that covertness is one crucial factor in the transformation of power and subject. Examining the subliminal complexities of institutional agents, he ascertains that

> *ideology* and the *unconscious* ... conceal their own existence within their operation by producing a web of *"subjective" evident truths*, "subjective" here meaning not "affecting the subject" but "in which the subject is constituted." (147)

What then remains verbally obscured but symbolically articulated by the *we* of subjective "objectivity" seeks to dominate and colonize the psyche through the vehicle of learning and envisioning. This process therefore strives to homogenize ways of knowing and types of knowledge that accord with hegemonic systems. By hegemonically manipulating metalanguage and creating "evident truths," numerous (neo)colonial discourses can be expressed, circulated, and rationalized in a variety of c/overt ways, with the interlocutor's accountability of agency hidden behind the (un)specified *we*. About hegemonic articulation, Lawrence Grossberg theorizes:

> It is the struggle to articulate the position of "leadership" within the social formation, the attempt by the ruling bloc to win for itself the position of leadership across the entire terrain of cultural and political life. Hegemony involves the mobilization of popular support, by a

particular social bloc, for the broad range of its social projects. In this way, people assent to a particular social order, to a particular system of power, *to a particular articulation of chains of equivalence by which the interests of the ruling bloc come to define the leading positions of the people.* (Grossberg 162; emphasis mine).

Consequently, academic discourse ideology with its (un)specified *we* continues to be conventionalized through current and ongoing usage; it continues to be played out (un)consciously in classrooms, (dis)appearing and reappearing, becoming reified as reality through utterances in (dis)course rituals. These rituals progress as follows: professors lecture; students listen, wait, interiorize theory, internalize vocabulary, debate intrasubjectively, and then respond—offering opinions and criticism with *we's*, *us's* and *our's* as modifiers of their own experiences and personal perspectives. Occasionally, these terms may also be (interpreted as) representing hegemonic Canadian nationalism. Thus, universalizing the subjective often occurs and recurs impalpably whenever persons gather and interact in a classroom environment; and, again, it becomes more refined by virtue of being unconsciously activated through articulation. In this light, the use of these terms in academic contexts is perpetuated partly by a lack of critique concerning their ethnocentric referencing to the speaking subject, partly by subliminal persuasion and militant conditioning, and partly by the facility in lingually surrendering and conforming to the expressions used by the majority.

Thus from my perspective, these personal and possessive pronouns in academic discourses—which again, at times, concurrently represent national and dominant cultural discourses—frequently displace, delete or dominate the *we's*, *us's* and *our's* of Other(ed)s groups in Canadian classroom settings. If Canada is presumably multicultural, and if the student bodies in university classrooms are a microcosmic reflection of this multiculturalism, then who exactly is an academic interlocutor addressing when uttering "we" in theoretical, experiential, subjective, or historical contexts? Not only, then, does the (un)specified *we* in speech acts trivialize the cultural/existential diversity of listeners; its allegorical codification of "western" also underhandedly belittles and recolonizes diasporic and multi-ethnic experiences and histories.[8]

First-hand experience of the we

I especially remember an incident I experienced as an undergraduate in an art-history class. One lecturer used a stream of collective terms when she spoke of the founding of Canada. "Look at what *we* did to the Natives to form *our* civilization," she began. I vaguely recall the rest, for again, I was too busy trying to decypher the context of her "we." On the one hand, it seems that the essential explicit message in this statement was her acknowledgement of the massacres and devastation suffered by the Natives at the expense of the founding of imperialist Euro-Canada. But it was the "we did"—uttered with such ease, and which had veiled numerous particularities—that was unsettling. Also, by virtue of the circumstance (her being a guest lecturer), I felt somewhat obligated to engage with her words.

On the other hand, the implicit meanings suggested by the "we" were perturbing. As an active interlocutor, I sat there unravelling many intimations. Within this "we" was the possible assumption (or rather her projection) that I am, or willingly identify as, "Canadian" as *she* defines it, that I see historical colonizers as my political affiliates, and that I consider Canada (my) "civiliza-tion." And the "our" was problematical too; for in Canada, being called nigger-Black, Black bitch, fucking nigger, nègre, Black and Decker, shit face, choco-late face, savage, immigrant, and Black pussy, I quickly learnt that there was an exclusivity implicit in the expression "Oh Canada, *our* home and native land." But then I am not the only one here. Millions of Others before me, beside me and around me, in the past and now, have (had) their own stories to tell of oppression, discriminatory violence, resistance and survival.

But it was perhaps a moment later, after the lecturer had uttered the statement about the colonization of Natives—a statement that had propelled me into the we-Hypothetical mode—that I became acutely aware of her differences—her Whiteness, the Anglo-Saxonness of her accent, her colonial Canadian patriotism, and more frighteningly, her position as an up-and-coming educator. I remember looking around at the rest of my classmates; most of us present were visible minorities. I wondered what they had thought of her statement, if they too had felt invisible, excluded, deleted, transparent.

As I continued looking at the speaker, she was not only a lecturer who was perhaps inebriated from her power position behind the lectern; by way of actual circumstances and a series of projections—both hers (verbally) and mine (interpretively), she transformed into a sign, a sign signifying academic smugness, Anglo-Saxon hegemony and White western elitism. The lecturer's momentary use of these small utterances was therefore revealing; it revealed her (want of) consciousness, her political (in)sensitivity, and her national imperi-alist-identified narcissism. Her speech acts also resulted in an invisible intangible domination, a verbal/psychical domination of telling colonial history from her own perspective, universalizing it through the *we* and *our*, and thus naturalizing her experience as a White mainstream authoritarian—which is how I eventually came to perceive her. So it follows that using these terms in academic discourse gnaws away at some of the listening subject's discretional autonomy. Uttering these pronouns additionally displaces and obscures specificities—the specificity of histories, national identities, realities, personal experiences; the specificity of alterity and differences within the web of bureaucratic power and authority; but more importantly, the specificity of self-location within the context of agency, resistance, and complicity.

Similar incidents have occurred in courses I have taken in Women's Studies, Translation, English Literature, Religion, Communication Studies, and French Studies. Once in a sociology course, the professor, a White woman, refused to adopt a more inclusive gender-neutral language while lecturing. Standing behind the lectern, she would use male normative modi-fiers—"he" this, "him" that—and mix them with the collective terms. To make matters worse, most of the theories she was delivering were western, ethnocentric, and heteropatriarchal. I wondered, though, if that professor ever saw herself in her "we" of male normative discourse, a "we" that was subliminally representing and universalizing straight White male experiences of the presumable "first world," and (in)visibly dismissing many Others. This problem, as I shall later discuss, is not limited to White heterosexual/women lecturers, nor to professors.

The hegemonic we filtered through marginal discourses

In numerous cases, the *we* of vagueness, uttered by many academic interlocutors, tacitly represents "first-world straightdom." In other words, the concept intrinsic to the *we* ideology/discourse takes for granted that all listening subjects are western heterosexual citizens from the middle/upper classes. By the term "straightdom," I am not merely referring to sexual preference. I am also talking about the aspects of sexual identity that transcend corporeal/genitalic practices, that materialize as passive/active culture through their societal desexualization in theory, ideology, institutional(ized) privileges, rights and laws, and that become exclusionary and potently influential by virtue of being politicized. I am especially referring to political hetero/sexist notions that stagnate and gestate in belief systems while repeatedly becoming finely and minutely dispersed, normalized, automated, and (re)enacted in sociocultural and sociopolitical performatives, on an epochal/daily basis. Of individuals' symbolic interaction with discourse, Jacob Mey writes:

> ... the language of the law, or legal language; the language of the church, or religious language, the language of institutionalized aggression, or military language; and so on. In these languages, people have seen fit to standardize certain linguistic symbolizations in order to perform certain, appropriate functions that are pertinent to the existence and survival of the institutions and their members. (147)

So long as these auto-(re)generative auto-transformative belief systems necessitate language to become active in institutions, actively performed and thus imbibed in culture; so long as they require a sociopolitical mode of communication and verbal/textual expression to instigate and maintain the sociopolitical homogenization of sociocultural heterogeneity, straightdom's appropriation of the pronoun "we" *will* doubtless ensure that (hetero)sexual politics, hegemonic hierarchies, types of discrimination, and exploitive power asymmetries continue to be recreated and psychically reinscribed in utterances and contexts.

De-eroticized and disseminated, heterosexual notions as "mainstream" culture subliminally influence the way in which the uttered (un)specified *we* is (expected to be) received in group contexts. In this regard, the *we* affects a wide range of individual/collective cultural dynamics: from discriminatory ideas about "normal" behaviour as "straight" behaviour in public and private—if ever and whenever those categories exist, and prejudicial suppositions about heterosexuality as the uniquely ideal model for family and parenting, to oppressive heterosexist preconceptions about subcultural alternative experience(s) and world(s) as inconsequential. Not to comply to all the *we* of straightdom includes and touches (which seems to be everything), is to be (in)visibly (dis)placed into the outside of Other experiences and realities (which is actually the spacial/symbolic inside of various power-contested centres and peripheries), where different forms of oppression and political struggles are occurring. All the aforementioned aspects resurface in classroom situations, albeit microcosmically. All these forces inure, in fractional proportions, through academic texts, interaction, and dialogue.

In speech acts, the (un)specified *we* of straightdom, which is still closely linked to androcentric suppression, reactionary patriarchy, and compulsory heterosexuality, also stems from the recurringly phobic want of/for obedience, uniformity, fixity, and order; for it is a thing that cannot acknowledge its rigidity, that cannot unhinge itself, that cannot encompass too many differences. It sooner latches onto the faction in nuance that symbolizes and forces conformity, than onto the fragment that deviates and signifies change. The (un)specified *we* is therefore an oppressive verbal/allegorical unit that thrives politically on the insularity of limits, boundaries, and restrictions within given contexts.

It follows that, on a personal level, I have also at times had difficulty identifying my/Self with *we's, us's,* and *our's* of some of my Black and Asian university-educated colleagues from the supposed "first-world." For instance, certain comrades are Black British, and others Black Canadian. When they begin their sentences with the homogeneous "in *our* society" or "in *our* culture," my we-Real fragments, oscillates; and some of it—the parts of my Other Selves that are not identifying, that are recalling and psychically magnifying subcultural/non-occidental experiences—becomes displaced in the we-Hypothetical. This happens as I am realizing that the Black heterosexual and/or western experience is being subliminally universalized, and colonially (re)denying Other experiences.

In academia, another example of identity oscillation lies with the *we* uttered by certain Black men in group discussions. To particularize, I must say that it is the *we* of numerous Black West Indian/Canadian male scholars that I have found perturbingly exclusionary. Granted, a desperate want exists in Canadian culture for positive Black male role models; and there is also a need to address racial violence against Black males in Canadian society. In fact, these needs likewise apply to the Black female counterpart. But for numerous Black male scholars, the idea of *we*, of a normative "community," is that of a comfortably-homophobic Black heterosexual brotherhood in which Black women are meant to occupy fringed positions of objectification and subserviency, and their sociopolitical/sociocultural concerns taken as afterthoughts. It seems as though for some, Black women's needs are considered less pressing, inferior, and can thus afford to fall onto deaf ears.

Within certain Black brotherhoods, the straight Black man gains power as normative subject through sharing certain sides of his identity with those of dominant cultures—namely male, heterosexual, and possibly first-world. These sides, in turn, become codified in discourse and politically naturalized into verbal invisibility. Because of this invisible interlocutory normalization, any alternative *we's* become non-subject, especially if they are understood in these groups as gendered or introducing a gender(ed) problem—a problem which might actually be referring to a crisis in Black male-female collective/cultural dynamics. The *we* as gender(ed) non-subject, or object, is then classified as part of Black "women's issues;" it thus becomes depoliticized and rendered into conversational naught. In this case, gender is automatically equated to female-ness, and femaleness as alterity must be subordinated, controlled, and forced into triviality in order for it not to threaten, or interfere with, Black male heteropatriarchal power. This denotes that, to find a place in the Black fraternal "community," Black women must be ready to accept an inferior location where their experiences and identities become (in)visible, and their exercizing of agency minimal or nil. In such a context, the scholarly brotherhoods' *we* is a pronoun resembling that of the White-male heterosexual hegemony; but the crucial difference is in its being politically and historically racialized as Black.

For some other Black men, their articulation of *we* implicitly disenfranchises Black women, and is based on the reductionist/essentialist assumption of Black women's issues consisting primarily or uniquely of menstruation, childbearing, and "finding a man." The androcentric reductionism of Black female roles works ambiguously to glorify Black women as m/Others, yet to restrict them to the realm of nurturing, under male governance. Inside these cliques, difference rather than similarity in experience or identity is stressed. And with the insistence on re/seeing difference, male authority can be reconfigured, reColoured from White to Black, reclaimed, and justified through the essen-tialization, objectification, and subjugation of Black women. Here, in these racialized subsets of heteropatriarchy, lies the (un)conscious tendency to distinguish Black male culture as more important and more valid, than (the brotherhoods' constructed (mis)conceptions of) Black women's culture. There is a strong tendency or desire to ensure that Black heterosexual men will domi-nate—and thus negotiate power—within the psychical/experiential we-Real. With this monopolization achieved, all Others would immediately fall outside of this mode, and downwards in its hierarchy. In such a situation, it appears as though no, or very little, attempt to change androcentric, sexist or misogynist attitudes is being incited; and no deconstructivist movement towards Black female inclusivity, or towards *comprehending* Black women's experiences as di-versified and political, is being encouraged in these groups.

The same situation occurs with certain White gay/lesbian/queer col-leagues. Using the *we*, they tend to universalize and make hierarchically primal the White western/"first-world" queer experience, thus interpretively subju-gating or discounting experiences of non-straight diasporic Others. Irrespec-tive of its location from the margins, this *we* is likewise charged with exclusionary and oppressive power, given its naturalization of Whiteness and first-worldness. Also, the pronoun temporally simplifies experience, especially for the diaspora, by insinuating that what should matter most is the West's assimilatory here and now, although the "modern" situational present, sandwiched between plural histories and imagined futures, relies heavily on past experiences for sense and meaning in the contemporary. How, then, should the diaspora reintegrate their substantial past as part of their identity if it is not "western" or considered as such by Canadian Others? In excluding diasporic Colour from its implied membership, the (un)specified *we* of the queer subaltern demonstrates its historical connections to colonial ideologies that continue to beget oppressive Canadian thought and to construct, in the collective imaginary, Canadian identity as fixedly Colourless and "indigenous." In fact, this *we* represents the imposition of what I call a (dis)location in identity for Others of Colour.[6]

As a *double entendre*, the (dis)location of identity signifies the simultaneity of suppressing or concealing parts of Self (dislocating) and finding kinship with Others (locating). Ostensibly, to experience a sense of belonging, Other listening subjects of Colour and of non-straight orientation may feel pressurized, or the disquieting need to overlook crucial sides of their politico-historical/ethnic/cultural identity for the sake of fostering connections and "community." Still, even within this context, their position in "community" becomes volatile, uncertain, and sub-secondary, based as it is on an/Other's idealization of "we." Says Paul Gilroy:

> The tension between chosen identities and given identities appears in a very stark form in the history of the Black Atlantic diaspora, where the obligation to engage in self-discovery has always involved an act of refusal, and the conventional understanding of what it means to be an individual has been either imposed on its subordinated Others, or premised on their exclusion. (19)

I draw attention to this imposed (dis)location in identity for diasporic Others, not to ignore the White lesbian/queer/gay political resistance now taking place in academia against compulsory heterosexuality and racism, nor to minimalize the acts of academic subversion, performed by many heterosexuals (be they Black, White, of Colour, upper-class, diasporic or first-world), that help to spark political inclusion and to stop types of oppression, but to emphasize the ongoing crisis in politically situating the multi-marginalized Selves of the diaspora in Other occidental yet subaltern groups that share certain discourses and ideologies with dominant culture.

It is therefore significant to highlight the strong ties and the replicating of systemic oppressions that, through collective terms and their presence in linguistic performatives, exist between and within the margins and the mainstream. The *we* that contingently creates a collectively envisioned community is always (in)visibly racialized, stratified, nationalized, enumerated, gendered, and sexualized. Even in subcultures, discriminatory power structures from the outside—meaning from the overlaps of hegemony, patriarchy, and the western mainstream—can trickle in through the *we* which, in certain contexts, would (in)advertently micro-hierarchize and determine, according to an/Other set of prejudicial criteria, the order of subjects and the degrees to their privilege. Robert Stam claims that: "The oppressed, because they are obliged by circumstances and the imperatives of survival to know both the dominant and the marginal culture, are ideally placed to deconstruct the mystification of the dominant group" (259–260).

But as the previous examples illustrate, this is not always the case. Evidently, subcultures can personify the "dominant group" in variables and increments. The marginalized/oppressed can, on a small scale, transform into the dominant/oppressor.

What now? The (non) conclusion

So then, what would be a viable solution or replacement for the (un)specified *we* that has been so widely appropriated in English Canada's *lingua franca*? The *I* that is psychoanalytically loaded with egotism and self-absorbtion? The conceited pro-structural *I* that promotes hegemonic classifications and (di)visions? Or the *i* which contextually puts certain speakers in an ever-reducing space of alienation, marginality, and subordination, where they become the Other majority? Although there are likewise problems with the *I*/ *i*, the conscious use of it begins to break down dichotomies, to expose complexity, subsets, and contested intersections in individual agency negotiated between a subject's internal-external worlds. It therefore begins to interrogate the dilemmic overlaps and multi-positions of the speaking Self/ subject within the dynamic social matrices of power and vulnerability, of status-quo compliance and defiance.

Expressly using *I*/*i* could thus demonstrate an interlocutor's lucid state of occupying positions that are interstitial, ambiguous, and paradoxical, compared to the automatic utterance of the (neo)colonial *we*, which signals either an unawareness in auditively oppressing listeners, a want to conceal Self as autocratic subject, or a denial of subject-/self-location and its contra/dictions in agential and oppressive positionality. Says Trinh T. Minh-Ha:

> Power therefore never dies out: tracked, pursued, wornout, or driven away here, it will always reappear there, where I expect it least. And language is one of the most complex forms of subjugation, *being at the same time the locus of power and unconscious servility. With each sign that gives language its shape lies a stereotype of which I/i am both the manipulator and the manipulated.* (1989, 52; emphasis mine)

The acknowledgement of conflictual and problematical power stances becomes less apparent in using the terms "we," "our" and "us." For in addition to their homogenous vagueness and effective masking of position and identity, they succeed in (un)intentionally infantilizing and thus suffocating Other voices.

Behind the *we* screen of veiling and artificial homogeneity manifest, during the decoding phase, complex lopsided power dichotomies which sporadically (re)surface in the core of abstraction, in the intermittently concrete, and in the lucidly understandable. The *we* screen collapses when listeners, marginalized or Other/wise, are able to see through its translucent illusion of homogeneity and perceive in the utterance the polarized colonial constructs being (re)produced and (re)presented, such as the often privileged/historicized discourse of the hegemonic self and the usually un(re)marked narrative of Others, the heard colonizer and the ignored colonized, the ruler/model and the ruled/modelling. Insofar as these binaries contain a multiplicity of ambi/valent positions, they nevertheless (re)create (neo)colonial patterns of communicating in dynamic classroom situations. This in turn evokes and perpetuates, in the contemporary, colonially historical (di)visions in interpreting, learning, self-locating, and knowing.

Moreover, the passive structure as a solution to or replacement for the (un)specified *we* is not without its share of difficulties. For to say "Look at what was done to the Natives to form this civilization" is to mask, once more, the location of the speaking and/or (syn)tactical subject, and to displace, once again, the issue of accountability. Similarly, to say "*I* must do this," "*We* must do this" and "This must be done" involves three different perspectives in subject representation, responsibility, and agency, all inherently having varying degrees of subject (in)visibility and dis/guise. The third phrase is especially

ambiguous, in that it creates authority or urgency through a mitigated imperative which, when idiomatically reversed (see Levinson 268–276), absorbs the
syntactical subject and thus the accountable fragment "done by *who/m*."

Still, passive structure begins to address the trouble of a speaker gener-
alizing, talking for and verbally (mis)representing Others through the *we*. Its
absence produces a marked interlocutory difference in that it potentially
leaves room for listeners to interpret the speaker's utterances as individualis-
tic, as opposed to "objective," to negotiate their own identity/identities in
terms of what was said and inferred, and to choose alternative positions (of
alliance, ambiguity, dissent, neutrality, and so forth) in relation to that of the
speaker's. Also, the absent *we* comes across as less patronizing and less
auditively oppressive. It can therefore signify an interpretive space of/for
possible decolonization. I use the adjective *possible* cautiously, recognizing
that psychical/cognitive/linguistic decolonization is not unflawed, and cannot
always be achieved through syntactical absences. In fact, these absences may
themselves constitute further forms of indirectness which could recolonize
and re-exclude Others in different, more complex ways and cause greater
proliferating modes of identification in what would be considered real and
hypothetical.

Conversely, an additional dilemmic subthought is that verbal subjective
mystification, if and when strategic, can be a positive subversive thing. Subject
masking can be used to counter-attack an idea or issue that has, itself, already
been mystified subjectively. But then, *who decides* when, where, how and why
to use it? Who will claim, or be given, the power position of making decisions?
The initiative of deciding comes full circle to the matter of subject, self-
location, responsibility, and accountability.

Yet trying to find a responsible problem-free way of expression means a
speaker would most likely end up wordless, or rather speechless; for it would
seem that in most modes of linguistic communication exist inherent limits and
exclusions with/in speech-act conventions. The challenge, then, is to keep
striving for different means of verbal expression that are more inclusive,
particularist and non-homogenizing. This may entail stopping a speaking
interlocutor to ask for a subject elaboration of the (un)specified *we* (something
I have done (im)politely on several occasions) as well as finding more
disambiguated ways of creating and referring to subjects in discourse and
context.

I my/Self, though trying hard to erase these problematical collective terms
from my personal vocabulary, still fall back on them. I still use them, perhaps

too frequently. The contours of my psyche have been presubjectively colonized by them; I am an insider to them from the outside, and they are familiar to me, slipping through my breath in between words, sometimes uncontrollably, to convey thought and idea. Easy to pronounce, easy to access, they are etched and stored, there in my memory, like huge hurdles that my tongue cannot, at times, leap over and run free from. But I am conscious of uttering them, conscious also that they need more of me, more Self, more *I/i* contextualization so as not to exclude and recolonize and universalize, so as not to perpetuate the refined passive/active violence that occurs with their utterance. And I believe that being aware of all this, and *acting* on this awareness, is perhaps just a beginning, is just one small step forward in lingually and cognitively collapsing (neo)colonial (di)visions.

[1] The ideas for this essay gained force in an undergraduate course in Art History that I took with Professor Joan Acland. It appears abbreviated in the 1997 *Institut Simone de Beauvoir Institute Review/Revue*, volume 17. This expanded version is an elaboration of certain ideas—old and "new"—provoked by a deeper understanding of discourse dynamics. For this, I want to thank Professor Doina Lecca. Her course on discourse theory has made me aware of the complexities and implicit/explicit ambiguities in pragmatic/linguistic interactions. I must as well thank Professor Christine Ross whose course on nationhood and art in Art History led me to another level of awareness about national/identity politics. Also to thank is Professor Catherine Mavrikakis who took the time to read, and give important feedback on this essay.

[2] This problem, however, is not unique to Canada, nor to the English language. The use of these pronouns is a general phenomenon in North American and European English. The *nous* in French discourse poses similar problems.

[3] Please note that, hereafter, the common-letter "self" denotes my generic use of the word, while the capitalized "Self" or "Selves" is used emphatically to refer to the individual subject.

[4] My terms "we-Real" and "we-Hypothetical" are inspired from the "Hypothetical-Real relation." See Allison 379-380.

[5] I thank Professor Catherine Mavrikakis for pointing out, in this section, the ever-present link between the subjective *I/i*s and the we-Real(s)/we-Hypothetical(s).

[6] A theoretical development of the (dis)location of identity is forthcoming.

References

Allison, Desmond. "Textual Explicitness and Pragmatic Inferencing: The Case of 'Hypothetical-Real' Contrasts in Written Instructional Scientific Discourse in English." *Journal of Pragmatics* 15 (1991): 373–393.

Bhabha, Homi K. *The Location of Culture.* London: Routledge, 1994.

Gilroy, Paul. "Roots and Routes: Black Identity as an Outernational Project." *Racial and Ethnic Identity: Psychological Development and Creative Expression.* Eds. Herbert W. Harris, Howard C. Blue, and Ezra E.H. Griffith. New York: Routledge, 1995. 15–30.

Grossberg, Lawrence. "History, Politics and Postmodernism: Stuart Hall and Cultural Studies." *Stuart Hall: Critical Dialogues in Cultural Studies.* Eds. David Morley and Kuan-Hsing Chen. New York: Routledge, 1996. 151–173.

Levinson, Stephen C. *Pragmatics.* 1983. Cambridge: Cambridge University Press, 1992.

Messer-Davidow, Ellen. "Know-How." *(En)Gendering Knowledge: Feminists in Academe.* Eds. Joan E. Hartman and Ellen Messer-Davidow. Knoxville: University of Tennessee Press, 1991. 281–309.

Mey, Jacob L. *Pragmatics: An Introduction.* 1993. Oxford: Blackwell Publishers, 1994.

Pêcheux, Michel. "The Mechanism of Ideological (Mis)recognition." *Mapping Ideology.* Ed. Slavoj Zizek. London: Verso, 1994. 141–151.

Shi-xu. "Ideology: Strategies of Reason and Functions of Control in Accounts of the non-Western Other." *Journal of Pragmatics* 21 (1994): 645–669.

Spivak, Gayatri Chakravorty. *The Spivak Reader.* Eds. Donna Landry and Gerald MacLean. New York: Routledge, 1996.

Stam, Robert. "Bakhtin, Polyphony, and Ethic/Racial Representation." *Unspeakable Images: Ethnicity and the American Cinema.* Ed. Lester D. Friedman. Urbana and Chicago: University of Illinois Press, 1991. 251–276.

Trinh, T. Minh-Ha. *Women, Native, Other: Writing Postcoloniality and Feminism.* Bloomington: Indiana University Press, 1989.

Vivian, Charles H. and Bernetta M. Jackson. *English Composition.* New York: Barnes and Noble, Inc., 1961.

The Evaluation of University Teaching
Exploring the Question of Resistance

Jamie-Lynn Magnusson

T he evaluation of university teaching has many political and ideological dimensions that have not been sufficiently explored in the literature dealing with evaluation practice. The problem I raise in this paper concerns how students can use the evaluation process as an expression of resistance to curricula that challenge them. In my faculty development practice, I found instances of this type of resistance in courses that challenged dominant paradigms and ideologies: courses dealing with feminist issues, anti-racist issues, and issues of sexuality, for example. Although the literature on student evaluation of teaching does not deal with this topic, the question of student resistance has been explored quite extensively in the critical pedagogy literature (e.g. Hoodfar; Manicom; Ng; Simon).

This literature attests to the frequency with which university professors who "teach against the grain" (to appropriate Simon's term) have to endure stressful circumstances in their academic environment as a result of hostile reactions toward the course material. Various writers point out that in addition to the professor, other students may become the object of hostility. Moreover, this type of resistance may be implicitly or even explicitly supported within departmental power structures and departmental culture. The following quotes from articles published in peer-reviewed journals illustrate how resistance is enacted in the classroom.

Although anger aroused by curriculum in women's studies is a response familiar to me as a feminist, my most difficult and worrisome moments as a feminist teacher concern the anger that comes from the classroom—including teacher/student and student/student dynamics—rather than from the course content. In the extreme, this anger lead to an encounter during which unbridled emotion on the part of a handful of students threatened to create divisions within the class difficult to remedy through appeals to "reason." As we shall see, I do not view this anger as a problem to be resolved simply through "proper" technique or teaching method. Rather, I view it as arising from contradictions inherent in the endeavor to bring feminism into the classroom. (Currie 342)

In discussing male resistance to feminist material Orr writes:

Many male students drop out in the early weeks of the course, and among those who remain there is a contingent clearly hostile to the course for sexist reasons. This hostility manifested in a variety of ways, ranging from sulky silence in class and/or poor attendance; to a superficial "going along with it," "saying what the prof wants to hear"; to overt anger exhibited in sexist comments, put-downs of women students, and attempts, all too often successful, to silence them." (242)

The phenomenon of resistance discussed by these authors can escalate when the issues arising from the course interrogate intersecting categories of privilege and entitlement, and particularly when the professor embodies these dimensions. Social critical scholars Ng and Hoodfar have examined their own experiences teaching material that deals with complex issues of gender and race in their courses, the former within the context of anti-racist education and the latter within the context of feminist anthropology. As they point out, the resistance one would expect in these courses will be different depending on how "entitled" and "authoritative" a student perceives the teacher to be. In our culture, racism and sexism are aspects of hegemonic relations of ruling within our social institutions, including academia, and can be problematized in terms of everyday lived experience (e.g., Smith). The lived experience of women of color teaching "against the grain" is captured in the following quotes.

At the conclusion of a course I taught on minority groups and race relations, a male student brought a complaint against me, charging that

I had used the class as a platform for feminism.... On at least two other occasions, complaining (male) students have physically threatened me. Indeed, complaints of this kind about my courses' contents and my pedagogical methods have recurred during my ten years teaching in the university.... I am a feminist and a member of a racial minority. My scholarly work focuses on integrating analyses of gender with those of race, and vice versa. My insistence on teaching ethnic and race relations within a feminist perspective, and on challenging Eurocentric assumptions in feminist theorizing, has consistently got me into trouble throughout my university teaching career. (Ng 189–190)

Hoodfar explains how resistant students were calmed when a white guest lecturer was invited to one of the class sessions:

I invited a white female colleague to give a guest lecture on women in Uganda. In her talk she discussed some of the same issues [author's note: here Hoodfar is talking about the issues students had resisted in previous class sessions] ... To my surprise, much of the tension had evaporated by the following session.... I could not help but to suspect strongly that the discussion by my colleague, who was a white woman with very acceptable scholarly credentials had legitimized my position in class. (313)

These testimonials and scholarly analyses suggest a need to review how resistance can be enacted in the evaluation of teaching. Although I examine resistance within the context of student evaluation of teaching, I should make clear that other evaluation approaches, such as peer review or dossier assessment, are also vulnerable to resistance but in different ways and from different constituencies. I should also emphasize that although I problematize some features of student evaluation of teaching, I am not recommending removing student input from the evaluation process. However, student evaluation of teaching represents a particularly important theoretical location at which to begin examining the political dimensions of institutional evaluation. It reveals the ideological implications of conceptual practices associated with evaluation methodologies.

Minimizing testimonials of resistance: an institutional response

In presenting these quotes I must admit that my first encounter with this type of resistance was through my instructional development practice in a research university, listening to professors' stories about their teaching experiences.[1] My initial reaction was that they must have been doing something wrong, perhaps by not handling sensitive situations with sufficient delicacy and diplomacy, or otherwise not using good pedagogy. This is a typical reaction from someone like myself, who was trained in psychology, a discipline that has had virtually no tradition of scholarly social criticism, and that has been associated with supporting social institutions through its research, rather than challenging and transforming them (see Magnusson 1997). The literature I was bringing to bear on my instructional development practice in universities had been developed within a psychological paradigm of inquiry. In my own teaching of psychology as a beginning lecturer, I had never presented anything more radical than a series of scientific studies into a number of topic areas concerning the individual within social life: structuralist representations that depict people apart from their relational and institutional contexts, but at the same time capture within the structuralist conceptual categories the ways in which social life is institutionally mediated. As will be discussed later, this style of research is committed to a vision of social science as social engineering (e.g., Habermas), and when applied to the project of "instructional development," it supports the ways in which educational practice has come to be institutionalized in our universities (Magnusson 1997). Thus, in my teaching and instructional development practice at that time, I had never known what "teaching against the grain" involved in terms of a scholarly tradition embedded within social equity concerns. The training and institutional position that I had taken up within universities had supported a very orthodox conception of teaching, learning, and scholarship that, in effect, characterized an inequitable system that excluded or marginalized many groups. Much like the sociological intellectual traditions examined by Dorothy Smith, psychological research practices associated with the functioning of social institutions, including higher education evaluation methods, support and reproduce relations of ruling. The evaluation of university teaching, then, in terms of the conceptual practices by which effective or ineffective teaching is defined and measured, supports and reproduces an inequitable system of knowledge production.

My reaction to stories of resistance was embedded within a moral and conceptual framework that devalued the intellectual traditions associated with scholarly social criticism. The epistemological characteristics of this framework were carved from discursive practices that regulate knowledge production in the social sciences, and psychology in particular; the regulation of knowledge production achieves reproduction of relations of ruling that manifest in patterns of domination and oppression that often go unquestioned because they have become hegemonic (Smith). Within the academy, critical scholarship that had evolved within feminist inquiry, anti-racist inquiry, or queer inquiry, for example, could not merely work within the existing intellectual frameworks, but required changing those frameworks in a way that legitimated different epistemologies grounded in ways of experiencing social life that had been marginalized or excluded altogether from institutional discourses. Hence, my response in terms of minimizing testimonials of resistance was an aspect of how I, through the ways in which I participated in my scholarship, teaching, and instructional development practice, supported the reproduction of inequities in the academy. The disbelief I originally experienced reflected how my personal psychology supported my own resistance to the challenges posed by marginalized groups struggling for legitimation. The manner in which I personally had discounted these experiences reproduced the manner in which these experiences were discounted from the social texts and official discourses of our universities.[2]

Gradually I began to reframe my approach to higher education "teaching and learning" to include a more critical perspective. I had to abandon the approach I had been trained in to become a professor and instructional developer. This training had involved graduate courses in math, statistics, computer programming, psychometrics, and techniques of positivist empirical validation. These were the methods upon which an extensive psychological literature had evolved within the specialized area of higher education teaching and learning.[3] And these were the traditions within which methods of evaluating university teaching had developed. These methods have now become institutionalized within our universities and can work against efforts to achieve equity in the academy, at both the level of undergraduate and graduate studies.

In developing these arguments I would not wish to leave the impression that they lead to the conclusion that teaching should not be assessed, or that students' voices in an assessment process should be excluded. I am suggesting that an evaluation process that is grounded in the positivist psychometric paradigm is not appropriate for universities committed to principles of equity. In order to address questions of equity the assessment paradigm must include conceptual practices that interrogate issues of power in the production and regulation of knowledge, including how the assessment process itself interacts with these power dynamics. Before articulating such an assessment philosophy, I will present a case that shows quite clearly that student evaluations can become enmeshed in a politics of resistance and play a role in regulating knowledge production.

Student evaluation of teaching and the politics of resistance

In the previous section I introduced the notion that our methods of evaluating university teaching have evolved within a positivist psychometric paradigm that supports the manner in which educational practice has come to be institutionalized within our universities. One could say that it reproduces these institutionalized practices and aims toward perfecting a kind of technical control over university teaching. Although there is a wide range of assessment practices available to evaluate university teaching, many academic units use student evaluations as the primary, and often exclusive, source of information about teaching. The student evaluations are collected using psychometrically designed ratings forms that have an underlying factor structure. This means that effective teaching is defined in terms of structural categories that are ostensibly empirically grounded and validated. The technical discourse of psychometrics, situated as it is within a positivist framework, is closed off from a scholarly examination of these definitions of effectiveness as socially constructed and institutionally mediated categories. Similarly, there is no scholarly examination of evaluation as a social practice within academic organizational culture, with meanings that are constituted socially and politically.

In this section I present a case that clearly indicates the need to problematize student evaluations as a process that has social, political, and ideological implications.[4] The case involved an associate professor teaching a graduate course in an educational administration department in an American research university. However, in presenting the specifics of this particular case, it is important to examine how the incident is situated culturally. Feminist scholars of education understand that educational administration departments have traditionally been the training ground for entry into administrative positions within governments and schools, and most of these positions have been held by men. This particular region is similar to others in North America in that most teachers in the primary public school sector are women, whereas most principals of these schools have been men. Representation of women in administrative positions is higher in the primary schools compared to secondary schools and is now approaching a more acceptable gender balance than in the past; representation of men in teaching positions is higher in secondary schools compared to primary schools.

Within the department in question there were more female than male students (about 70 per cent women and 30 per cent men), but the academic staff were predominantly men. Two women had been hired into faculty positions in the past six years in a conscientious effort to aim for a more inclusive academic unit. Interviews with the male faculty suggested a sophisticated understanding of issues of inclusivity and a desire to support initiatives to promote equity. Some pointed out the necessity of addressing these issues within the graduate curriculum, within graduate supervision relationships, and within the departmental culture. It seems, then, that the department had been moving toward what many academic staff felt to be a transformation in terms of addressing systemic inequities, especially along dimensions of race and gender.

However, inequities are not erased quickly or easily, and there were many elements of the academic life of the department that continued to reflect its patriarchal origins. Interviews with the two female faculty members and with some of the graduate students revealed incidents of sexual harassment, and several interviewees observed that although women occupied a majority position in most courses, the men often dominated much of the discussion. Three of the female interviewees independently reported sexual harassment from the same male student; each interviewee felt that the culture supported this type of behavior and that there was little they could do about it. Two female graduate student lecturers, and one of the female professors independently reported difficulties associated with presenting feminist perspectives in their classes. These difficulties were attributed primarily to male students who would engage in tactics such as rolling their eyes and expressing hostile comments, but sometimes were associated with female students who were opposed to feminist scholarship. When asked about their experiences in presenting feminist perspectives in class, the male professors all reported positive student reactions. It was not possible to determine whether these male professors were presenting feminist perspectives that were more culturally palatable (e.g. essentialist approaches extoling the virtues of women admistrators as more nurturing, caring, and so on), or whether they were presenting more troubling kinds of perspectives, but were seen as more authoritative and entitled to present such perspectives than were the female professors.

It did seem, however, that the experiences of the women in the department differed according to how closely aligned their scholarship was to social critical perspectives. Women who did not associate themselves with social critical perspectives reported feeling supported by their professors and/or colleagues, and generally had positive experiences. Women situated within social critical perspectives, on the other hand, appeared to have more difficult experiences: one ruptured advisor/advisee relationship was reported; difficult classroom experiences were reported; and difficult collegial relationships were reported. The same did not seem to be true of the men in the department in that male students and faculty alike appeared to feel supported within departmental culture regardless of their scholarly orientations. Although I do not think this pattern can be generalized beyond this particular department, the overall pattern makes sense given the patriarchal history of most educational administration departments: it should be easier for men to develop positive collegial relationships within patriarchal academic cultures, and successively more difficult for women to fit into such a culture to the extent that their scholarship problematizes patriarchal relations of ruling. I am aware, though, of men in other such departments who experience difficulties through taking up anti-racist or anti-homophobic scholarship, for example; the details of this case must therefore not be seen as trying to capture generalizable findings but rather as trying to examine the specific details of one case in terms of broader themes. That is, the validity must be articulated in terms of an abductive rather than an inductive logic.

This was the departmental context within which the case involving student evaluations was situated. The professor in question, a white women in her mid-forties, arrived as an immigrant to the U.S. about 15 years earlier. She speaks with an accent that reveals her country of origin, which can be described as a country that has struggled through political instabilities within a developing nation state. Oftentimes, in my research involving this department, I had the impression that her sophisticated range of philosophical thought around feminism, power, oppression, critical theory, and such, was not taken seriously because it was confused in the minds of some of her colleagues and students with an ideological orientation associated with political struggles within her country of origin: "she is Marxist," or "she is ideological" were examples of comments I heard. Certainly her own experiences of oppression must have informed her work as a scholar, as has been the case for any feminist scholar, anti-racist scholar, and so on. But there seemed to be an assumption that her scholarly orientation was not really an intellectual labour but rather an ethnic attribute. Interestingly enough this woman had received her doctoral training in an American university, attesting to the degree to which her colleagues and students were often unable to distinguish good training in social critical theory from their own indoctrination into a social mileau that is suspicious of any discourse that seems "leftist." Anyone familiar with social critical theory could appreciate her intellectual contributions; she had in fact published scholarly books that were favourably reviewed by important academics in her field. However, the students and many of the professors in the department had little or no familiarity with this literature.

In one graduate course the professor was teaching, a group of four male students became openly hostile toward the professor when she was presenting feminist material. The feminism this professor taught was not of the essentialist variety, which students often find acceptable and even commendable because it celebrates attributes such as caring, connectedness, and so on as natural qualities of women. The feminism taught by the professor was more troubling to students in that it problematized essentialist perspectives and required students to come to terms with scholarly analyses that raised questions about aspects of their everyday lives that they had never seriously examined: capitalist culture, patriarchy, racism, homophobia, to name a few. The tension in the classroom environment escalated and these men stopped coming to a number of class sessions. On the day that the department had organized student evaluations of this professor's teaching, the four men showed up as a group. As one of the men sat down he pointed at the professor and stated "Today is the day we're going to get you." The student evaluations were collected and submitted to the central office for scrutiny. At a certain point the professor was held accountable to these evaluations.[5] The other department members were unaware of the critical pedagogy literature on resistance, and were only familiar with the psychometric literature on student evaluation of teaching which claimed that these evaluations were valid and reliable indicators of teaching performance. Indeed, the university had been actively promoting the psycho-metric narrative of student evaluation validity through workshops, dissemination of literature, senate activities, and the like. The administration was unable to give her evaluations a political reading, and to appreciate how many students participated eagerly in her courses and became themselves targets of hostility.

Even though the academic staff of the department participated enthusiastically in initiatives around "inclusivity," they had not been prepared to deal with these kinds of disruptions. In the case of sexism, it was one thing to hire women into the department, but quite another to understand what this change meant in terms of addressing systemically sexist features of the academic environment. It is important to understand, for example, that the kinds of evaluation practices that had evolved and become institutionalized within patriarchal academic cultures involved defining excellence according to the terms of that culture. In this particular case, the process of evaluating teaching had the effect of reproducing, and even technically perfecting, the regulation of patriarchal elements of the graduate education.

Evaluation practices, generally speaking, whether in the context of evaluating students or in the context of evaluating professor's teaching, have the effect of regulating knowledge production: they are discursive practices of academic cultures that legitimate certain conceptual practices and delegitimate other conceptual practices. In order to address the question of equity in graduate education, then, one must understand how our evaluation practices tend to delegitimate precisely those conceptual practices grounded in the epistemological frames of groups that have been marginalized or excluded within the academy.

Power and method

Although I have presented the details of one case, it is important to understand that this type of scenario is enacted many times over in universities. I chose this case over others because I was able to embed the particulars within a broader context as a result of the study of the department I had undertaken. To the extent that this case, and others that I am aware of, point to a systemic equity problem involving the use of psychometric tools to evaluate professors, it is astonishing that this problem is not addressed in the academic literature attesting to the validity of these instruments.

My own attempts to raise awareness within the community of scholars that deal with postsecondary evaluation has been met with comments such as "this is advocacy and not science," or "this is anecdotal evidence only."[6] In addition to the privileging of positivist inquiry—which has the effect of regulating the research literature dealing with evaluation of teaching—many of the researchers are stakeholders in the evaluation industry. Some have developed their own student evaluation instruments that are available commercially; some have developed evaluation instruments that are available in the public domain through peer-reviewed journals; many have university positions within which their duties involve implementing and maintaining student evaluation systems. The student evaluation systems within universities are data engines that underpin the volumes of psychometric studies that are published in journals that in turn generate income and/or legitimize academic careers. These researchers are central contributors to the literature on student evaluation of university teaching, and they form a significant constituency within the pool of peer reviewers who decide which studies can be published in academic journals or presented at meetings. Many concerns that are raised within the academy related to evaluation are delegitimized or minimized by refering to this regulated literature on the evaluation of university teaching.

In addition to the resistance represented by stakeholders, there is the resistance that is embedded within the denial that I discussed earlier. Many academics refuse to believe that the Arthur Jensons and Philip Rushtons[7] within academia often enjoy greater academic freedom and more vigorous institutional protection than scholars who are committed to anti-racism, or are otherwise engaged in transformative scholarship and teaching.

The gatekeeping discussed above and the denial that is played out individually and institutionally are supported by how "academic" knowledge is socially organized within relations of power. The character of the conceptual practices associated with evaluation research has been shaped through its formation within these relations of power. As has been discussed by many who are involved in transformative scholarship, these relations are characterized by patterns of domination and oppression that are experienced in terms of intersecting axes of race, gender, social class, sexuality, ableism, and so on. These patterns of domination are linked to material practices that support inequitable social formations such as capitalist culture and its modes of production. The conceptual practices associated with evaluation methodology are aspects of these power relations and affect how these methodologies become institutionalized and function to support how organizations socially construct categories of "goodness" and "badness." In the following points I draw attention to some of these features of evaluation methodology.

1) Evaluation methods are characterized by discursive practices that complement those of the institution, and are socially, economically, and politically situated. For example, the positivist psychometric forms of evaluating university teaching, when they were developed, were consistent with the then popular philosophies of scientific management. These were embedded within a process-product conception of teaching, in which effective teaching is defined in relation to "production"; that is, effective teaching was articulated in terms of "teaching behaviors" corresponding to structural dimensions (e.g. "enthusiasm," "clarity," "organization," "rapport," etc.) that were purportedly empirically linked to quantifiable student achievement outcomes. These teaching behaviors are organized theoretically into structural categories that are consistent with the manner in which educational practice had come to be institutionalized within undergraduate programs of large research universities:

multiple section courses that accomodate a few hundred students in each section and that are held in large lecture theatres. These evaluation methods have become integrated into the organizational culture of research universities, and are often inappropriately transferred to graduate teaching contexts as illustrated by the case presented in this paper.

It is interesting that as management philosophies have changed, so have conceptual practices associated with evaluation research. For example, the "scientific management" philosophies have given way to managerial strategies that are consistent with flexible production within our current corporate environments. Likewise, corporate evaluation practices are also changing: "personnel performance assessments" using behavioral checklists within hierarchical managerial relationships have given way to "dossiers" and "portfolios" that are managed by the individual workers who usually have short term contracts associated with particular projects; scientific surveys using psychometrically validated instruments are not as popular as focus groups and quality circles that can be formed quickly and efficiently around specific projects. Interestingly, these corporate methods are becoming popular practices in educational evaluation research and social science notions of what constitutes valid knowledge have shifted to accomodate these changes. Within the universities, however, the student evaluation of teaching methodology is still very much ingrained within the organizational culture.

The point I wish to emphasize is that these discursive practices form the social environment of research universities, and these social environments are characterized by systemic inequities. To the extent that our evaluation research methods complement or blend with these discursive practices, it is highly likely that the evaluation systems themselves will be inequitable. Before introducing an evaluation system into higher education contexts we should be asking many questions about why we want to buy into this culture of evaluation in the first place, and what it means to set up the system in certain ways.

2) The manner in which psychometricians attempt to deal with racism, or other inequities, is inadequate. "Race" is entered as a variable into a regression equation, and if this variable does not contribute to variance, the evaluation is deemed fair with respect to race, or whatever variable is being tested. If "race" is found to contribute to variance, the items that are most sensitive are removed, thereby removing this "bias." The case presented in this paper demonstrates that inequities such as sexism or racism within assessment situations can not be addressed in this technical manner because racism and sexism are systemic within the entire organizational culture. The notion that

206 | Jamie-Lynn Magnusson

things should be evaluated, and the ideas we have about how things should be evaluated, are expressions of our racialized, gendered social reality, and not, as positivist narrative would suggest, separate from that reality. As I have written previously:

> If evaluation is, instead, viewed as an expressive, social process that manifests in an assessment practice that expresses social and cultural reality, then it becomes clear that the assessment results can reflect many things other than good teaching. For example, if the university is a racist culture, the assessment results will reflect racism. That is, the evaluation in its construction, application, and interpretation will reflect the social reality of the evaluation context. By limiting evaluation research to a technical discourse, for example, by insisting that we can eliminate racism in measurement by carefully examining the variance attributable to race, perpetuates a modernist myth that social science can achieve an evaluation that is free of culture and free of ideology. Rather than achieving a culture-free test, we have merely achieved a contradiction in terms: evaluation of social reality is free of social reality. Keeping this contradiction veiled serves the purpose of occluding the main function of evaluation, which is to maintain the basic institutional framework that shapes the social reality of the university. (1996,10)

What this passage conveys is that the evaluation system is an aspect of the organizational culture, and is linked to each of the elements of that culture. For example, the case presented here shows how the evaluation system, seemingly an assessment of teaching performance, interacts in complex ways with the relational context within which learning, as a social and cultural production, takes place. Similarly it interacts in complex ways with administrative decision-making in terms of decisions as to who teaches what courses, who deserves more time for research, salary decisions, and other markers of privilege and entitlement within the academic world.

3) Once the social meanings of evaluation are constituted within the organization, it is very difficult to challenge the imperative to evaluate, and it is very difficult to change how evaluation gets done. At this point we are not merely discussing academic definitions of effective teaching, but also legal definitions of what constitutes grounds for dismissal or other disciplinary action, material entitlements within the organization that become written into

labour agreements, and so on. In this manner, psychology as a discipline has been woven into the fabric of our social institutions, including universities, through its psychometric evaluation practices. We have psychologists in our public schools, hospitals, legal systems, social welfare systems, for example. It is not surprising, therefore, that of all the social sciences, psychology has been the most resistant to changes that have altered the intellectual terrain of other knowledge communities, including the challenging of structuralist, modernist suppositions and, in particular, within an emancipatory, transformational framework. For example, reflexive scholarship committed to social equity considerations currently has no legitimate scholarly place in academic psychology. As I have discussed elsewhere:

> It seems that my training as a psychologist has somehow missed, or ignored, important intellectual and cultural events that have occured in other scholarly communities that would have allowed me to apply the same critical eye to ... structuralist notions that scholars in other social science areas have applied to structuralist suppositions within their own domains. I believe these kinds of oversights in training reflect the nature of knowledge regulation in my discipline, and further reinforces my practice as a social engineer. For example, training in research psychology that has higher education teaching and learning as a focus is considered suitable preparation for institutional positions such as "instructional development officer," and would involve setting up evaluation systems to assess quality of teaching (e.g. student ratings instruments), and developing workshops to improve lecturing and other skills deemed necessary for teaching large undergraduate classes. On a humorous note, I observe that instructional development offices are blossoming in Canadian universities, and have for some time now been a phenomenon of American universities, but I have yet to find a burgeoning of "Offices of Emancipatory Pedagogy" in our higher education systems. I present these illustrations because I think it is important to understand that the metaphors and forms of theoretical models I use in my research practice are more than cognitive manipulations; they are supported by a broad range of social and cultural experiences and find their way into institutional applications that serve institutional interests. (1997, 207)

4) Psychometric evaluations, in conjunction with instructional develop-

ment programs, achieve a kind of colonization of academic life. The evaluation process and the conception of teaching captured within the psychometric categories of the evaluation instrument are grounded in a particular philosophical/cultural perspective that becomes the basis for changing one's educational practice. There is an imperialist posturing in the manner in which psychologists engineer a program of evaluation and development grounded in psychological paradigms, and then impose this program on other academic cultures (Magnusson 1997). There are chilling themes of colonialism and violence that dominate this scenario, and these themes need to be recognized by those undertaking the task of implementing teaching evaluation systems within universities. Implementing standardized, institution-wide evaluation systems is disrespectful of diversity in terms of how other academic cultures think about education and knowledge.

Summary

I have a few suggestions for those considering implementing an evaluation system within universities. First, situate the assessment within intellectual traditions that value reflexive, interpretive scholarship and that foster conceptual practices that interrogate and interrupt oppressive aspects of academic culture. I recommend, for example, authors such as Schwandt who has tried to develop a conception of evaluation as practical hermeneutics. However, the particular framework he develops, if applied to the university setting, presumes much more possibility for equitable participation and dialogue than actually exists. We must not forget that we are dealing with actual violence: Aboriginal students taunted with racist slurs in campus parking lots, gay students physically assaulted, racist graffiti etched into elevator walls and hallways, women sexually assaulted, the case of the business administration dean who developed an agenda to rid his accounting department of "third world mathematicians," the women engineering students who were gunned down, and so on. The assessment philosophy, therefore, must acknowledge at the outset that these oppressive conditions exist, and that evaluation practices must work to transform these conditions.

Second, teaching evaluation systems are often housed and maintained within "teaching centres." These teaching centres, through their various activities, can be set up to address educational practices that reproduce systemic inequities. One example of such an activity would be the development of evaluation practices that are nested within equity imperatives. At the moment, teaching centres usually operate within the mandate of a central administration that controls the purse strings and determines which initiatives will be funded and which will not be funded. These funding and reporting lines often have the effect of severing connections between teaching centres and grassroots movements mobilized by groups that lobby around equity issues: women's groups, Aboriginal and anti-racist networks, gay and lesbian groups, and disability activists, among others. The ways in which teaching centres are structurally and operationally situated within universities could be altered in such a way as to nurture rather than discourage these connections. In this way "teaching centres" would indeed be fostering excellent learning environments.

Third, those in administration must be educated to read faculty evaluations with a political eye. In the case of teaching evaluations, it is not sufficient to glance only at mean scores. These scores gloss over the polarized reactions that students often have to social critical scholarship. Evaluations that reflect these polarities often result in low overall impressions of the professor; however, a closer reading of the individual evaluations will often reveal a cluster of students who were very enthusiastic about the course. The same political eye should be used when reading curriculum vitae, interpreting peer evaluations, and so on. Furthermore, university teachers who are experiencing hostility due to sexism, racism, or homophobia must have support within the classroom.

Finally, in this paper I have focused primarily on the question of student resistance within the context of evaluation. However, this resistance is only one small aspect of a larger question of institutional resistance that is manifest in multifarious ways within academic culture. We need, then, to fit the discussion I have presented here within a much larger context and develop an orchestrated agenda for change.

This article will also be published in Resources for Feminist Research's Fall/Winter 2000 issue (Volume 27, Number 3 and 4). Reprinted with permission.

[1]Instructional development involves assisting universities in improving the quality of teaching, and often involves instituting and maintaining student evaluation data systems, in addition to hosting workshops, providing personal assistance to professors, and so on. In recent years, most instructional developers have specialized doctoral training in psychology, educational psychology, and psychometrics, and are knowledgable in the specialized literature dealing with higher education teaching and learning, most of which has evolved within a psychological paradigm of inquiry. The position I held as an instructional

developer was fairly typical in that I was a full-time faculty member with graduate teaching responsibilities, in addition to administering an instructional development program.

[2]If it seems as if I am pressing this issue it is because each time I have taught this material in graduate courses dealing with higher education teaching, or in workshops hosted for university faculty, I encounter the same reaction: denial. Students and university faculty who teach within the mainstream often feel that these testimonials of resistance are exaggerated, and the teaching skills of the professor are questioned. It is important to understand that these reactions are themselves instances of resistance.

[3]McKeachie and his colleagues at Michigan's National Centre for Research into Postsecondary Teaching and Learning provide an excellent review of this literature (McKeachie, Pintrich, Lin, and Smith). Reviews dealing with psychological research into postsecondary teaching are also available in the various editions of the *Handbook of Research on Teaching* (McKeachie; Trent and Cohen; Dunkin). With respect to the special topic of student evaluations of teaching, there is an extensive body of literature spanning several decades. For a sample, I would suggest literature reviews or meta-analyses by Marsh and Dunkin; Abrami, d'Apallonia, and Rosenfeld; Murray; Feldman. These provide a flavor of the technical, psychometric discourse within which the literature is embedded.

[4]Although I use the case of one professor, the enmeshment of the student evaluation process within a politics of resistance is more widespread. In a discussion group of academic women at the 1996 Canadian Society for the Study of Education (Learned Societies Meetings), the topic of student evaluation of teaching became one of the discussion items. Several feminist professors provided testimonials related to student evaluation of teaching and resistance.

[5]Although the professor was questioned about the evaluations, and requested to be more sensitive to students such as these, she was in fact awarded tenure and promoted.

[6]These are samples of reviewers' comments I have recently received. One of three reviewers was very enthusiastic about my contribution; two of the reviewers provided me with the lowest possible ratings accompanied by comments such as the ones I have presented here. They clearly were opposed to the scholarly genre represented by this work, and engaged in a gatekeeping legitimized within a framework that privileges positivist inquiry. This pattern represents the very same issue I am discussing in this paper: overall low

evaluations as a result of a polarized reaction to scholarship that problematizes inequitable features of academic culture.

[7]Philip Rushton and Arthur Jenson are psychologists who use psychological inquiry methods to support their claims that there exists a racial basis for differences in intelligence.

References

Abrami, P. C., S. d'Appolonia, and S. Rosenfield. "The Dimensionality of Student Ratings of Instruction: What We Know and What We Do Not." *Higher Education: Handbook of Theory and Research Volume 11.* Ed. J. C. Smart. Memphis: Agathon Press, 1996.

Currie, D. "Subjectivity in the Classroom: Feminism Meets Academe." *Canadian Journal of Education* 17 (1992): 341–364.

Dei, G. J. S. *Anti-Racist Education: Theory and Practice.* Halifax: Fernwood Press, 1996.

Dunkin, M. J. "Research on Teaching in Higher Education." *Handbook of Research on Teaching.* Ed. M. C. Wittrock. New York: Macmillan, 1986.

Dunkin, M. J., and B. J. Biddle. *The Study of Teaching.* New York: Holt, Rinehart, and Winston, 1974.

Feldman, K. A. "The Association Between Student Ratings of Specific Instructional Dimensions and Student Achievement: Refining and Extending the Synthesis of Data from Multi-Section Validity Studies." *Research in Higher Education* 30 (1989): 583–645.

Habermas, J. *Theory and Practice.* Trans. John Viertal Boston: Beacon Press, 1971.

Hoodfar, H. "Feminist Anthropology and Critical Pedagogy: The Anthropology of Classrooms' Excluded Voices." *Canadian Journal of Education* 17 (1992): 303–320.

Magnusson, J. "Higher Education Evaluation: Social Science in a Political Arena." Pres. at the Canadian Society for Studies in Higher Education, Learned Societies, St. Catharines. 1996.

Magnusson, J. "Higher Education Research and Psychological Inquiry." *Journal of Higher Education* 68 (1997): 191–211.

Manicom, A. "Feminist Pedagogy: Transformations, Standpoints, and Politics." *Canadian Journal of Education* 17 (1992): 365–388.

Marsh, H. W., and M. J. Dunkin. 1992. "Students' Evaluations of Teaching: A Multidimensional Perspective." *Higher Education: Handbook of Theory and Research, Volume 8.* Ed. J. C. Smart. Memphis: Agathon Press, 1992.

McKeachie, W. J. 1963. "Research on Teaching at the College and University Level." *Handbook of Research on Teaching.* Ed. N. L. Gage. Chicago: Rand McNally, 1963.

McKeachie, W. J., P. R. Pintrich, Y. Lin, and D. A. F. Smith. *Teaching and Learning in the College Classroom: A Review of the Literature.* Ann Arbor, MI: National Centre for Research to Improve Postsecondary Learning, 1986.

Murray. H. G. "Effective Teaching Behaviors in the College Classroom." *Higher Education: Handbook of Theory and Research, Volume 7.* Ed. J. C. Smart. Memphis: Agathon Press, 1991.

Ng, R. "'A Woman Out of Control': Deconstructing Sexism and Racism in the University." *Canadian Journal of Education* (1993): 189–205.

Orr, D. J. "Toward a Critical Rethinking of Feminist Pedagogical Praxis and Resistant Male Students." *Canadian Journal of Education* 18 (1993): 239–254.

Schwandt, T. A. "Evaluation as Practical Hermeneutics." *Evaluation* 3 (1997): 69-83.

Simon, R. "Teaching Against the Grain: Texts for a Pedagogy of Possibility." Toronto: OISE, 1992.

Slaughter, S. *The Higher Learning and High Technology: Dynamics of Higher Education Policy Formation.* Albany: SUNY Press, 1990.

Smith, D. *The Everyday World as Problematic: A Feminist Sociology.* Toronto: University of Toronto Press, 1987.

Trent, J. W., and A. M. Cohen. "Research on Teaching in Higher Education." Ed. R. M. W. Travers. *Second Handbook of Research on Teaching.* Chicago: Rand McNally, 1973.

"I Never Really Thought About It"
Master/Apprentice as Pedagogy in Music

Roberta Lamb

M entoring has been suggested in recent years as a means for achieving equity in education, professions, and business. The idea is that, for example, if women are mentored, if people of color are mentored, then they will be successful and gain status (particularly in white, male-dominated fields) more quickly than if they are not mentored. But from my position as a musician-scholar trained in the classical western art tradition, it is more complicated. Mentoring has been educational practice in universities and conservatories, choir schools, convents or monasteries, and royal courts through hundreds of years of western art music, where the practice of the master teacher or mentor who guides, trains or molds the student apprentice or protégé continues to function as a common and vibrant pedagogical model. Yet the music discipline remains a male-dominated and Eurocentric field. Recent statistics suggest that women make up about 28 percent of professors in music (but much more than 50 percent of those on part-time and term contracts); about 40 percent of doctoral students, about 60 percent of Master's level and about 75 percent of undergraduates.[1] Even for those of us in the field, it is difficult to name more than a handful of symphony conductors, music directors, recording company executives, and so forth, who are not male, not white, not able-bodied, not straight or closeted. In fact, is was only in February 1997 that the Vienna Philharmonic Orchestra voted to allow women to audition for positions within the orchestra, while a "whites only, no Jews" policy remains tacitly in effect (see Duncan).

While the academic mentoring of graduate students in music may not be unlike that found in other fields, mentoring in music is set within a context where very likely both the professor and the graduate student have been part of this mentor-apprentice tradition since childhood. The master teacher/student apprentice has a centuries-long tradition in both western art music and Indian classical music.[2] Historically, it is tied to religious belief and practice, and to patronage through a highly stratified class system. These systems are racialized and gendered. The master, mentor, guru is accorded great privilege, being near to god, genius, or otherwise exceptional, while the apprentice (and the common musician) occupies a position subservient not only to the mentor, but to others in society. The apprentice's training is long, arduous, and begins at an early age. Most cannot hope to gain greater status than a competent, qualified craftsperson. While other kinds of musical traditions (jazz, pop, rock, folk) are not as regimented as the classical tradition, they are often even more commodified, or have taken on some of the characteristics of classical tradition as part of a legitimating process. As one of the senior scholars who participated in this research put it,

> *The model for teaching music is to replicate the text of the master with exactly the proper nuances. To absolutely efface who you are as a human being in order to become the voice of this other person from another period. Every belief we have in the authority of the composer, the originator, tells us to do that. And so much of the training in music is rooted on great respect for the master composers, the right way of doing something. Of course, that's true cross-culturally to some extent.* (female mentor 1)

These contradictory images of the benefits of mentoring caused me to question mentoring as an equity solution in graduate education and, consequently, led me to this research project of examining professors' and students' perceptions of mentor/apprentice pedagogy in music.

Relevant research

Studies concerning the mentor/apprentice relationship in educational or professional settings are numerous, although few studies deal with the arts (Heywood; Shuster), or more specifically mentoring or role models in music. Gould reviewed literature on role models in music in relation to sex-typing of occupations; Hamann and Walker surveyed African-American high school students to determine if music teachers served as role models. Stroud studied five exemplary university band conductors (all male) who are prestigious mentors. Prather focused on three instrumental conductors/music educators in order to identify and analyze musical patterns as well as teaching patterns evolving from one musician to another. While two of her participants were women and one male, Prather did not discuss gender differences or similarities. Two biographical studies of women music educators include mentors and role models as an aspect of the biography (Baker; Hatch).

Among the nearly four dozen mentor-in-education studies located, many focused on gender and/or race as significant issues in relation to success in education (Chao; Chew; Cooper; Eldridge; Infante; Kahn; McShane; Metcalfe; Wright) or academic career (Abney; Clemens; Crawford; Eubank; Fleming; LaCroix; Lemberger; Lewis; McGaha; Matczynski and Comer; Papalewis; Robinson; Schneider; Specht; Wilson; Woodlee). In addition to these studies there is a healthy body of literature addressing formal, prescribed, institutional mentoring programs. With the exception of those studies that engage positive and negative effects of mentoring and have specific applications to equity in graduate studies, research on formalized mentoring programs is not considered herein.

Redmond examines the effectiveness of planned mentoring to increase cultural diversity in North American universities. She notes the exclusivity of informal mentoring:

> Because natural mentoring most often occurs between persons who feel most comfortable with each other, those students who are culturally different from their predominantly European-American male faculty are least likely to enter into mentoring relationships with faculty. (189)

A successful formal mentoring program to address social injustice would require faculty, student, and institutional commitment, and be planned with goals and a structure that includes training for mentors and monitoring.

Holdaway, Deblois, and Winchester, the only Canadian study in this literature review, aim to identify problems with respect to completion of graduate degrees and graduate degree program quality by evaluating responses from 736 supervisors of graduate students in Canadian universities. Holdaway *et al.* note that the relationship of many supervisors with their graduate students is more like project manager than mentor and that graduate supervision is highly variable and idiosyncratic. Ten valuable supervisory practices were identified: give prompt feedback; have a balance between direction and independence; regular progress report meetings; have supervisors who are expert in students' specific research field; help students revise research design; ensure that thesis project does not become too large; ensure steady progress; provide opportunities for students to present research-in-progress and receive feedback; provide a graduate student handbook; and assign supervisors at the beginning of the students' programs. Many of these important practices could be considered a mentor's responsibility.

Copious and thorough studies of mentoring and role models in business education and career development exist; therefore, only those relevant to mentor/ apprenticeship as a form of education were considered for the current research (Gaskill; Kram; Kram and Isabella; Noe; Ragins and McFarlin). Most of the studies focus on the following problems in the mentor/ apprentice model for women: lack of access to information networks; tokenism; stereotyping; socialization practices; norms regarding cross-gender relationships; reliance on inappropriate power bases; limitations of role-modeling; intimacy and sexuality; public scrutiny and peer resentment; and the politics of an organizational culture as barriers to implementing educational reform of the mentor/apprentice model. Nevertheless, it is difficult to superimpose business studies onto graduate education, and even more difficult to superimpose them onto music education; yet the importance of business studies to this project derives from their direct engagement of power issues in mentoring. Few studies in education and none in music examine these power issues.

Mentoring problems

Several empirical studies discussed problems found in mentoring, although these were seldom statistically significant. This insignificance may, in fact, be due to the framing of the research question in such a way that problems become "noise" in the system rather than issues of concern. As an example, one of the studies finding no significant difference in cross-sex or same-sex mentoring mentions that in follow-up interviews women indicated a preference for a same-sex mentor (LaCroix), yet the way the survey instrument was constructed and analyzed did not uncover this fact. Two studies explicitly identify problems in cross-sex mentoring that relate to power differentials between men and women: one mentions the safety factors for women who did not like working late night hours or the socializing requisite with male mentors

(Matczynski and Comer); another mentions the intimidation and negative behavior modeled by male professors towards female university students (Boyle 1989).

Auster (1984) identifies both positive and negative characteristics in mentorship, saying the negative characteristics have not been thoroughly studied. He calls mentorship a "dyadic role set in a power imbalanced exchange" (150), where sex, race, and age may affect the dynamics of the relationship. He particularly notes that the male mentor/female apprentice often is to the disadvantage of the female because of skepticism about the woman's career commitment and sexual innuendo. Auster concludes that these characteristics have been found cross-culturally.

Bowman, Hartley, and Bowman examined "faculty and student perceptions regarding dual relationships in mentoring, friendships, monetary interactions, informal social interactions, and romance-sexual relationships" (232). They found that there was a lack of consensus regarding ethics of such relationships, although women were more likely to rate activities as unethical and there were differences of perception between students and faculty. According to Bowman *et al.*, many women who mentor believe that close personal relationships where personal struggles are shared and examined are unethical.

On the other hand, Fitzgerald, Weitzman, Gold, and Ormerod discovered that 26 percent of their sample of male faculty reported sexual involvement with students, and considered such relationships permissible provided they were not evaluating the student, the student initiated the relationship, it resulted in a continuing commitment, the student was older or there was mutual consent. The researchers conclude that the positive responses to each of these factors misrepresent the power dynamics of faculty-student relationships. Representing a 30 percent return rate, 235 male faculty of a prestigious, research intensive university responded to Fitzgerald *et al.* Women faculty were also surveyed and had an equivalent (30 percent) response rate, but could not be analyzed because the numbers were too small.

Redmond suggests that the following philosophical and practical questions must be considered when thinking about planned mentoring as a means of promoting equity:

> Can mentoring improve retention rates by addressing only some of the reasons for attrition among culturally diverse students? Is it fair to expect faculty, normally without additional compensation, to help

remedy the social and racial problems that have been produced by society? Is it fair to expect students to help teach professors what they should have learned before becoming professors? Is mentoring simply another fad which, in time, will disappear as funding for such programs dwindle? Is it rational to expect persons from different and often opposing cultures to develop the close personal relationships needed for mentoring to succeed? (192)

Methodology

A 40–90 minute semi-structured interview with optional follow-up was used to collect anecdotal data from female and male students and professors directly involved in music instruction in universities and conservatories at the graduate level and in their final year of undergraduate Bachelor of Music degree programs. Several methodological choices parallel Collins' research into mentoring in social work. First, mentors described their experiences with their own mentors, as well as with students they mentor. Second, no definition of mentor or role model was imposed on the participants; rather the definitions came from the participants. Third, none of the participants had been involved in a formal, institutional mentorship program.

This article reports only on the graduate level data from 35 of the participants (21 women and 14 men). Participants were volunteers from schools of music, resulting in an interesting female/male ratio across the mentor and apprentice categories.

Of the 23 graduate students and 12 professors interviewed, only two were people of color; two identified as lesbian and two as gay; all were able-bodied. Participants teach at the university or secondary school level while several are primarily performing musicians. All the participants were either in musicology, performance (including conducting) and/or music education; while 69.5 percent of the graduate students were women (16 female, 7 male) only 42 percent of the professors were women (five female, seven male).[3]

North American music schools and conservatories, being based in a western European art music tradition, have primarily white populations, although recently the numbers of Asian students have increased. Because the methodology for this study involved the "snowball" technique it resulted in a rather homogeneous group of participants. In addition to the racism that is built into the definition of music in a university or conservatory, class privilege is a major factor: a student cannot get into a music school or conservatory without an audition. A student who has not had one-to-one applied instruction is not likely to demonstrate competence (and talent) at these auditions. Music instruction is not inexpensive, yet in Canada the average annual salary of musicians (not employed by institutions) is less than $20,000.

It was much more difficult to find men who were willing to participate than women. In order to keep the ratio of female/male participants similar to the ratio found within the general population of music schools and conservatories I had to decline to interview some of the women who were willing to participate. I am assuming that this snowball selection process has resulted in a sample where the men could be classified as sensitive and the women as those who have stories to tell. The basis of this study, therefore, is not predictive to a general population, or even to a wider population of musicians and music scholars, but rather descriptive and analytical of these particular cases. Yet, I have found when presenting small sections of this work at conferences to colleagues in music, the stories resonate with their experiences.

Results

The interview seemed to provide an opportunity for participants to reflect on mentor/apprentice music pedagogy in ways that had not been available previously and to think about their own pedagogical processes in music. Comments such as, "I haven't really thought about it much, and maybe I'll think about it a bit more now," were common to both male and female participants. Some of the women suggested a therapeutic value to discussing the issues, while both women and men stated they had learned something by talking about the mentor/apprentice process.

The categories of the results were pulled from the interview transcripts through Kirby and McKenna's extension of Glaser and Strauss' grounded theory with intersubjectivity, critical reflection, and "hurricane thinking." Definitions of mentor and power issues within the mentorship became the major categories. Several subsidiary categories emerged under the power issues: self-esteem, "my way or the highway," conducting, harassment and sexuality, institutional hierarchy, motivator or coach. While these categories are discussed in detail below, no attempt has been made to establish "significance." The analysis is presented in terms of participants' quotations and the understandings I have gleaned from their interviews in comparison with the previously cited literature and my experiences as a musician-scholar, all set within the context of graduate education at universities.

Definitions of mentor

The definitions of mentor presented by male and female participants differed in interesting ways, while maintaining certain common features. Throughout the interviews, and without exception, the participants emphasized their own identity as musician. As one woman apprentice said, "It's really hard to take the instrument away from that person's concept of themselves." Neither did this centrality of musician identity differ between professors and students, both groups applying this identity definition to "mentor" also. It might be that the role of musician identity is one factor that distinguishes graduate studies in music from other disciplines. Further, both males and females, professors and students, commented on the following as important characteristics of a mentor: the mentor's musicianship (i.e., subject knowledge or competence and prestige within a community of musicians); her/his ability to bring out the best in students; the personal interest a mentor takes in her/his student, demonstrating that she/he has the best interests of the student at heart; and the significant trust that develops between a mentor and student.

Male participants made a clear distinction between a role model and a mentor, whereas female participants often did not differentiate between the two or label them, but began to describe these relationships directly and immediately, mentioning names of mentors and places of study. Male participants were less likely to mention such details. Female apprentices, in particular, were the most resistant to labeling their experience with music teachers. Female participants appeared to prefer role models to mentors, in the ways they defined the concepts. Several males used the word "idol" to describe a role model, but no female used that word. Males most frequently cited academics and their piano teachers as mentors. Female participants named family members as mentors more frequently than any other, although academic mentors and piano teachers were next. Both refer to the intimacy of the mentor/apprentice relationship; some liken it to a marriage, but only women compared mentoring to parenting. Consider these examples by two women mentors and one apprentice:

I think a role model I would see as somebody who was working in an area that I could see myself in, so I could read myself into the kind of work that they did. Mentor to me has connotations of somebody whose philosophy, with whom you really have a spiritual connection. (female mentor 1)

... part of what I really enjoy about my mentor relationship ... is that it's a one-to-one and I am intensely observing and interacting with this individual. I mean I'm consciously trying not to have that intense one-on-one with my students. And yet I have chosen to adhere myself very closely with one person, align myself. (female mentor 2)

I would say that the mentor is responsible for your long-term musical development.... The mentor is more responsible for a plan of action that says: O.K., this year you will learn this repertoire; you will work through this set of studies; when you get up in the morning you will play these pieces. (laughs) I mean it can get quite specific. (female apprentice 1)

Contrast with these the comments made by two men:

... I think it would be difficult to choose a mentor who you didn't feel was a role model; however, I think a role model can be one even though you're not in their presence.... But I can see mentoring as having some type of ongoing encouragement, ongoing rapport, a person that you can really let loose with.... (male apprentice 1)

... A role model doesn't take any particular interest in you or your career. I mean, the role model doesn't necessarily demand anything. I see a mentor as much more intimate kind of, you know, relationship, where you're actually interested in each other's careers and helping each other out.... The mentor is somebody you respect and takes a personal interest in your development, and who fosters that development in a personally connected kind of way, within a hierarchical situation because they're still the teacher and you're still the student. (male apprentice 2)

Several male mentors named the importance of the apprentice accepting the mentor, in connection with their definitions of mentoring.

... I think if there's a good match, that is, the mentee accepts being mentored. There's the respect and the faith and so on, and the mentor is really a benevolent mentor who has the best of the other person at heart, and doesn't simply want to turn the person into a disciple for the sake of being a disciple.... He admired stuff about me and I about him and it was a very powerful teaching and learning situation for me. (male mentor 3)

One female apprentice in her early 20s provided this eloquent description of the parenting characteristics she saw in her mentor:

> *A mentor can also carry on some roles of parenting in some respects, even though you are usually out of that age. There's guidance—they know more about that life than you do. They've lived their whole career in the music field and they know what it is that they are talking about, and maybe they do have some suggestions. They taught a love for the instrument, also. People really thrived under their care, but ... I think that passionate vision to go that one step further which I would consider makes a mentor a mentor. And I'm wondering if maybe [my mentor] has become the person that she has been through the whole reality of bringing up a family and, the reality of having a child that needs a different kind of care, that has made her into the human being that she is. In a way her playing is charmed, but her life is not necessarily charmed.* (female apprentice 2)

A male apprentice in his 30s also uses the family/marriage metaphor, while another likens a failed mentor/apprentice relationship to divorce:

> *It's a very intimate relationship that's probably somewhat like a very close family member or a close friend, or a spouse even, someone that you can come to and you can let it all hang out and not be concerned of judgment or negativity and the type of understanding where you really feel that they have your best interest in mind and so you trust them.* (male apprentice 1)

> *... But again, if you have a falling out with your mentor ... then basically it's like a very ugly divorce and you end up with everything taken away and a lot of emotional scars....* (male apprentice 2)

Gay and lesbian participants criticized the family/marriage metaphor when describing their perceptions. A gay male mentor nearing retirement reminisced: "... It was almost a kind of patriarchal thing that existed in the Victorian marriage, you know? And so that was detrimental to my development as a person" (male mentor 4). A younger lesbian, recently graduated, described her mentor as someone she "... belonged to body and soul.... It's like a love relationship, it's like you have to be musically monogamous.... You couldn't go and play for another teacher. Oh, no! That would be like musical adultery" (female apprentice 1).

Overall, it appeared to me that women were conflicted about the role of mentoring in their lives, whether as a professor or a student. Some women consciously chose not to have a mentor due to these misgivings and believed that their success was the result of family and peer support or help and their own self-reliance and independence.

> ... *I think, for me the whole term mentor is problematic in that it implies submission, and rewards for favors granted and benevolence from on high, superiority. And those are concepts I have trouble with....* (female apprentice 3)

> ... *I think that's one of the really difficult things about mentor/student, which frankly may have been one of the reasons I didn't want a mentor. I'm very independent; I'm very self starting.... I like to collaborate rather than work in a hierarchical system. On the other hand, to be pragmatic, it is a hierarchical system, so I find that a real conflict in how I respond to many of the things I have to respond to. It can lead to the student being told what to do and you must do it my way—my way or the highway....* (female mentor 4)

The European mentor model, called "Viennese School" by some participants, was mentioned by both male and female professors. Most called up this historic archetype as a fairly negative example of mentoring, but allowed that it had shaped western art music and produced great musicians. The students were less likely to use this terminology but did identify an older, stricter, authoritarian style that was not comfortable for them. Participants contrasted these models with their desired traits in a mentor. Students, both male and female, mentioned a friend or guide, although the women, especially the younger students, put more emphasis on friendship and the men put more emphasis on career guidance. Women professors and students identified an emotional or deeply personal connection, as well as crediting the mentor for helping her to "see strengths I didn't know I had." Women also emphasized the importance of a mentor's honesty and the need for safety in the relationship. Both men and women thought a mentor's enthusiasm and love of music were crucial, but the men went on to define this in more technical terms related to the discipline and skills necessary to succeed as a professional. Male professors and students also described a mutuality to the relationship, whereby the mentor, as well as the apprentice, gained.

Self-esteem

Women brought up self-esteem and lack of confidence in their abilities or talents as on-going issues. One apprentice wondered if she is "good enough" and has difficulty seeing herself as a "grown-up musician," even though she is over 30, while the men appeared confident in their knowledge and position and did not question their talents. The questions the men asked that revealed some insecurity focused on "doing the right thing" in their teaching, on being aware of and dealing appropriately with difficult issues.

> ... *I've had some real, some real serious worries, thoughts, about the ethical dimension of even forcing your children to take piano lessons or music lessons from age five on ... for the convergent, obedient, submissive child, who does it well, and starts to define themselves in terms of their musicality and their musicianliness, I wonder about a lot of the people that we have walking around here and what happened to their souls and their spirits and their self-identity in relationship to being musicians.* (male mentor 3)

Most women participants linked "voice" to positive power, empowerment, self-esteem, and functioning mentor relationships, and the absence of voice to negative experiences with power or lack of self-esteem. The concept of voice was not mentioned by the men, although one male professor identified how he uses language as an important factor in mentoring relationships. A woman professor, reflecting back on her experience as an apprentice, still feels she has no "place or voice" in music except perhaps as a performer. Another more senior woman mentor states that in traditional music education, the student must "absolutely efface who [they] are as a human being in order to become the voice of this other person from another period." One young woman, intent on becoming a composer, hoped that in studying contemporary art music she would be "hearing a voice that was mine." These two examples discussing self-esteem in relation to their mentors are from a musicology and performance student, respectively:

> ... *there was this wall, and it seemed that the object of my work was to please him. It was to please him more than it was to please me. And that all of my self-esteem and all of my self-recognition was through his words, which is a completely dangerous game, but one which I think a lot of women fall into.* (female apprentice 5)

... I think one of the things about this whole model is that you are not your own self in that kind of a situation. You become that person's student. And I felt like I remained nameless. So when you go to a competition, you are not your own name, but you are so-and-so's student or you are from that studio.... You "perform" the musician you think "they're" trying to "create." Looking back, I now know that the degree of manipulation was very strong. It seems to me that to succeed with this kind of manipulation, one first needs to suppress any sense of autonomous "self"—make one feel dependent, which is what I think happened in my case.... (female apprentice 6)

This male graduate student has carefully avoided a mentor relationship because he has concerns about its effects on his mental health:

... There's an imbalance in accomplishment. And I suppose in the best cases there's a mutual respect and a sense that you will eventually overcome that imbalance, that the purpose is to help you get to where the mentor is, or at least at some place that's equivalent to where the mentor is, so then it'll dissolve into like a lifelong friendship or whatever. I'm realizing now if you want to build a career, it's positive to have a powerful ally which is what mentors seem to become.... So, you know, it was this positive and negative, asymmetrical relationship, I didn't feel like I wanted. I don't know for myself how healthy mentoring is at all. (male apprentice 2)

"My way or the highway"

The status of one's self-esteem was often contrasted with the demanding authority and discipline of a mentor who insisted that things be done *his* way (and most often, but not every time, participants used the male pronoun). More men than women talked about this specific experience in great detail, yet not all participants saw this authority as negative. One male mentor saw such authority as a distinction between "the relationship of your knowledge to your teacher's knowledge. One doesn't challenge one's master."

In allowing that there might have been positive aspects to the authority of the mentor, an older female apprentice speaks to the relationship as a kind of contract:

I do believe that the learner has to believe to some degree that the teacher is in a position to impart information in a way that inspires confidence, in a

> *way that is professional, that is, I want to say authoritative, and by that I don't mean that the teacher has to hold a hand over the disciple. I don't mean something where there's superiority/inferiority or anything like that. I think it's really a kind of contract relationship, where each party agrees that they're going to do certain things. (female apprentice 7)*

A different male mentor laments that the performance majors still had little choice as to whether they would participate in the authoritarian mentor model:

> *Especially within the performance world, this master relationship, I think is very strict.... I think for any of them to deviate from the path once they get here would be very difficult. They have to be followers and they have to go with that teacher.* (male mentor 5)

A younger male mentor is distraught over the prevalence of the disciplinarian mentor in music education:

> *All we do is criticize and demand and ... cajole and shape and, and so on, excellence, and make them the best musicians we possibly can—regardless of the cost to the person. And if they fail, well, "out!" ... And that tension between demanding excellence and not demanding more than is ethically responsible is hard ... to find where that point is.* (male mentor 3)

Conducting

Conducting apprenticeships were most frequently mentioned by students as the sub-discipline within music where they were most likely to experience a loss of self, where it became necessary to please the mentor in order to succeed. Applied performance was mentioned second most frequently. Male students were likely to express some identification with the conducting professor—in only one case was the conducting professor female. All the participants identified the conductor as the locus of musical power.

> *... The conductor controlling the orchestra, the composer controlling the conductor. That's [the] top to ... bottom model for industrial society. Master/teacher, it's definitely top/bottom.... Well, women don't get to be conductors, even today.* (male mentor 1)

An older male apprentice who is concerned with becoming the kind of conductor who can mentor young musicians in a respectful way observes differences between the "Viennese School" discipline demanded by the older male conductor and the more mutual mentoring demonstrated by the woman conductor.

> *... There's a male conductor who is, I think, 70, and has a long tradition of choral music in this particular city. The woman conductor is well known as a professional, has a high degree of academic accomplishments and so on, but fosters a more, in my opinion, mentorship approach. One of the differences I perceive is I think the kids fear the man. And I think sometimes that that fear is misinterpreted as respect.* (male apprentice 3)

Women apprentices often expressed anger at dealing with the conductor's demands.

> *There's a particular conductor in this city—who shall remain unnamed— who is known for ruining several flutists' lives on the East coast ... people that won't even touch their instruments, professional players will not touch their instruments!* (female apprentice 3)

A male apprentice, while displeased with the conductor's demands, had an entirely different response:

> *I've worked with a few conductors over the years and a few music people who've had very set determined ways where there's no giving. And in all honesty, if I've had the choice to be there or not, I just don't. I take the highway. If it's their way or the highway, I cruise.* (male apprentice 1)

Sexuality and harassment

The most controversial power issue revealed through these interviews had to do with sexuality within a mentor/apprentice relationship. According to the women participants, sexuality issues seem to be more prevalent in the music field because of the personal nature of music studies, the personal identity constructed through performing, and the private side of music instruction where many sessions take place behind closed doors. Women spoke bluntly.

...When I started teaching ... I used to have this saying, and I was still really mad. I was really angry that if you were a promising young man ... you find a mentor. And if you are a young woman you get literally fucked.... (female mentor 3)

Inappropriate sexuality is still a concern of graduate students today. The concerns around the issue of intimidation are not unlike those identified by Boyle and Auster and the sexual involvement as reported by Fitzgerald *et al.* Further, the women participants in this research expressed views coinciding with the women in Bowman *et al.*, who were more likely to rate such activities as unethical.

All the male participants demonstrated concern to deal with potential sexuality/harassment situations appropriately. As mentors, they make sure they keep their office doors open during consultations, they present themselves properly to all their students, not to be seen as one who would even inadvertently misuse his position, and remain aware of appropriate routes to assist students.

These concerns parallel the difficulties surrounding norms regarding cross-gender relationships, reliance on inappropriate power bases (Noe), sexual concerns and intimacy (Ragins and McFarlin; Kram), including the perception of a sexual relationship even though one may not exist. For several male graduate students the issues are also significant in terms of the impact a male professor/female graduate student relationship has on other students, as well as what such a relationship says about masculinity. One male graduate student identifies sexuality issues as one of the reasons he did not want to have a mentor.

Maybe another reason that I haven't had mentors, as such, is that I've always been on the fringes one way or another, although in a very privileged kind of way but, you know, on the fringes. It's often been women who have been into the same kinds of things that I'm interested in. I suppose that there's ... would be very much a less common thing for a young man to have a woman as a mentor. And then there's the other thing of the situations where a woman is with a male mentor. It either has turned into a sexual thing or ... that energy is always there. You know, there's all this, "Are they or are they not sleeping together?" kind of thing. And the assumption that they're thinking about it, like nothing but doing it, but that it's always an issue. In terms of male/male mentor, it's probably one of the reasons, again, I've pulled away from it, that whole homoerotic kind of overtone. (male apprentice 2)

The place of sexual orientation within the mentor/apprentice relationship has not been discussed in any previous research located. Accordingly, the presumed sexual orientation in the research appears to be heterosexual. Adding homoeroticsm to the issues does complicate the picture, but a homosexual orientation increases that complication for both mentor and apprentice even more, as this mentor explains.

… I don't say, "Keep your problems to yourself. I don't want to hear about them." I want them to get it out and go find somebody to listen to them.… Now I think, also, perhaps for some of us it's a little bit more difficult. Being a gay man I don't, I'm very cautious that I don't want people to think, including the student himself—if it's a male student—that the interest that I have in him is a sexual one. (male mentor 4)

Institutional hierarchy

The structure of the academic institution itself presents difficulties in relation to equitable mentoring. One male mentor echoes the concerns expres-sed by Redmond in terms of mentoring occurring between those who feel com-fortable with each other because they are similar. His thoughts relate to Auster's observations that sex and race may affect the mentor relationship dynamics:

I think that certain of the male students have it pretty easy.… These people are mentored, and really mentored in a sort of, looked after way and gotten through, in some cases by hook or crook … nearly always white, practically all our students are anyway so it doesn't mean anything, but they have a look, you know, sort of clean cut, if they weren't playing the trumpet they'd be on the football team. (male mentor 6)

Women mentors express different concerns regarding institutional hier-archies, noting the intimidation and negative behavior cited by Boyle as effects on women of prevalent attitudes.

I think the women that are in [positions of power] now—to the extent that they are—are basically women who are injured, who are unable to operate in a way that they would have liked.... (female mentor 5)

A male mentor summarizes all the hierarchy issues with the single comment, "Obviously the power is within the university; the power is with the professor, generally."

Motivator or coach

In general, when participants were describing positive mentor relationships, rather than the model predicated on the old mentor/apprentice, they described an empowering, more egalitarian relationship in which the mentor functioned as motivator, facilitator, or coach (at least one of these three words appearing in almost every interview). Apprentices in Prather's study of instrumental music educators also preferred to describe their mentor as a coach. Some of the participants' descriptions were based on positive experiences and wanting to re-create such experiences with their own students; others were based on negative experiences and fantasies of what would be an ideal mentor. "... The mentor's relationship, perhaps, starts off as a direct questioner and begins to teach a student how to ask those questions and then suggesting, so that the mentor is becoming more of a coach, more of a guide" (male apprentice 3).

A female apprentice sees the positive mentor-as-coach experience as, "moving on a more professional level at that point." A male mentor remembers his apprentice experience with a coaching mentor as follows:

The fact that he would show me how to do it and then I would try and then we would be able to talk about it—what worked and what didn't work. I think coaching in the sense of specifically assigning tasks to me and then watching it and then debriefing after. It was certainly beyond what he need have done; it wasn't assigned.... (male mentor 3)

Both male and female participants resisted the old concept of apprentice as disciple to the mentor, paralleling the definition by one of Stroud's conductors who named the conflict between the mentor as guide and the mentor who demanded a disciple. Mentors in this research take the word "mentor'" and redefine it in a new paradigm:

the motivator, the person who, who'd like to see people go, you know, inspire them and enthuse them, motivate them.... My teaching style is not one where I would make them be something in the sense of "you need to do it the way I do it." I think that's the sort of approach I associate with mentoring. (male mentor 3)

This female mentor describes the mentoring model she has developed out of a cathartic response to one very damaging "non-mentor" in her history and one very stimulating mentor:

This is the model that I learned from my mentor. And I think this is a woman's way of knowing.... A very positive model of the idea of inducting into a practice. I think the most positive thing about a mentorship is being validated in the sense that you see somebody doing what you want to be able to do, what you know, what you think is right, and you see what you think is important, what is right, what is valid being done. And so you know that at some level A) that it's being achieved and B) that it's possible to achieve it yourself because you actually have the opportunity to have that model in your mind's eye. (female mentor 5)

Some discard the word completely and look to different ways of teaching students wherein they hope to promote both artistry and equity.

... "mentor" makes me squirm a bit, I think, because of the connotations of what that means. It seems to me that my role is to enable people to find their strongest way of doing whatever they are doing. And that's a very difficult role. For instance, that often will mean, with a conventional female student, that they have bought into all of the stereotypes of gender, and there's got to be a very sort of gentle consciousness raising with them, or else they'll just turn off from you completely, in my view, and be satisfied with this kind of straight jacket.... So you've got somehow to gently make them aware of where their attitudes come from, where their aspirations are. Then if they choose to hang on to some of them, at least that's conscious. They're then doing that out of strength and out of power. That's the only thing that interests me.... (female mentor 1)

These alternatives include facets of the ten valuable supervisory practices identified by Holdaway *et al.*; however, two further suggestions are more imaginative and could lead to very different models for graduate music education.

It's popular now to say mentoring is important, and there are ways in which it is, but at least as important is people having their own power in their own realm which is why I see the chamber music thing, and when I say chamber music I mean without a coach! I mean a group of four people or ten people working together without the boss. (female mentor 4)

I can't stand the sort of "training only superstars" that goes on in our education system, the conservatory model. And I guess one of my big things, the biggest thing that drives my teaching is respecting different personalities, traditions, and learning styles. It's the thing that motivates me as a teacher and it is so hard. And we have absolutely no idea, in society with all the talk through the years of postmodernism and feminism, we still have not admitted how hard it is to respect difference. I think that's the huge challenge of teaching. (female mentor 1)

Conclusions and implications

The mentors and apprentices in music who participated in this research have a variety of experiences with the mentor/apprentice model of pedagogy in graduate music education. There are positive, negative, and indifferent experiences. While this paper presents only a snapshot of the interviews (which, also, are only a snapshot of the participants' experiences), the results can be grouped into conclusions about age and experience, alternatives to mentoring, and the role of gender.

Age and experience emerge as rather consistent patterns in the mentor/ apprentice relationships described here. This conclusion parallels Auster who suggests that age as well as sex and race may affect the dynamics of the mentorship. Among the younger women apprentices all indicated more identity involvement, a sense of being chosen, a certain awe of her mentor in relation to self-esteem. The older female graduate students acknowledge caution and care in choosing a mentor; indicating specific requirements for a mentorship due to insight gained from earlier experiences with a mentor. The performing musicians have a very strong sense of self evident throughout these interviews. While their identities are most strongly tied to the idea "musician," they seem to negotiate a more fluid movement among the subject of music, their mentor, their work in the field, and their musician identity. All the male participants appear to occupy this position of strong self and musician concept, whether or not they were performers. Among both males and females, the mentor participants, but especially the older ones, sustained more conflicts about the nature, purpose, and benefits of the mentor/apprentice relationship.

The overall discomfort of all female participants with the term mentor and the interest of several of the men in the motivator/coach model, implies alternatives to mentoring might be explored. One of the male apprentices imagines an anarchist approach where there are no mentors; however, he acknowledges that such a model would do nothing to change current institutional structures. Several of the women apprentices suggested a kind of mentoring based in feminist principles that respect individuals and understand the potential for power to corrupt or disrupt a teacher/student relationship. Kram and Kram and Isabella suggest a model of peer mentoring which seems to me to be similar to the reforms to music coaching suggested by some male and female participants.

It was not a secret to the participants that I was particularly curious about gender in this pedagogy. In general the younger graduate students, both male and female, did not see gender as having a particular effect on their experience; however, as the interviews continued, situations where gender politics came into play were acknowledged. For example, two young women were very pleased to have a female mentor who is prominent in their field. One woman noted that her male mentor may not have given her as much attention as he did his male apprentices. Among the women, the mentors and doctoral-level apprentices all acknowledged the role of gender politics in their experience of music pedagogy in some way, often in great detail and frequently noting a detrimental effect. At least six female apprentices commented on sexuality as a tool of the mentor's power, in their own experience. One gay man recalled a similar negative experience when he was an apprentice. Two heterosexual men mentioned concerns in relation to sexual orientation in connection with a mentor. Others, both male and female, were aware of situations where questions of sexuality or harassment affected mentoring relationships. Since many studies mention the impact of gender and/or sexuality (Ragins and McFarlin; Noe; Kram; Matczynski and Comer; Boyle; Auster; Bowman, *et al.*; Fitzgerald, *et al.*), it seems these issues must be considered, studied further, and solutions provided prior to adopting mentoring as a formal means for improving equity in graduate education. It seems to me that the salience of gender and sexuality, even where participants would rather see equality, parallels the experiences of women musicians with gender in Kimberlin's study, while Kram's cross-gender mentor research provides a point of departure, especially for analyzing the mapping of heterosexuality within the mentorship model.

If we acknowledge the roles of class, race/ethnicity, sexuality, and gender in past and current practices of the mentor/apprentice model of professional music education, then we might be able to learn from the hundreds-year-old mentoring tradition in music, in order to avoid a similar model for other areas of higher education. The complex and varied responses by participants in this research reinforce Redmond's point that a successful program to address social injustice in the university setting, with goals and a structure that includes training for all involved, would require faculty, student, and institutional commitment. We could then work with the complexities to enhance what is beneficial and challenge those limiting aspects of the political structures of our academic institutions in order to ensure that the pedagogical focus may move towards empowerment and peer models of learning.

This research received funding from the Social Science and Humanities Research Council of Canada

[1]See directories of the College Music Society and the Canadian University Music Society.

[2]See Walker for one description of past mentoring practice in music. See Tait for a description of current characteristics of "good" pedagogy. Kingsbury analyses pedagogical practices in his controversial case study of a prestigious conservatory. Nettl examines university music schools.

[3]These numbers add to greater than 100 percent and/or the total participants because participants often were involved in two sub-disciplines of music.

References

Abney, R. "The Effects of Role Models and Mentors on Career Patterns of Black Women Coaches and Athletic Administrators in Historically Black and Historically White Institutions of Higher Education." Diss. University of Iowa, 1988. *Dissertation Abstracts International* 49 (1989): 3210.

Auster, Donald. "Mentors and Proteges: Power-Dependent Dyads." *Sociological-Inquiry* 54.2 (1984): 142–153.

Baker, K. M. "Significant Experiences, Influences and Relationships in the Educational and Professional Development of Three Music Educators: Gretchen Hieronymus Beall, Eunice Louise Boardman, and Mary Henderson Palmer (Educational Development, Beall Bretchen

Hieronymus, Boardman Eunice Louise, Palmer Mary Henderson)." Diss. University of Illinois at Urbana-Champaign, 1992. *Dissertation Abstracts International* 53 (1993): 3466.

Bowman, Vicki E., Lesa D. Hatley, and Robert L. Bowman. "Faculty-Student Relationships: The Dual Role Controversy." *Counselor-Education-and-Supervision* 34.3 (1995): 232–242.

Boyle, T. P. "A Naturalistic Examination of Influential Variables, Especially Faculty Mentoring and Modeling, Affecting University Attrition (Tinto)." Diss. Brigham Young University 1988. *Dissertation Abstracts International* 50 (1989): 82.

Chao, G. T. "A Comparison of Informal Mentoring Relationships and Formal Mentorship Programs." ERIC Microfiche No. ED 333 784. 1991.

Chew, C. V. "A Case Study of the Characteristics and Functions of Female Mentor Relationships (Mentoring)." Diss. Virginia Polytechnic Institute and State University 1991. *Dissertation Abstracts International 52* (1992): 2367.

Clemens, J. B. B. "The Influence of Mentors on Career Development of Women in Educational Administration in Leon County." Diss. Florida State University, 1989. *Dissertation Abstracts International* 51 (1990): 353.

Collins, Pauline. "The Interpersonal Vicissitudes of Mentorship: An Exploratory Study of the Field Supervisor-Student Relationship." *Clinical-Supervisor* 11.1 (1993): 121–135.

Cooper, D. L. "Case Studies of Mentors and Gifted High School Students: The Role of the Relationship in Academic and Emotional Success." Diss. Mississippi State University, 1991. *Dissertation Abstracts International* 53 (1993): 2245.

Crawford, S. H. "Perceptions About Workplace Factors that Affect Professional Growth of Female Faculty in Traditional and Nontraditional Disciplines." Diss. Bowling Green State University, 1987. *Dissertation Abstracts International* 48 (1988): 2770.

Duncan, S. "Vienna Philharmonic to Admit Women" *Orange County Register* [California] 28 Feb. 1997 Distributed by Monique Buzzarte on "Zap the VPO" at http://www.dorsai.org/~buzzarte/zapvpo.html.

Eldridge, N. S. "Mentoring from a Self-In-Relation Perspective." ERIC Microfiche No. ED 350 494. 1990.

Eubank, R. K. "The Effects of Same-Gender and Cross-Gender Mentoring on Personal Development, Career Advancement, and Job Satisfaction of Female Administrators in Higher Education." Diss. University of South

Dakota, 1987. *Dissertation Abstracts International* 49 (1988): 670.

Fitzgerald, Louise F., Lauren M. Weitzman, Yael Gold, and Mimi Ormerod. "Academic Harassment: Sex and Denial in Scholarly Garb." *Psychology-of-Women-Quarterly* 12.3 (1988): 329–340.

Fleming, K. A. "Mentoring. Is It the Key to Opening Doors for Women in Educational Administration?" *Education Canada* 31.3 (1991): 27–33.

Gaskill, L. R. "Same-Sex and Cross-Sex Mentoring of Female Proteges: A Comparative Analysis." *Career Development Quarterly* 40.1 (1991): 48–63.

Glaser, B.G., and A. Srauss. *The Discovery of Grounded Theory: Strategies for Qualitatieve Research.* Chicago: Aldine Press, 1967.

Gould, E. "Gender–Specific Occupational Role Models: Implications for Music Educators" *Update* 11.1 (1992): 8–12.

Hamann, Donald L. and Linda Miller Walker. "Music Teachers as Role Models for African-American Students." *Journal of Research in Music Education* 41 (4) (Winter 1993): 303-314.

Hatch, D.G. "An Examination of the Piano Teaching Skills of Master Teacher, Joanne Baker." Diss. University of Missouri—Kansas City, 1987. *Dissertation Abstracts International* 48 (1988): 2270.

Heywood, W. M. "Mentoring: Midlife Resolution for the Male Fine Artist." Diss. The Fielding Institute, 1988. *Dissertation Abstracts International* 50 (1989): 1133.

Holdaway, E., C. Deblois, and I. Winchester. "Supervision of Graduate Students." *Canadian Journal of Higher Education* 25.3 (1995): 1–29.

Infante, R. A. "Gender and the Mentoring Process: Comparison of Men Who Choose Male or Female Mentors (Male Mentors)." Diss. University of Texas at Austin, 1989. *Dissertation Abstracts International* 51 (1990): 972.

Kahn, S. R. "Male Graduate Students' Evaluations of Their Dissertation Advisory Relationships: A Comparison of Same-Sex Versus Cross-Sex Mentoring Experiences." Diss. City University of New York, 1990. *Dissertation Abstracts International* 51 (1990): 3174.

Kimberlin, C. T. "'And Are You Pretty?': Choice, Perception and Reality in Pursuit of Happiness." *Music, Gender and Culture.* Eds. M. Herndon and S. Ziegler. Wilhelmshaven: Florian Noetzal Verlag, 1990. 221–239.

Kingsbury, H. *Music, Talent, and Performance: A Conservatory Cultural System.* Philadelphia: Temple University Press, 1988.

Kirby, S., and K. McKenna K. *Experience, Research, Social Change: Methods From the Margins.* Toronto: Garamond, 1989.

Kram, K. E., and L. A. Isabella. "Mentoring Alternatives: The Role of Peer

Relationships In Career Development." *Academy of Management Journal* 28 (1985): 110–132.

Kram, K. E. *Mentoring at Work*. Lanham, MD: University Press of America, 1988.

LaCroix, M. L. "Relations Among Gender, Years of Experience, and Preferred Mentoring Functions of High School Assistant Principals." Diss. University of Massachusetts, 1992. *Dissertation Abstracts International* 53 (1992): 1748.

Lemberger, D. "The Mantle of a Mentor: The Mentor's Perspective." ERIC Microfiche No. ED 346 088. 1992.

Lewis, C. L. "Mentors and Mothers of Successful Women." Diss. The Wright Institute, 1991. *Dissertation Abstracts International* 52 (1991): 2283.

Matczynski, T. J., and K. C. Comer. "Mentoring Women and Minorities in Higher Education: An Anecdotal Record." ERIC Microfiche No. ED 331 376. 1991.

McGaha, B. J. "An Exploratory Analysis of Factors Associated With Underrepresentation of Women as High School Principals in South California." Diss. University of South Carolina, 1992. *Dissertation Abstracts International* 53 (1992): 1010.

McShane, A. M. "Perceived Affective and Behavioral Characteristics of Mother–Daughter Relationships and Subsequent Mentoring Relationships (Affective Characteristics)." Diss. Utah State University, 1990. *Dissertation Abstracts International* 51 (1990): 437.

Metcalfe, H. E. "The Impact of Mentoring on the Educational and Occupational Aspirations of Female Elementary School Students." Thesis, University of Windsor. 1989. *Masters Abstracts International* 30 (1992): 436.

Noe, R. A. "Women and Mentoring: A Review and Research Agenda." *Academy of Management Review* 13 (1988): 65–78.

Nettl, B. "American Midwestern Music Schools of Music as Venues of Musical Mediation and Confrontation." *Music-Cultures in Contact: Convergences and Collisions*. Eds. M. J. Kartomi and S. Blum. Basel, Switzerland: Gordon and Breach, 1994. 169–185.

Papalewis, R. "Preparing School Administrators for the Culturally And Linguistically Diverse. A Formal Mentor Training Program in Progress." ERIC Microfiche No. ED 333 094. 1991.

Prather, B. W. "Are There Identifiable Patterns of Personal and Professional Mentoring Relationships Between Instrumental Music Educators." Diss. University of Arkansas, 1993.

Ragins, B. R., and D. B. McFarlin. "Perceptions of Mentor Roles in Cross-Gender Mentoring Relationships." *Journal of Vocational Behavior* 37.3 (1990): 321–339.

Redmond, S. J. "Mentoring and Cultural Diversity in Academic Settings." *American Behavioral Scientist* 34.2 (1990): 188–200.

Robinson, R. W. J. "Through Their Eyes: Reflections of Pennsylvania Female School Administrators Regarding Career Paths, Mentoring and External Barriers." Diss. Temple University, 1991. *Dissertation Abstracts International* 52 (1992): 2357.

Schneider, A. M. "Mentoring Women and Minorities into Positions of Educational Leadership: Gender Differences and Implications for Mentoring." ERIC Microfiche No. ED 344 843. 1991.

Shuster, S. "Mentor Relationships of Women in the Visual Arts." Diss. California School of Professional Psychology—Berkeley/Alameda, 1989. *Dissertation Abstracts International* 50 (1990): 4236.

Specht, J. S. "A Qualitative Investigation of Eighteen Mentor/Protegé Relationships: Factors Affecting Career Development of Women in New Jersey Public Education." Diss. Seton Hall University, School of Education, 1989. *Dissertation Abstracts International* 50 (1989): 1171.

Stroud, S. L. "An Examination of Five Active University Band Directors Selected as Exemplary Conductors (Mentorship)." Diss. University of Illinois at Urbana—Champaign, 1991. *Dissertation Abstracts International* 52 (1992): 2456.

Tait, M. J. "Teaching Strategies and Styles." *Handbook of Research on Music Teaching and Learning.* Ed. R. Colwell. New York: Schirmer, 1992. 525–534.

Walker, R. *Musical Beliefs: Psychoacoustic, Mythical and Educational Perspectives.* New York: Teachers College Press, 1990.

Wilson, S. A. "The Effect of Race and Gender on the Formation of Mentoring Relationships for Black Professional Women." Diss. Case Western Reserve University, 1992. *Dissertation Abstracts International* 53 (1992): 557.

Woodlee, B. W. "Factors Relating to Retention of Women as Presidents in Higher Education Leadership (Women Administrators, College Presidents)." Diss. Peabody College for Teachers of Vanderbilt University, 1992. *Dissertation Abstracts International* 53 (1992): 1377.

Wright, K. S. "From the Odyssey to the University: What is This Thing Called Mentoring?" *ACA Bulletin* 79 (1992): 45–53.

Be like who?
On Race, Role Models and Difference in Higher Education

Warren Crichlow

One person's desire can bring a role model into being. In this respect, the process of taking and making role models is like falling in love.
(Fisher 1988: 220)

We were in love at first sight.
(Als 1996: 122)

In the wake of persistent demands for social justice and equality, the term "role model" has become ubiquitous within North American university affairs. Glib responses to equity such as the institutionalization of cultural diversity programs, affirmative action, and multicultural curricula have produced a narrow educational prescription for real or imagined role models. While critical academic theorizing has challenged the essential unity of race, class, and gender, bureaucratic equity achievement in the university tacitly requires "positive images" of success within these same "naturally" binding categories. Despite recognition that identities are partial and contradictory, "role models" are politically constituted along racial, gender, and other socially and historically constructed lines of difference. In this context, role model positions function as idealized identity boxes where ascribed characteristics become literally employable. Blacks, gays, women, physically challenged persons and so on are positioned (or im-position themselves) as representatives of success. They doubly serve as fixed images of achievement and pedagogues of "academic" (or conversely ideologues of "politically correct") socialization. Here the institutional "role" function and the primacy of physical or imagined identity attributes of individuals are artificially fused. The role model thus performs an officially designated expectation which takes on a pedagogical life of its own.[1]

In performing the authorized role, however, the "model" can come perilously close to losing his or her sense of identity and individuality. That is, both are subject to displacement by irresistible illusions of institutional power, authority, legitimacy, and job mobility. Vested with normative institutional identifications, expectations of "role" conformity consequently structure university and classroom protocol in forced and often alienating ways. The results are usually disastrous for the process of teaching and learning, both for the subjected student and the person who carries the burden of *perfect* model expectation.

This conundrum which invariably attends role modelling in the university—in curriculum, administration, teaching, advising, and supervision—lies with the cynical illusion that primary lines of difference determine, as Mary Helen Washington notes, who can have something in common with whom: that diversity "is like having so many crayons in your crayon box ... their colour is their identity, their substance, their uniqueness" (228). Within this dubious economy of likeness, students are blithely provided role models whom they resemble or with whom they are assumed to intrinsically share a collective interest and will therefore automatically "be-like."

Fortunately, this simplistic "be-like" scenario is more complicated than first meets the eye. On one hand, the institutionalized nature of role models cannot ensure identifications rigidly along lines of race, sex, or any other presumption of essentialized difference. The premise of automatic comformity to legitimated role models is also countered by extant forms of dissent and resistance observed in the classroom and in the everyday environment. On the other hand, the restricted availability of models of behaviour accepted within the narrowly construed narrative of university culture represses possibilities for open-ended communication and fluid identifications that are essential to realizing more substantive academic goals of intellectual exchange and knowledge production.[2]

Rescuing role modelling from cliche and narrow preconceptions requires a more complex awareness of its machinations. Role model processes involve, of course, interrelationality and intersubjectivity. How such relations are made and unmade, however, derive from both conscious and unconscious motivations and life choices. In this view, even the willing role model is not in charge! These processes are not fixed or natural in any strict consensual sense, as a "role model" is not a person who simply models or impersonates an abstract role.[3] Rather, a role model is a person chosen and created by another, an unpredictable attachment which emerges from spoken and unspoken forms of fantasy, pleasure, and desire. The non-linear processes of relationship formation endemic to role model choosing are open-ended and can arouse unexpected forms of identification and meaning. Contrary to the obligatory institutional mandate for linear identificatory or "become like" arrangements, role modelling is conceived here as a dynamic process which can foster the exercise of individual agency. Indeed, role model processes share in the vitality of everyday life. That is, the social striving for productive self-fashioning is integral to multifarious forms of problem solving, creative endeavours and cultural resistance struggles. Rather than restricting agency, the conflict and change embodied in role model relationships should ideally open individuals to the possibilities of the unimagined.

The role model process I posit is one that escapes normative university categorization. To more fully approximate this departure, I turn to the two juxtaposed epigraphs which began this text. Read together, they indicate the possible complexity of role model relationships, constituted both formally and informally. The first quote is from feminist scholar Bernice Fisher. In "Wandering in the Wilderness: The Search for Women Role Models," Fisher (1998) explores her considered ambivalence toward idealistic enthusiasm among liberal feminist professionals for role models: "if women merely follow the lead of so-called role models, we all, everyone of us, can succeed." Eschewing these reductive, celebratory prescriptions for university models, she meditates instead on the multiplicity of "meanings of role models as personal heroes" (212).[4] Fisher's analysis is striking because she intently embraces the slippery contradictions of model making and model taking to open consideration to more complicated yearnings that bring individuals together despite social realities of difference and conflict. For Fisher, taking and making role models is akin to the process of falling in love. Role model relationships entail feelings of longing which, she contends, "come from … not only what has not been given but also for what can be—the kind of passions we need to carry us over into the future, to the realization of vaguely perceived ideals" (Fisher 1988, 220; see also Fisher 1980, 1981).

The second quote, from writer Hilton Als's recent collection of memoirist essays, *The Women*, emphatically underscores the importance of Fisher's analysis: that desire can bring another into being as a role model. His first-person account implicitly interrelates the fraught and fragile nature of falling in love with the workings of private, unpredictable desires. He endeavours to show that choosing, loving, criticizing, and ultimately "moving on" from a role model is a significant, though painful, process of self-discovery. To explore the contradictory truths love-role model relationships reveal, Als deploys the caustic trope "Negress"—a metaphor for the price paid for living life in an intolerable condition of puritanical self-sacrifice and self-denigration. Through-out his slim study, Als insistently offers a critical reading of the consequence of modeling roles that disable individuality (Lee 7); relational situations that, as Barbara Houston puts it, "prevent other more useful identifications" (155). In Als's hands, retrospective portraiture serves as a critical device for unpacking the stultifying and tragic ways role models become trapped and often trap themselves in a role performance that empties the self.

Each of the role models on whom Als meditates serves to reveal moments of both significance and dread, passion and commitment, desire and betrayal (of self and other) in the struggle against conformity to externally-defined expectations of behaviour. He reflects forthrightly to define his voice as a writer and as an individual. Als writes, in fact, to remember joys and tragic despairs in the lives of three role models. He writes also to expunge the self-imposed limits each lived so self-destructively. Working through vulnerabilities of self-other disclosure, Als provocatively models what he has learned from the implication of loss in each of their lives and, in turn, what these role models collectively contributed to his intellectual formation. At the same time, Als's melancholic defense of his individuality must be understood as a performance of both his deep connection to and autonomy from these models. He is eager to demonstrate how he, in fact, resolved their contradictions in his own life. Central to Als's project is a personal (is political) act of writing beyond reflexive politics of socially-circumscribed identity.

It is not insignificant that Als's depictions render role models who are enigmatic, difficult, and lamentable but who nevertheless remain complexly influential through the instabilities and tragic contradictions of their identities. Contrary to the popular "simple version" of the role model idea (Britzman 25–42), a desire for a perfect example of who, how, and what to become like, I recognize in Als's portraits a mutable view of the role model process. This perspective takes seriously the workings of passion, identification, and love as vital categories through which to understand the ways role models are com-plexly taken and made in and outside the university.

Indeed, the overlap between Als and Fisher confirm the contravening notion that role model relations do not work simply through mimesis: "the process of model making approaches copying or imitation ... [but never] exactly" (Fisher 219). Fisher's critical analysis identifies celebratory role model discourses as forked because the real conditions that have produced these relationships are elided. Role model discourse works well because it obscures a context of inequality that refuses to change: "Capitalist and patriarchal structures prevent us all from succeeding, no matter how many role models or heroes we acquire. Success cannot be attained by everyone: it depends on access to social, economic and political resources" (212). Fisher's blunt critique of role modelling as mimesis has its parallel in analyses of difference in colonial discourse illuminated by Homi K. Bhabha. The concept of mimicry in colonial discourse, like role model mimesis, operates as a strategic compromise. Both occupy an unstable place between what Bhabha (addressing limitations in Said's analysis of "orientalism") describes as "the demand for identity, stasis ... and the counter pressure of ... change, difference" (86). Mimicry in this sense works through tensions of ambivalence. I suggest that mimesis in role modelling also works through ambivalence. Here role modelling can be understood as an illusionary vehicle of reform and equity: there is the appearance of levelling the playing field, but only through the production of a "recognizable Other, *as a subject of difference that is almost the same but not quite.*" To quote Bhabha at length, mimicry "is constructed around ambivalence; in order to be effective, [it] must continually produce its slippage, its excess, its difference ... an indeterminacy ... the representation of difference that is itself a process of disavowal ... a complex strategy of reform, regulation and discipline, which appropriates the other as it visualizes power" (86). I will not pursue the implications of this line of thought here. Rather, I suggest it as a critical method for further examination not only of how conventional role model discourse helps to sustain inequity, but also how its limitations may reveal subversive possibilities in role model relationships.

As Fisher points out, role models can neither provide "neat, uncontradictory selves [nor guarantee] a nonproblematic relation to the world." The specifically untidy processes of discovery engendered by role model relationships reveal serviceable yet "unpalatable and contradictory truths about the world and ourselves" (Fisher 227, 228). Before returning to Fisher's useful reconsideration of models and heroes, I will probe Hilton Als's account of his first encounter and subsequent friendship with the poet, novelist, dramatist, and professor Owen Dodson.[6]

In the third and final essay of his collection, Als reflects on the strong residual effect Dodson had on his earlier life. Through both intellectual history and literary criticism, he pensively maps the constructed and highly contested nature of a role model relationship. The contentious contradictions at play in Als's melancholic portrait of Dodson indicate the imprecise character of the term "role model." He demonstrates how extraordinary role model relationships result from complex, difficult, and uncertain experiences rather than the standardized, linear, and predictable emulations assumed in the university press to service diversity, affirmative action, and multiculturalism.

Als and Dodson first met in 1974 in Dodson's Brooklyn home, not in a customary site of higher learning. Thirteen-year-old Als was under the tutelage of a long-time woman friend of Dodson's. The woman taught poetry and piano to "gifted" initiates who were either self-interested or had parents like Als's mother who, with upward mobility in mind, deemed exposure to extracurricular arts important.

Als recalls that he received a scholarship to study with this teacher. But instead of learning poetry, Als remembers that he studied the teacher's dishevelment, her "intractable bewilderment." It was a bewilderment that, Als thinks, was as much about her ruffled life as it was about "young people like myself, whose ambition would consume what she had to offer and carry them on to the next person they would need to consume in order to become something other than themselves" (Als 121–122). Recognizing that Als's ambition required something greater than she could impart, the teacher sent him on to that next person, her friend Owen Dodson.

Als does not use the term "role model" to describe the formative yet ultimately failed intellectual and sexual liaison he claims to have shared as an adolescent with the older man for six years.[7] In fact, he curiously states that Dodson was neither a "father" figure nor was his literary work "an immense liberation for me."[8] The Dodson that emerges from Als's cool, irreverent, and unsentimental analysis is a rather impulsive nurturer and a pedantic teacher who nevertheless "made the world less common through exposing people to many things they had never known before" (139). Als says that Dodson made it possible for him to come close to a "curiously shaped" world of literary personalities, gossip, and history of the Harlem Renaissance at a time when "I had just begun to be confused by my attraction to reflection (writing) and to being social" (122). With Dodson as a conduit, Als temporarily moved beyond the thrall of his mother and sisters: he traversed further into parts of the world and himself that he had only begun to imagine possible.

Making the strange approachable and the familiar again difficult is perhaps the more common adage for what transpired between them. Providing access to a larger world of idiosyncratic people and ideas is the implicit task a role model performs in relation to the inchoate desires of an inquisitive and ambitious student. The afternoon Als first encountered Dodson was marked by immediate recognition and identification. Each immediately recognized in the other flirtatious skills in dissemblance, the ability to mask and falsely charm. Talk of books and looking at old photographs, finding shared resemblances, discovering cross-cutting interests and curiosities combined to unleash fluid psychological needs and suppressed desires. Seduced and energized in a mutual pedagogical gaze, Als says he and Dodson fell in love. What fascinates is how Als's desire, like falling in love, brought Dodson into being as a role model.

The relationship eventually failed, eroded in fact by the very desire that initiated it: the passionate need to fulfill ambition and love. Als's ambition was to learn about literature and writing. He was intrigued by the marvelously close association Dodson's experience provided to that larger world of language and culture. Despite the admiration which initially mediated this relationship, the dangerous lesson learned by the ambitious student is how to think in ways perhaps unintended by his teacher. As Als states:

> our relationship was that of the pedant and his student consumed with ambition. What the pedant knows: his ambitious student will stop at nothing in order to learn to be himself...to become a self without the burden of the pedant's influence. (133–134)

Thinking leads Als to recognize the frailties of his mentor; that social pressures to conform had already moved Dodson "away from the expansive interior places writing could have taken him to" (127). In one sense, the linked life of the mind and writing that Als's ambition preciously sought outgrew what Dodson, in his senior years, was capable of giving. At age 19, Als left his aging teacher and lover in order to find the next person who would help him to accept his right to individual vision—a right whose ambitious possibilities he had only momentarily glimpsed in the chic literary world of Dodson's archaic memory. In another, more telling sense, Als confesses that he too betrayed the friendship (and his own vision) by succumbing to the terror of individuality he had so hoped to vacate: that place where kinship and fear "had the power to displace my love and confusion for men like Owen" (143).

Reading Hilton Als's essays foregrounds tensions that are often suppressed in role model arguments, especially those in higher education where the term role model typically refers to a rather contrived and often disingenuous sense of what constitutes relationships between students and faculty of the same race or gender (Allen). Although generated through reflexive literary means, Als's insights into the limits of the joined terms "role" and "model" illuminate knotty issues about race, gender, and difference that university-based discussions often evade. His reflections suggest questions generally held in abeyance by institutional quests for positive role models: roles filled by persons who are expected to both conform to and piously reflect social standards and conventions of success authored by the dominant group. Queries that challenge such idealized desires for model behavior and attendant assumptions of piety include: what roles are role models supposed to model? Are there fragilities that role models cannot *not* avoid modeling? What fascinations, desires, needs draw the young person, the student to take and make a role model? What aspects of the positive role model's narrative are important/unimportant to what the role model might mean for different students in changing times—and where and when do shifting aspects of biographical narrative produce the "negative role model?" (Austin 539–578). What do we covet, admire, and deny in the role model idea? And finally, can role models assure gender and race equity in the university?

In a variety of ways critics of the role model argument have commented on similar questions from fields as diverse as women's studies, critical legal studies, critical race theory, multicultural education, black studies, and queer studies (see also Dyson; Lopez; Morgan; Munoz; Richards). Though there are important theoretical and pedagogical differences among critical scholars, their common point of contestation clusters around the problematic nature of the positive role model idea. Writing at the intersection of multicultural education and gender, for example, Deborah Britzman argues that a desire for an idealized, stable, and positive role model displaces the contradictions and controversies which actually construct and set individual identity into perpetual motion and change. Britzman's analysis problematizes the assumption that the role model can serve as the guaranteed "transitional object" to unique gendered (or normatively "successful") identities. Given that role models are also fashioned through existing circuits of dominant-subordinant social relations, Britzman asks whether, in fact, "a copy can be unique?" (25). Her inquiry does not suggest that role models should not be offered in educational settings. Rather, she specifically pushes for an account of gender that understands its contextual particularities and for a radical conception of role modeling practices beyond normative frameworks of power and domination.[10]

As I have suggested above, neither gender, race, or other stable construc-tions of social difference can be the final arbiter in choosing a role model. While consciously chosen practices of oppositional "difference" are important and demand careful contextual consideration, I argue that conceptualizing radical role modeling requires an engagement with the more complex ways individuals achieve such relationships. Specifically, the larger question concerns the concious and unconscious search for role models and what this reveals about self-fashioning desire. I consider Hilton Als's portrait of Dodson as but one of the myriad instances in which role model relationships are experienced. Passion, identification, and love are vital to the creation of role models. And, as Als poignantly writes, role models can also be consumed by a creator's ambition. The need for role models is not simply about binding identificatory expectations. Rather, the powerfully felt desire to become "something more," albeit something only vaguely envisioned, is the dynamic factor that urges a person to go in search of what another might offer.

Bernice Fisher's explication of role models and heroes also foregrounds the individual's search for the adoption of another as a role model. Most significant is the individual's quest to forge a new life that markedly differs from the present: to redefine the self in a way that is (or will become) at odds with kin, community, or dominant modes of thought. Often there is no known prec-edent for the life one imagines (say, the dual inconceivability of a viable life as a gay man and writer as Als recalls in his immediate familial context). In fact, such a life, as mere fantasy, may constitute a threat to traditional sustaining social supports. Taking on a new life necessitates change—and tensions of change "rend" the self. Fisher argues that this process of "rending" of the self and the intricate social fabric in which we participate constitutes "the [mean-ingful] context for our quest for role models and heroes" (Fisher 1988, 217).

At issue is the transition from the present imagined self (lack and all), to the future self only vaguely perceived. For Fisher, this anxious search for role models—the creation of idealized persons—"is an attempt to find support, validation and guidance in changing historical circumstances" (217). In a volatile social context, Fisher observes, the inadequacies of selected role models may have less to do with individual imperfections than with the fact that "no authority figures can provide definitive answers or solutions to the problems that change poses" (217). Neither the individual nor corporate role model can impart definitive guidance; no one can guarantee a contradiction-free transi-tion to an imagined future. Crossing borderlands of change is indeed lonely work, as the destination is elusive and assurance that the immense struggle to arrive is worth *the price of the ticket* similarly escapes foreknowledge (Fisher 1988, 217–218).

Change in uncertain times manufactures powerful feelings of longing for guidance through the historical contradictions that mark everyday life. I think Fisher is correct in pointing out that "the people we find to help us in this struggle, and the models we [subsequently] make of them are not the same" (218). Role models, as Fisher puts it, can be anyone alive or dead whose voice (spoken or written) speaks "to ways of acting not yet [generally] embodied in our social realities" (Fisher 1988, 219–220). In this sense, then, the role model simultaneously arouses passion and helps to clarify a vision through an arduous transitional period. But as Als's account vividly demonstrates, the accumulation of deepening insights wrought by change brings about an attendant disappointment: the irreconcilable difference between the model's fragilities (as well as the sloppiness in our own life) and the idealized features that once made that model's life so compelling to follow. Perhaps the role relationship's end is that untenable moment of dissatisfaction when illusion painfully unravels. Als's portrait articulates both an unnerving will to move on and the awful cost of suppressing creative ambition.

Fisher is critical of feminists who unproblematically view the role model process as simply choosing "images of women who have survived and who therefore in some sense negate [historical and political] contradictions" (217). In order to formulate an alternative to this rigid "be-like" idealism she questions memories of her own encounters with role models and their larger-than-life representations. The valuable lessons Fisher draws from re-thinking her experiences serve to confirm that a radical conception of role modeling must be sought in the context of the commitments the relationship entails and the passions it expresses (Fisher 1988, 217, 225). Relatedly, Als's transgressive act of memoir interrogates the problematic of role modelling, particularly the debilitating costs individuality pays for modeling externally defined values. Als's "raced" Negress figures are destroyed by self-sacrifice. To exorcize this tragic inheritance, Als sifts through the ruins of his mentors' silenced lives. He finds salvation only in the public exhumation of their failures and, in so doing, surmounts socially-imposed limits antithetical to individual agency and artistic freedom.

Despite their distinct critical strategies, both Als and Fisher valorize passion and elements of individual choice that ideally should inform role model practices. Within the context of narrow norm-laden prescriptions that dominate hierarchical educational and political institutions, this commitment to the passionate and selective nature of role model making reasserts a radical respect for the various choices and desires individuals may express in forming these relationships. Of course, as Fisher reminds us, role model taking is "rarely, if ever, a solely individual or completely social matter.... [W]hat seems to be a deeply personal act takes place in a profoundly political environment" (Fisher 1988, 221). Inequality in material conditions and social justice within and across communities profoundly differentiate access to role models and other kinds of supportive social relationships. Clearly racism, sexism, and other exclusionary practices require redress through ongoing political struggle and collective action. In community and university contexts, however, where social and political demands for solidarity with a specific identity position are so pervasive, sustaining individuals' capacity to choose and shape their own political values is a necessary interventional measure for radical role model practices.

My reading of Fisher and Als suggests that role model relationships must be evaluated by their capacity to model practices of living and thinking beyond reflexive identity politics and ideological confines. Hilton Als finally rejected the style of literary celebration he felt Owen Dodson had eventually adopted. He did not, however, relinquish his own ambitions to engage the larger world of intellectual pursuits so dramatically opened by Dodson. I have utilized Als's reflections to extend the criteria of responsibility in role model relationships: the nurturance, sustenance, and extension of individuality. In this sense, then, the ethos of role model relationships is to "model" disciplined self-reflection that enables complex judgements and critical action independent of larger social pressures. I imagine that this commitment to the multiple ambitions, desires, and pleasures that inform agency can only be supported in those interpersonal spaces that consciously and cognitively resist coercive forms of authority and conformity which are all too pervasive in the politics of universities.

Can role models assure gender and race equity in the university on the edge of the millennium? My immediate response is a negative one, particularly if the goal of equity is dependent upon role models understood within the banal administrative discourses of cultural diversity, multiculturalism, and affirmative action. Inscribed in these institutional arguments for role models lie questionable premises of "race" and "gender." This produces an odd tension, given we can no longer believe (at least within some intellectual work on the complexities of identity categories) in consensual categories like race and gender. Under the rubric of institutional rhetorics, inequalities will be reproduced, modeled in a ghettoized matrix of endless difference and political identity.

Of course, this is dangerous territory. On the one hand, I agree with Anita L. Allen who correctly argues that raising critical questions about role models is not meant "to cripple activism" for equity—it is a given that this fight is ongoing. On the other, it is politically important to contest the assumption that "role model capacity" is specifically reducible to a race or gender determination (Allen 195). That is, the contribution a person can make as a role model is simply incommensurable with such socially constructed categories. Moreover, role modelling is certainly not the *only* reason for diversifying university faculties or the only tactic in the struggle to achieve equity. Professors, teachers and other professionals are traditionally often held up as role models, but this elevation does not reflexively mean that all professors and teachers are good role models, nor should they be expected to be. "Raced" professors have the right to pursue their commitment to scholarship and teaching duties as "cosmopolitan intellectuals," who, as Phillip Richards puts it, necessarily engage university politics with an "outsider's detachment" (Richards 75, 80). And students of any identity persuasion have the right to adopt non-traditional commitments to a life of the mind beyond a limiting "be-like" scenario.

I have asserted the individual here as the center of a radical conception of role model practice. Obviously this view does not solve the complex problems that surround role modelling as pedagogy or as strategy for equity in the university. As Bernice Fisher insightfully points out,

> contradictions surface as we try to embody values like equality, justice, compassion, and freedom in our ongoing relationships. Because our social order systematically undermines these relationships by destroying connections necessary to realize them, experience often teaches us to go it alone. (1988: 223)

Despite this paradox, in its deepest sense, I believe the search for role models is about the need for relationships that can help us become something more, creatively and productively. Role modelling in the university has the unrealized capacity to engender new vitalized ways of relating individually and collectively, to thinking and to living differently in a world of difference. But like matters of love, to institutionalize this highly idiomatic attachment will foreclose insight into the more difficult work we do in the name of finding something more.

The author would like to thank Kass Banning, Winston Smith, Deborah Britzman, and Rinaldo Walcott for their invaluable insights and suggestions on this article.

[1]This does not deny any commitment to political redress of existing inequities, expansion of multicultural democracy access, and access to economic opportunity. I am committed to interesting and provocative role model relationships in the university that cannot be predicted in advance. With other critics, however, I affirm the need to sustain critical dialogue on the institutional presumptions and discourses surrounding this term—especially in the present atmosphere of intense public and governmental conflict over the future of "diversity" efforts in higher education. Along with Bernice Fisher, I want to claim "the possibility but also the importance of criticizing the role-modelling process, not despite, but because ... [it is] so powerful and meaningful" (1988: 227).

[2]For example, see Barbara Houston's reading of Mary Helen Washington's account of the tensions of interracial co-teaching in a women's literature classroom (154–155). In addition, Valerie Smith interprets Washington's discussion to focus on the difficulties and possibilities of building an academic community in a racially diverse classroom in "Split Affinities: Representing Interracial Rape."

[3]Recently, studies of impersonation and performativity have advanced important insights into the processes of pedagogy, teacher/student relations, and performance practices in everyday life and academic disciplines. Relevant to the examination of role models, these studies expand understanding of the ways identities are constructed through complex human relations known as performance. See Gallop; Parker and Sedgwick.

[4]Fisher's title is in part inspired by the phrase "wandering in the wilderness," written by Alice Walker in her meditation on Zora Neale Hurston. See Walker.

[5]See Bhabha 1994; for a useful critique of Bhabha see Young.

[6]Als unsparingly portrays two other significants in his life. First his mother, Marie, a proud immigrant from Barbados and resourceful single mother who nevertheless yearned betwixt and between hopeless longing for love always just beyond her reach. Second Dorothy Dean, the unfulfilled 1950s Radcliff/Harvard educated black American woman mostly known for her social impetuousness in the heady world of New York's gay white elites during the 1960s and 1970s. For Als, Dodson shared with Marie and Dorothy a commitment to "the experience of pain" and to the tragedy it affords. The three are also marked by important differences. Dodson's life and his relationship to Als is as different

from both women's as Marie's is from Dorothy's. They are linked, however, in a stoic Negress stance Als describes as living "while trying not to experience" (15).

[7]*The Women* may be considered an eclectic work of memoir. As such the reader might heed Samuel Delany's insightful caution regarding the autobiographer and, more so, the would-be memoirist: "I hope to sketch, as honestly and as effectively as I can, something I can recognize as my own, aware as I do so that even as I work after honesty and accuracy, memory will make this only one possible fiction among the myriad ... anyone might write of any of us, as convinced as any other what he or she wrote was the truth" (14).

[8]Here Als makes a rather presumptuous attempt to differentiate his relationship to Dodson from James Baldwin's famous relationship with his "mentor" Richard Wright. Als writes, I think, to settle accounts and to emphasize his own trajectory from Dodson that, in an unwarranted manner, thematically parallels Baldwin's troubled essays on Wright. Nonetheless, I read Dodson as a role model for Als. In a sense by no means "metaphysical," the typical "role," Dodson played for Als is similar to the example Wright initially provided Baldwin: "he was a writer. He proved it could be done—proved it to me, and gave me an arm against all those who assured me it could *not* be done." See for example, Baldwin's "Eight Men," "The Exile," and "Alas, Poor Richard."

[9]The title of James Baldwin's last collection of essays associated with his mediations on the value of a life's struggle. Was the cost worth the price of the ticket?

[10]Other critics, like Kathryn Pauly Morgan address contradictions in authority and norm-ladened behavior inscribed in role model mediated socialization in feminist pedagogy. Conversely Barbara Houston adopts a view of role modeling as a more active and contingent process, focusing on possibilities cultivated in relationships rather than what might be jeopardized.

References

Allen, Anita L. "On Being a Role Model." *Critical Multiculturalism: A Critical Reader.* Ed. David Theo Goldberg. Cambridge, MA: Basil Blackwell Ltd., 1994. 180–199.

Als, Hilton. *The Women.* New York: Farrar, Straus, Giroux, 1996.

Austin, Regina. "Saphire Bound." *Wisconsin Law Review* 3 (1989): 539–578.

Baldwin, James. *Collected Essays.* New York: Library Classics of the United States: 1998. 247–268.

Bhabha, Homi K. "Of Mimicry and Man: The Ambivalence of Colonial Discourse." *The Location of Culture.* New York: Routledge 1994. 85–92.

Britzman, Deborah. "Beyond Rolling Models: Gender and Multicultural Education." *Gender and Education: Ninety-second Yearbook of the National Society for the Study of Education.* Eds. Sari Knopp Bilken and Diane Pollard. Chicago: University of Chicago Press, 1993: 25–42.

Brown, Sterling A. *A Son's Return: Selected Essays of Sterling A. Brown.* Ed. Mark A. Sanders. Boston: North Eastern University Press, 1996.

Delaney, Samuel. *The Motion of Light in Water: Sex and Science Fiction Writing in the East Village: 1960–1965.* New York: Richard Kasak Book Edition, 1993.

Dyson, Michael Eric. "'Be Like Mike': Michael Jordan and the Pedagogy of Desire." *Reflecting Black: African-American Cultural Criticism.* Minneapolis: University of Minnesota Press, 1993. 64–77.

Fisher, Bernice. "Wandering in the Wilderness: The Search for Women Role Models." *Signs: Journal of Women in Culture and Society* 13.13 (1988): 211–233.

Fisher, Bernice. "The Models Among Us: Social Authority and Political Activism." *Feminist Studies* 7.1 (Spring 1981): 100–112.

Fisher, Bernice. "Who Needs Woman Heroes?" *Heresies* 3.1 (1980): 10–13.

Gallop, Jane, ed. *Pedagogy: The Question of Impersonation.* Bloomington: University of Indiana Press, 1995.

Houston, Barbara. "Role Models: Help or Hindrance in the Pursuit of Autonomy?" *The Gender Question in Education: Theory, Pedagogy, and Politics.* Eds. A. Diller, B. Houston, K. P. Morgan & M. Ayim. Boulder, Colorado: Westview Press, 1996. 144–160.

Lee, Andrea. "Fatal Limitations." *New York Times Book Review* 5 January 1997: 7.

Lopez, Ian Haney. "Community Ties and Law School Faculty Hiring: The Case for Professors Who Don't Think White." *Beyond a Dream Deferred: Multicultural Education and the Politics of Excellence.* Eds. Becky W. Thompson and Sangeeta Tyagi. Minneapolis: University of Minnesota Press, 1993. 100–130.

Morgan, Kathryn Pauly. "The Perils and Paradoxes of the Bearded Mother." *The Gender Question in Education: Theory, Pedagogy, and Politics.* Eds. A. Diller, B. Houston, K. P. Morgan, and M. Ayim. Boulder, Colorado: Westview Press, 1996. 124–134.

Munoz, Jose Esteban. "Famous and Dandy Like B. 'n' Andy: Race, Pop and

Basquiat." *Pop Out: Queer Warhol.* Ed. J. Doyle, J. Flately, and J. E. Munoz. Durham: Duke University Press, 1996. 144–179.

Parker, Andrew, and Eve Kosofsky Sedgwick, eds. *Performativity and Performance.* New York: Routledge, 1995.

Patterson, Orlando. "The Moral Crisis of the Black American," *Public Interest* 32 (Summer 1973): 52.

Richards, Phillip M. "A Stranger in the Village: Coming of Age in a White College." *Dissent* (Summer 1998): 75–80.

Smith, Valerie. "Split Affinities: Representing Interracial Rape." *Not Just Race, Not Just Gender: Black Feminist Readings.* Ed. V. Smith. New York: Routledge, 1998. 1–34.

Walker, Alice. "Saving the Life That is Your Own: The Importance of Role Models in the Artist's Life." *In Search of Our Mothers' Gardens.* San Diego: Harcourt Brace Javoanovich, 1983. 3–14.

Washington, Mary Helen. "How Racial Differences Helped Us Discover Our Common Ground." *The Dynamics of Feminist Teaching.* Eds. Margo Culley and Catherine Portuges. Boston: Routledge and Kegan Paul, 1985.

Watts, Jerry Gafio. *Heroism and the Black Intellectual: Ralph Ellison, Politics, and Afro-American Intellectual Life.* Chapel Hill: University of North Carolina Press, 1994.

Young, Robert. *White Mythologies: Writing History and the West.* London: Routledge, 1990.

Contributors

Kay Armatage (Associate Professor, Cinema Studies and Women's Studies; Director, Graduate Collaborative Program in Women's Studies, University of Toronto). Co-Editor, *Gendering the Nation: Canadian Women's Cinema* (University of Toronto Press, 1999); author, *Nell Shipman* (in preparation). Research: women filmmakers of the silent era.

Kofi Asare (M.A. candidate, Drama, University of Toronto). Research: post-colonial studies, third cinema. Associations: Third World Publishing, Kwama Nkrumah House Collective, Globe African Theatre Inc.

Warren Crichlow (Associate Professor, Faculty of Education, York University). Co-editor, *Race, Identity and Representation in Education* (Routledge, 1993); *Cultural Studies: Special Issue on Toni Morrison and the Curriculum* (co-editor, 1995).

George J. Sefa Dei (Associate Professor, Dept. of Sociology and Equity Studies in Education, OISE/UT). Author, *Anti-Racism Education: Theory and Practice* (Fernwood, 1996); co-author, *Reconstructing "Dropout": A Critical Ethnography of the Dynamics of Black Students' Disengagement from School* (University of Toronto Press, 1997).

William Haver (Director, Asian and Asian American Studies Program, Binghamton; Member, School of Social Science of the Institute for Advanced Study, Princeton). Author, *The Body of This Death: Historicity and Sociality in the Time of AIDS* (Stanford, 1996); *Extremity: The Arts of Perversity and the Political Constitution of Being* (in preparation).

Jodi Jensen (M.A. candidate, Women's Studies, Simon Fraser University). Author, "Isn't Just Being Here Political Enough? Feminist Action-Oriented Research: A Challenge to Graduate Women's Studies," in *Graduate Women's Studies: Vision and Realities* (ed. A. Schteir; Inanna, 1996).

Roberta Lamb (Associate Professor, School of Music, cross-appointed to Faculty of Education and Institute of Women's Studies, Queen's University). Research: gender in music, and music education, community music, equity in academic unions.

Jamie-Lynn Magnusson (Associate Professor, Theory and Policy Studies in Education, OISE/UT). Research: equity in higher education.

Erica Meiners (Ph.D. candidate, Faculty of Education, Simon Fraser University; Education Commissioner, Teaching Support Staff Union, Simon Fraser University). Research: trauma studies, qualitative research methodologies, equity and education.

Patricia Monture-Angus (Mohawk, Six Nations Territory) (Associate Professor, Native Studies, University of Saskatchewan). Author, *Thunder in My Soul* (Fernwood, 1995). Associations: Task Force on Federally Sentenced Women, Government of Canada; Indigenous Bar Association.

Hildegard Maria Nickel (Professor, Sociology, Humboldt University, Berlin). Co-editor, *Women in Germany* (Bonn, 1993).

Terry Provost (Ph.D. Humanities, Concordia University). Research: visual culture, Black/Canadian/Cultural studies, postcolonial feminism, semiology, metalinguistics, and globalization.

Kathleen Rockhill (Professor, Sociology and Equity Studies, OISE/UT). Research: the normalization of bodies, focusing on physical disabilities and the production of "disablement" in everyday life.

Juanita Westmoreland-Traore (Dean of Law, University of Windsor). Employment Equity Commissioner, Province of Ontario, 1991–95; professor, Département des sciences juridiques, Université du Québec à Montréal, 1976–1991. Research: equality rights, anti-discrimination law, immigration law.

Allison Young (Ph.D. candidate, Political Science, Dalhousie University). Research: restructuring the labour market to combat structural unemployment. Associations: Employment Equity Council, CUPE (TAs and Sessionals), Dalhousie University.

Irina Zherebkina (Associate Professor, Head of Laboratory for Gender Studies, Kharkov State University, Ukraine). Research: gender sociology and philosophy; poststructuralism; Ukraine feminist movement.